The Man of Lawlessness

Also by Tom Davies:

Fire in the Bay
One Winter of the Holy Spirit
Black Sunlight
The Electric Harvest
Merlyn the Magician and the Pacific Coast Highway
Stained Glass Hours

The Man Of Lawlessness

Tom Davies

Hodder & Stoughton

LONDON SYDNEY AUCKLAND TORONTO

British Library Cataloguing in Publication Data

Davies, Tom, *1941–*
   The man of lawlessness: the media, violence and
   prophecy.
   1. Social conflict. Theories
   I. Title
   303.6'01

   ISBN 0-340-51290-3 Hbk
   ISBN 0-340-51291-1 Pbk

Published by Hodder and Stoughton,
a division of Hodder and Stoughton Ltd,
Mill Road, Dunton Green, Sevenoaks, Kent TN13 2YA
Editorial Office: 47 Bedford Square, London WC1B 3DP

Photoset by Rowland Phototypesetting Ltd,
Bury St Edmunds, Suffolk
Printed in Great Britain by Richard Clay Ltd,
Bungay, Suffolk.

Contents

Acknowledgments

The author would like to thank a number of people without whom he would have found himself standing on an extremely lonely cliff-top. They are Dennis Coggan, Orde and Flo Dobbie, Meryl and Malcolm Doney, David Grossman, Prabhu Gupthara, Carol and Stewart Henderson, Garth Hewitt, Jeffrey John, Christine Plunkett, Amanda and Iwan Russell-Jones, Owen Thomas, Michael Saward, Tim Shackleton, David Wavre, Martin Wroe, Peregrine Worsthorne and, of course – and always – my wife Liz.

The book is dedicated with great affection to all these, but principally it is dedicated to the memory of David Watson, who first taught me, as he put it, that I must always try to honour the fire that God had built in me.

1

The New Fear

In which we make a baleful survey of the rising tides of violence and crime in Britain and America – Discuss the surpassing power of ideas – Identify the Romantic nature of the zeitgeist of our times – And take the title Man of Lawlessness to represent our new metaphor for evil.

The Rising Tides of Violence and Crime in Britain and America

There was no set date as such, but, one day in the recent past, most of us began to feel unsafe when we left our houses. And more than a few of us began to feel unsafe actually *inside* our homes.

This new fear was difficult to come to terms with; the kind of gnawing feeling of anxiety we sometimes get when we are wandering through an old and overgrown cemetery – a formless panic, a slight but mounting terror that we have missed the bus yet again. The city streets were no longer safe and after dark they seemed quite dangerous. There was this continual threat of violence in our minds and rolling around deep inside us. Just what threat does that dark corner of the park hold? A mugger's knife or a rapist's lust? Just when was that window going to shatter and some pair of hands make off with our television? Why isn't it the way it was? Just what is happening to us?

As this fear began to take a deeper hold – as it became a more permanent part of our lives – some of us not only began acting fearfully but expecting to be feared. Just out walking in the park some of us found ourselves being careful who we were walking near. If it was a young girl or an old lady, we noted, as we walked closer to them, the way that they would throw a small fearful glance over their shoulder – just to check on what we were up to. As we were about to pass them they drew themselves away, their shoulders hunching up slightly as if in expectation of attack. We went to ludicrous extremes not to walk near them and we might even cross over to the other side of the park, in a direction in which we had not particularly wanted to walk, just so that we did not pose any sort of threat. We wanted them to enjoy their walk, too. We also then understood how perfectly fear casts out love. Why were we behaving like this?

Only in the last five years did the mining valleys of South Wales – where I was born – start becoming a home to this new fear. They began grilling the windows of all the shops. Doors in the welfare halls were fortified with steel bars – even the one-armed bandits were put inside cages at night when they were left unattended. Alarm systems began sprouting on the curving terraces. Safety chains and peep-holes were fixed on the front doors which had been left unlocked day and night for most of my lifetime. My people who had grown up in the shadow of the chapel and in the fear of the Lord were seeing the whole of their culture just disappear before their very eyes. They watched the decay of tenderness for which those valleys had once been famous; yes, the very death of love.

Cardiff, the capital of Wales, where I grew up as a child and to where I have just returned to live, has changed almost unrecognisably. By night it is no longer safe to walk through the city centre where gang brawls are frequent. Just the other month a youth was casually tossed off a central bridge and left lying on a pebble bank with a broken back. Most of the pubs now have large, dickey-bowed bouncers on the door – and they have only sprung up in the last two years or so. One night, with my friend The Major, we stood and watched a youth assault a bus shelter. He was well dressed, about 20 years of age and just kept attacking the bus shelter again and again, kicking and butting it with a quite chilling joy. Why was he doing this? *What* could be going on in his mind?[1]

In London, where I have lived for most of the last twenty years, the terror seemed to be multiplying almost daily. In the space of a few months I had my television and video stolen. A friend was brutally assaulted with a bottle in the middle of the afternoon. A man was violently mugged outside my front door. One evening, a young girl fell into my local pub saying that she had just been raped. And all of this was just what was happening around me or what I had seen. The one authentic sound of the inner city streets has become that of the police siren. Why are the times becoming so very violent and lawless?[2]

There are some who argue that life in London has always been a dangerous business, pointing to the footpads and highwaymen of old. Indeed it was the problem of criminality in London which first led to the transportation of convicts to Australia while, in the 1860s, there was such a vicious form of mugging, known as garrotting, that special protective collars were sold. The press generated a growing hysteria about the rising crime figures. Londoners should never walk home alone, the press said. Police were being attacked by 'booting' mobs and dared not blow their whistles for fear of attracting more assailants. Bayswater Road was declared as 'unsafe as Naples'.[3]

Yet, while we know that there has always been criminality in the city – and, indeed, that there has been violence since the very birth of man – we now know that the figures are booming in practically every field of criminal and violent endeavour. In the past decade recorded offences have gone up by an average of 6 per cent a year. In the past thirty years all recorded crime has risen sevenfold from one crime a year per 100 people to one per thirteen people.

According to a Home Office survey in 1985, one in two women and 13 per cent of all men feel unsafe in their area after dark. Some 40 per cent of women aged between 16 and 30 were 'very worried' about being raped. No fewer than 11 per cent believed that they were going to be raped within the year. Some 4 per cent of all women now carry an anti-rape alarm.

In a Gallup Poll in the same year 48 per cent of both sexes considered Britain 'fairly' or 'very' violent. Most thought that there was more violent crime than five years ago. Some 27 per cent believed that it was very likely that people would soon start taking the law into their own hands. In the summer of 1989, New York's Guardian Angels began patrolling London's Underground where there has been a 30 per cent increase in crime in the last seven years. A twenty-five-strong steaming gang, many armed with knives, robbed thirteen passengers on a late-night journey into King's Cross early in 1989.[4]

Many Britons have been changing their life style because of this new fear. The Home Office found that 58 per cent of all people who felt 'very unsafe' in their neighbourhood had not been out at night alone in the week before they were interviewed. Of these, 81 per cent said it was because they *never* went out alone at night. This new fear particularly affects the elderly, like one widow, 82-year-old Florrie Strudwick of Peckham, who has not been out on her own for ten years. She runs a wool shop from her home and reported that customers came to her with their money hidden in their underwear for fear of muggers. One mother hid money on her babies.[5]

Nothing in the past has even remotely prepared us for the size and energy of the growth of crime over the last twenty years. Robberies have risen from less than 1,000 a year after the war to some 24,900 now. Since 1974 the figure has gone up by 11 per cent a year. More than 8,000 Londoners are mugged each year compared with just 1,454 ten years ago. Only one in seven offenders is caught. Rape went up by 6 per cent in 1988 and wounding has increased steadily from 60,740 a year to 111,628 over the past decade. One in twenty attacks is serious enough to endanger life.[6] In one year, reports of wife-beating to the police rose by 142 per cent.

The most depressing aspect of this crime boom is the youthfulness of the criminals. The peak age for committing a criminal offence is now 15. Today, almost one in four 13- to 15-year-olds commits an indictable crime. One-third of the population has been found guilty of a 'reasonably serious' offence by the age of 28.

And these official figures may be a massive understatement, since research has established that only 8 per cent of robberies and 11 per cent of sexual offences are actually recorded. Each new statistic induces communal outrage and helplessness. They add to our new fear.

Yet these same statisticians sometimes suggest, rather unconvincingly, that there is no cause for real worry since, on the evidence of the figures, each individual can expect to be injured in an assault once every hundred years and robbed once every five centuries. The same statistics show that each individual can expect to be burgled once in every forty years which, in effect, covers everyone.

But even if we repeated these figures to ourselves each morning like a mantra it would not have much of an effect on our fear, which is always fear whether it is based on reality or in our imagination. Fear is only ever like itself and it grows and grows until it has eaten into our very hearts and spirits. It is fear that floods us when we focus our eyes on the newspaper headline and think: 'Oh no, not again.' It is fear that can chip away at our desire to live and it is fear – and often only fear – that drives us to an excessive abuse of the bottle when, for a few concussed hours anyway, fear is driven out, only to return when we awake, more fearful than before. Fear eats deep into all our human qualities. Fear removes us completely from God and therein, perhaps, lies our first clue as to why it is now being so actively promoted in the world.

Nationwide the picture is even less encouraging. The Chief Constable of Surrey, Brian Hayes, told a conference that in Surrey alone, the previous year, there had been 1,718 crimes of violence, a rise of almost 25 per cent, and attacks on the police had risen by 36 per cent. One 1988 report found violence rising in *all* rural areas.

One in three teachers were victims of attacks by pupils or parents, according to a study by the Professional Association of Teachers. Some 86 per cent of teachers polled believed that violence was on the increase in the classrooms.[7] We are also beginning to hear the most horrifying stories of the sexual abuse of our children. Many of our travelling soccer fans have become psychopathic thugs wandering the cities of Europe looking for faces to break. Our cities have been the settings for increasingly ferocious race riots.

We have also, in the last few years, heard of some astonishing, unbelievable massacres of civilians. Young men have been donning uniforms and shooting the innocent in places like Hungerford, Higham Ferrers and Walsall. The civil war in Northern Ireland has continued with ferocious intensity for the last twenty years. There were ninety-three deaths through terrorism in Ulster in 1988, while shooting and bombing incidents are both way up on the previous year.

In America – a land forged out of a religious dream and whose primary energy was religious – this new fear is no less real, but the growth in crime is even more alarming. In London twenty-six people were wounded and nineteen robbed for every 10,000 people in 1984. In New York fifty-five people were wounded and 103 robbed for every 10,000 in the same year.

In Washington during 1988 some 365 people were shot dead largely during the 'crack' wars in the ghettos, while gang warfare claimed 353 lives in Los Angeles. The numbers of murders in Los Angeles were up 25 per cent on the previous year with the gang members reported to be using AK-47s, Uzis and other automatic firearms. The Americans have also had problems with young men dressing up in uniforms and massacring civilians.

Murder, once uncommon, has now become routine. Between 1958 and 1965 the US crime rate rose faster than the population. Some 22,000 people a year are dying from gunfire in American streets. Crime grosses close to 10 per cent of the American national income and virtually forms a state within a state. It is dangerous to walk through the streets of most American cities after dark. In April 1989 a posse of 13–15-year-old boys on a 'wilding' spree in Central Park, New York, stripped and gang-raped a 28-year-old Wall Street banker. Some twelve million out of forty-five million children are not living with both their parents.

These figures add up to portraits of two great societies which have been seriously destabilised; two societies which are drifting inexorably into a new age of barbarism as, barely understanding what is happening to them, they flounder around and cry out in the tightening grip of violence and fear. And even the dimmest know that we have seen nothing yet and are beginning to foresee that soon possibly every single one of us is going to be drowning in this rising tide of lawlessness.

If we are to deduce anything at all from these figures it is that a sharp growth is taking place of unstable disordered people with unstable disordered ideas – particularly among the young. The only really pertinent question everyone should be asking is: Where are these people getting their ideas?

The Surpassing Power of Ideas

Politicians, in particular, always miss the point gloriously on the matters of crime and violence. Faced with this dramatic growth in lawlessness they draw up new plans for more police, tighter gun controls, stiffer sentences and crackdowns on excessive drinking. They even from time to time urge the return of capital punishment.

But these are all defensive measures which do not actually attack the real causes of crime, which dwell where no policeman's truncheon or hangman's noose can reach – in the human mind. Crime exists squarely and simply in the criminal's ideas.

The Chinese are perhaps the only race in the world who have ever really understood the all-surpassing power of ideas. Hence crime is seen as a matter of disorganised ideas. They usually just talk to the criminal until he sees the wrongness of his ideas. If he still does not get the point they talk to him some more. And yet some more. Those who are imprisoned are there to be 're-educated' or have their ideas 'reformed' by hard work. But when new ideas do break out in China – as they did in the Cultural Revolution and again in the early summer of 1989 in the student demand for democracy – the whole of that society is shaken to its very roots.

Our ideas rule and control everything we do. They are central to our lives and very culture. They are the indivisible atoms of our thought processes; they are the objects of our thought or the perceptions and images by which we think and act. They dictate how we think about ourselves and our views of the world. So there is a sense in which we are no more than the sum of our ideas about ourselves. The world is no more than the sum of our ideas about it. The greatest gift parents can give their children is the priceless gift of their good ideas.

Ideas have legs. They can travel through the countries of the world at the speed of sound. Some are original, but most are received. Our received ideas on the law rule the land. Our ideas on what makes a proper home determine the standards of that home. Our ideas on dress help us to decide whether to wear sober suits or go around wearing yellow plastic noses and Mickey Mouse hats. Our ideas on food suggest to us whether to eat steak or organically-grown blue cornflakes. There might be an *idée fixe* somewhere – probably California if anywhere – that it is both good and proper to eat steak garnished with organically-grown blue cornflakes.

Our actions spring directly out of our ideas. If we receive our ideas from a systematic study of the Bible then the chances are that we shall act in a Christian way. We do not kill. We do not steal. We do not try to make off with someone else's spouse or pinch his goat. We do not bear false witness. We value truth, kindness, goodness, etc. We glory in the greatness of God's creation.

Alternatively, if we receive our ideas from, say, the modern cinema then the chances are that we are going to act in an altogether different way. Every film, just like a book, contains a series of ideas which, in turn, can frame our world view and reinforce our concepts of ourselves. So a modern film might provide ideas which would actually encourage us to make off with someone else's spouse. It would probably be a matter of no concern to the modern film-maker that he had encouraged you to pinch someone's goat – particularly if that someone had lots of goats – since there is a widespread notion, which is particularly rampant in the modern cinema, that crimes can actually perfect the world. We are routinely invited to admire killers, perverts and thieves. We can safely laugh at all notions of truth, kindness, goodness, etc. Any thought of God is usually introduced as a vehicle for humour.

Similarly, if we browsed a while in the world of the modern novel we should invariably find a world which had lost God. It would be a world riven with animalism and violence and, under such circumstances, according to your average punk novelist, the best possible idea is to become alienated – live in a hole in the wall as alienated man.

Ideas have winged feet and the very best are ageless angels who travel down through the centuries intact and bright while mere buildings fade into rubble and dust. The ideas of Jesus and St Paul led to revolutions in society and human behaviour; they gave rise to new and powerful communities and even religious tyrannies, exciting or dismaying almost everyone who came into contact with them. Truthful ideas always last and will, in the end, always prevail. Ideas are at the root of all national movements, fads and fashions. They are more powerful than any army. If you want to find out about a man then just examine his ideas. Similarly if you want to find out about any society then first isolate and examine its prevailing ideas.

At any one moment the whole world is governed with huge and often distinctive jungles of philosophies and ideas. Russia is still largely organised around Marxist ideas, while Indian society has its own style and flavour, governed, as it is, by its ideas on caste and religion. But in both Britain and America it is very difficult, if not impossible, to isolate and examine their ideas-jungles precisely because they really *are* jungles since the countries' very freedom allows for a wide variety of philosophies.

Important and influential ideas are often generated by certain philosophies; by minds which have certain ways of looking at the world. Thus a socialist politician, after an early conversion, builds up a body of socialist ideas throughout his life, giving him a certain way of looking at – and acting in – his society. Conservatives go through a similar process of intellectual accretion, acquiring many right-wing ideas (and even, perhaps, formulating a few new ones of their own). It is no accident that broad bodies of generally raucous individuals, albeit in opposing parties, share the same bodies of ideas.

Thus it might well be both reasonable and logical to assume that, somewhere deep in the jungle of ideas of the free world, there is one mind and one philosophy which is generating our current plague of lawless ideas and, in the process, making our lives so full of fear and the very futures of our children so bleak.

This enquiry will be arguing that there is such a mind and such a philosophy. Right at the very source of modern lawlessness there is, indeed, a mind which is clearly discernible and a philosophy which is simply analysed. And this philosophy supplies and informs the zeitgeist of our time: the intellectual and moral properties of our age.

The Romantic Philosophy and the Man of Lawlessness

The great problem facing us is how to unravel this mystery of lawlessness and expose the nature of its evil workings. So, for the purposes of this enquiry, let us first of all call this mystery neither mind nor philosophy but a man. We shall simply take the title Man of Lawlessness and use it as a convenient metaphor for the object of our investigation. We shall then see if we can actually build up a picture of this man and show how he is working as the active catalyst somewhere in our growing chaos. Hopefully, as our investigation continues, we can locate him precisely in our lives and define his characteristics and personality.

As the Man of Lawlessness is so clearly central to the zeitgeist of our time I want further to submit, at this early stage, that its essential philosophy and that of our Man of Lawlessness is Romantic. It is the mind of the Romantic which they both share and keeps them so closely together.

Now the word Romantic is not terribly satisfactory since it means so many different things to so many different people. Some think of love or sunsets or lace-cuffs or piles of Mills and Boon romance books, but I am not referring to anything of this kind. By Romantic I mean a system of ideas which emphasises the worth of the imagination and emotion over and above reason and intellect. A Romantic will strike an attitude and ignore anything that contradicts it. His vehicle is poetic emotion. His characteristics are individualism, primitivism, a fondness for the Middle Ages, the Orient and vanished and alien cultures. He has a paradoxical tendency towards free thought and religious mysticism; admires and practises revolution against political authority and social convention; exalts physical passion and sexual perversion. He cultivates sensation and emotion for their own sake.

A Romantic has a persistent attraction to the morbid, the supernatural, the cruel, the perverted and the violent.

Immoral in its ethics, barbarous in its aesthetics and destitute of what normally passes for rational thought, the Romantic philosophy has also been defined as being totally at odds with the mind, heart and the very ideas of God. Some academics like H. G. Schenk in his *Mind of the European Romantic* have identified the Romantic Movement as both the product and cause of the decline of Christianity.

Having entered these few caveats we are almost ready to begin this enquiry which will take us on many and diverse paths through such as literature, cinema, politics and television. The method I have chosen is that of a working journalist, travelling wherever possible to meet people and look at incidents where there were suspicions that the Man of Lawlessness has been around. From time to time he will be barely visible, but we are going to keep running across his philosophy again and again until the accumulated evidence of his incredibly destructive powers becomes harder and harder. All that we can be certain of at this stage is that he is not going to be hanging around waiting for his photograph to be taken. But that does not mean he is not there.

As an on-the-ground reporter I hope that my arguments, where appropriate, will always be illuminated by the cold truth of fact. Also as an amateur theologian I have been collecting evidence on the mystery of lawlessness for the last twenty years, making this book, perhaps, a new work of theological journalism, trying to marry, if you like, a certain theological insight to the cold claims of investigative journalism.

In a sense this work will also be a journey through some twenty years of journalism, largely conducted on behalf of the *Sunday Times*, the *Observer* and the *Sunday Telegraph*. It is a journey which will take us to many different parts of the world. We shall be meeting famous personalities and keepers of the world's culture; we shall be travelling to scenes of major disasters and attending to notorious murders. As much as a work of theological journalism this will also be a detective story since, as soon as you start looking, the clues to the Man of Lawlessness's activity and identity become more and more abundant since he has clearly been at work in such diverse events as the killing of John Lennon, the attempted assassination of Ronald Reagan, the Hungerford Massacre and the war in Northern Ireland. Wherever there has been a serious outbreak of evil it is a more or less safe bet that he will be found around somewhere for it is he and he alone who is now responsible for our new fear.

But, just for now, let us assume we know nothing and, before we go anywhere at all, we shall take a journey through literature which will provide a preliminary sketch of the basic features of our Man of Lawlessness.

2

The Holiness of the Imagination

In which we set out after our quarry following literary footprints – Learn how Rousseau packed off all his children to a foundling school – Attend to the asylum scribblings of the Marquis de Sade – Hear about Byron's antics in Greece – And evaluate these Romantics' contribution to our modern cultural imagination.

The Literary Roots of the Romantic Philosophy

Romanticism made its first forceful appearance in literature towards the end of the eighteenth century. In every sense it was a child of an epoch of flouted authority with the individual in open revolt against the conservatism of society. It is common to talk of the period as a gigantic blossoming of subjectivity. At the time it was defended as a return to freer fancies and interpreted as the reaction of an artist's mind to the growing complexities of an increasingly industrialised civilisation. Its leading thinkers were Jean-Jacques Rousseau, the Marquis de Sade, William Wordsworth and Lord Byron. In a few thumbnail sketches of their lives and works we can find much to explain the gestation of the ideas so beloved of the Romantic mind.

Jean-Jacques Rousseau

Jean-Jacques Rousseau (1712–88) was a vitally Romantic figure who shook the world with the lyrical explosiveness of his ideas. 'Man is born free, but is everywhere in chains', was bandied about from one revolutionary mouth to another and his work was seen as being absolutely central to the French Revolution. *'Le Romanticism c'est la Revolution.'*

Here was the original angry young man, more sinned against than sinning. Throughout his works – of which *The Social Contract* was the most famous – we find a recurrence of such key Romantic concepts as the cult of the individual – The Noble Savage – primitivism and the corrupting evil of society. He was one of the first to maintain that the child was born innocent and gradually perverted by society's evil; therefore a child should be left alone for as long as possible and then educated through the emotions. He was also a fervent advocate of breast-feeding and virtually invented the notion of the cold bath. He also set new fashions in long hair and foppish clothes.[1]

In his *Confessions*, finished in 1770, we find almost the beginning of modern introspective literature when the writer's self was fully exposed for public display. His recollections were indiscreet, detailed and shocking to the contemporary taste. Yet he was also the first intellectual to proclaim repeatedly that he was the friend of all mankind.[2] He was, he told us, the people's champion: the leading apostle of truth and virtue. He repeatedly taught the doctrine of love and was fêted by many of his contemporaries.

Yet he took up with and stayed for most of his life with, a hotel servant, Thérèse le Vasseur, who bore him five children. He said of her that he never 'felt the least glimmering of love for her . . . the sensual needs I satisfied with her were purely sexual and were nothing to do with her as an individual.'[3] He also fell out with her brother, accusing him of making off with forty-two of his fine silk shirts.

All five children were packed off to a foundling hospital – the first in 1746 – and none of them had been given a name. Two-thirds of all babies there died in the first year. Only an average of fourteen out of a hundred survived until they were 7 when most of them became street urchins. This was an act of extreme cruelty which he compounded in his *Confessions* by declaring that he felt no shame about it. But when he became famous as a moralist he became morbidly sensitive about his abandoned children – even making an effort to trace them – but the emotional guilt, in the end, drove him out of his mind.

Thus ended one of the first founding fathers of modern Romanticism, a man who, in the judgment of one academic, I. W. Allen, was a 'masochist, exhibitionist, neurasthenic, hypochondriac, onanist, a latent homosexual, afflicted by the typical urge for repeated displacements, incapable of normal or parental affection, incipient paranoiac, narcissistic introvert rendered unsocial by his illness, filled with guilt feelings, pathologically timid, a kleptomaniac, infantilist, irritable and miserly.'[4]

If we are to judge a man by what he does – as well as by what he says – then, just on the evidence of this one life, the prospects of the Romantic movement making any decent contribution to anything were not promising. And in the work of the next key figure we are already finding the movement taking a decided turn for the worse.

The Marquis de Sade

The Marquis de Sade (1740–1814) was a philosopher, politician, psychologist and investigator of sexual deviations. His name gave rise to the word sadism and his life was one long story of the glorification of perversion, for which he was imprisoned and finally sentenced to death. In prison he overcame his boredom by writing sexually explicit novels and plays in which he declared himself an atheist. He was both witty and a revolutionary *par excellence* being later locked up in the Bastille in 1784. There he wrote *The One Hundred and Twenty Days of Sodom*, a catalogue of every known sexual perversion. After the storming of the Bastille he was transferred to the insane asylum at Charenton. Later released, he wrote further plays before being sent back to the asylum where he continued writing until he died.

As an author, de Sade advocated the unleashing of instincts even to the point of crime. Desires were to be satisfied in all their forms. He is now seen as being one of the first of the 'damned writers'. His ethical contentions were simple: society was corrupt and all social virtues redundant. 'Everything is good, everything is the work of God' became in his work, 'Everything is evil, everything is the work of Satan.' It was therefore necessary to practise vice because it conforms to the laws of nature which insist on destruction. In his writing evil became the axis of the universe.

His style and the thread of his novels contain many of the picaresque scenes peculiar to Romanticism. There are threatening forests, wild landscapes, lowering cliffs and ponderous castles. The victims are always innocent and the persecutors always malicious. Virtue always loses and vice always wins: the one in misery and the other in luxury. For de Sade the world contained only the pleasures of transgression and destruction. His characters always became engaged in the so-called divine ecstasy of destruction. Violence in all its forms was a means of playing god.[5]

Yet the oft-cited paradox of his life was the part he played in the French Revolution. He had often written of the sadistic pleasures to be gained from upheaval – and with Rousseau they were both seen as playing an important role in it – but, when offered the chance to indulge in an orgy of blood, he refused and pleaded poor health.

Nevertheless, he managed to attract some powerful supporters, including Swinburne, who described him as, 'Our prophet, our teacher, our poet'. Petrus Borel called him 'a martyr'. Baudelaire said he was '*L'homme naturel*'. Guillaume Apollinaire called him, '*L'esprit le plus libre qui ait encore existe*'. Another of his supporters was William Blake, who believed that de Sade had been imprisoned merely because of his prophetic writings.

William Wordsworth

In Britain some years later William Wordsworth (1770–1850) was to imbibe of the spirit of Romanticism, his early loyalties divided between Britain and France. In his youth he was unreservedly to acclaim the French Revolution:

Bliss was it in that dawn to be alive,
But to be young was very heaven.
The Prelude

Wordsworth himself was in revolt against the conventional neo-classicism of the day, his works continually emphasising the value of imagination and emotion. 'Poetry is the most philosophic of all writing . . . its object is truth . . . carried alive into the heart by passion'; and that it is 'the spontaneous overflow of powerful feelings: it takes its origin from emotion recollected in tranquillity'.

These lines became the very talismans of the main English Romantic poets – Lord Byron, John Keats and Percy Bysshe Shelley – who all came to believe in the holiness of the imagination and the corresponding rejection of reason. The great and only instrument of the moral good was the imagination. It was Shelley who came to insist on the primacy of poetry, claiming that it was prophecy, law and knowledge. 'Poetry awakens and enlarges the mind itself by rendering it the receptacle of a thousand unapprehended combinations of thought. Poetry lifts the veil from the hidden beauty of the world.'[6]

But Wordsworth grew to denounce and renounce the bloody excesses of the French Revolution. Edmund Burke lamented that the 'glory of Europe had been extinguished for ever' and it took a Napoleon to return to the country some vestige of discipline and control. Thereafter Wordsworth returned to live in the Lake District where, celebrating the pantheistic glories of nature and founding the modern cult of nature mysticism, he became increasingly Anglican and Tory. Shelley, who had seven children by three different mothers, spent most of his life being hounded by creditors.

Lord Byron

But if ever there was anyone tailor-made for the Romantic dream it was Lord Byron (1788–1824), whose life and work captured the imagination of Europe. As a child with a club-foot he was taken to Scotland and educated at Aberdeen Grammar School. His nurse, May Gray, awoke precocious passions in him at the age of 9 and, after receiving an inheritance, he later went to Harrow where he became attached to other boys. After a term at Trinity College, he indulged in dissipation which put him heavily in debt. He also began writing poetry and, by 1808, had flung himself into 'an abyss of sensuality'.

He travelled extensively in Europe, falling in love with a married woman in Malta and discovering that he was very fond of Greece where he delighted in the people. Later he wrote his famous *Childe Harolde's Pilgrimage*, in which he expressed his melancholy and disillusion with the post-Revolutionary eras. On publication of the *Pilgrimage* his notoriety enabled him to be lionised in Whig circles and he proceeded to sweep into many more passionate liaisons, including one with Lady Caroline Lamb and another with his half-sister. Later he married and, plagued by debt and scandal, went into exile.

In Europe he met Shelley and, struggling with such reflections as man is 'half dust, half deity, alike unfit to sink or soar', he still chased other men's wives, writing in 1818, his other epic *Don Juan*, a picaresque verse satire. By 1818 Shelley found him fat, gloomy and sunk in promiscuity. In two years he had spent £2,500 on Venetian women and had slept with 'at least two hundred'. But he was still not slow in his sexual pursuits and soon, longing for some violent action, took up the offer of the London Greek Committee to act as their agent in their war for independence against the Turks. There, suffering from the strain of an emotional friendship with a Greek page-boy, he was to die, roundly cursing every last Greek in the world.

In Byron's life we have, perhaps, the most complete description of the Romantic fallacy: the longing for violent 'heroic' action, the gloom and the melancholy, one minute against society, another against God and the next himself. Transgression provided him with his very life-rhythms and he sought, particularly in incest, an added spice for love.

The first book to be written about Byron was *Astarte* by his grandson, the Earl of Lovelace. In one perceptive passage he wrote:

He had a fancy for some Oriental legends of pre-existence, and in his conversation and poetry took up the part of a fallen or exiled being, expelled from heaven, or sentenced to a new avatar on earth for some crime, existing under a curse, predoomed to a fate really fixed by himself in his own mind, but which he seemed determined to fulfil. At times this dramatic imagination resembled delusion; he would play at being mad, and gradually get more and more serious, as if he believed himself destined to wreck his own life and that of everyone near him.[7]

But those warped Byronic ideals are far from dead and are indeed festering in all sections of the mind of the media today. Byron was also credited with the invention of tales of vampirism, with Mary Shelley, leading to that enormously successful literary species 'the tale of terror' in which the postures of the macabre, the sickening and the horrible were persistently cultivated. The works of our most successful horror writers descend directly into the macabre, springing directly from Mary Shelley's original Frankenstein myths. Horror films, which form a part of the staple diet of our film industry, also draw their antecedents from such tales of doom and images of terror. Where once Mary Shelley terrified the world with Frankenstein we now have such indulgent eruptions of the Romantic imagination as *Alien*, *Nightmare on Elm Street*, *The Fly* and *The Predator*.

It was Byron's similar insistence on the ugly and obscene which was to inspire the cruel studies of physical torment by the painter Géricault, who specialised in madmen and corpses. From this it is but a short step to the contorted, perverted shapes of our own 'master' of that genre, Francis Bacon.

Byronic ideas even seeped into theology. In his later years Byron was to write: 'Passion is the element in which we live: without it we vegetate.' The theologian Søren Kierkegaard, seen as one of the founders of existentialism, was to write: 'The conclusions of passion are the only reliable ones.' Also in his final pursuit of the glories of violence and war Byron was anticipating the operations of our own news media which is nothing if it is not in pursuit of violence and war.

William Blake

Another key Romantic poet of the era was the visionary William Blake (1757–1827), who also exalted the powers of the imagination over and above the claims of reason, fervently supporting revolution in all its forms. His *Songs of Innocence and Experience* did much to shape this period of Romantic storms and he penned such seminal ideas to the Romantic experience as 'the road of excess leads to the palace of wisdom' and 'sooner murder an infant in its cradle than nurse unacted desires'.

The Romantic Legacy

After the death of Byron the Romantic cat was clearly out of the Classical bag and youth became increasingly eccentric, mooning over lost beauty and sending up the battle-cry of 'Impulse over Order'. The world, so they felt, had betrayed their nobility and intensity of purpose. Literary horrors fed imaginations in real life and so there were raging passions *à la Byron*, suicides *à la Chatterton*, and so on.[8] Few of the leaders of the movement lived long either. Keats died at 25, Shelley at 29 and Byron was extremely lucky to make 36.

By 1830 on the stage none of the decencies or silences of civilised convention was respected; every kind of lewdness and perversion from poisonings to suicides and assassinations was paraded before the public. 'Nothing succeeds like excess!' the Romantics screamed.

The movement continued to grow spasmodically under various talents and some writers tried to ring the death-knell on Romanticism on several occasions. The conservative Goethe saw the billowing tides of revolutionary ideas threatening to swamp his treasured civilisation and wrote *Hermann and Dorothea*, a beautifully-controlled epic which sought to restore fundamental simplicities. He proscribed Romanticism as disease and Classicism as health. He later wrote *Werther* as a warning to a lovesick generation about the Romantic aberration. In this novel the hero commits suicide for unrequited love, but Goethe did not make his intentions explicit enough and the young Werther became the hero of the Romantic ideal, provoking a further spate of suicides.

In *Madame Bovary* Flaubert made a comprehensive catalogue of the excesses and extravagances of the Romantic outlook; the yearning for happiness which the world can never satisfy, the desire to return to childhood and the disillusion which arises from the Romantic inability to distinguish between dream and reality. Emma Bovary saw life through the eyes of the popular novel and her hunt for the Romantic dream led to her adultery, a life of subterfuge and deceit and, finally, suicide.

More than any other nation it was the French who restored a sense of reality to literature and Romanticism began to die under a fusillade of yawns. The French, with their predilection for the clear-cut date, put 1845 as the internment year. Romanticism was posted missing, presumed dead. The artist had not been integrated into society but, at best, had effected an uneasy alliance.

Yet just in this rudimentary sketch of the ideas and lives of the early Romantics we are already beginning to see the first dark outlines of our Man of Lawlessness. We are beginning to see his destructiveness, his emphasis on the primacy of passion and the imagination, his insistence on the ugly and the obscene and his often tireless pursuit of violence and war.

We are also being given our first clues to the extent of his authority and influence in our own time, since, if we walk into a video shop, we are faced with the most comprehensive range of violence and perversion; if we open a newspaper we find a long catalogue of crime, savagery and war; if we turn on our television news there is more of the same; our mass-marketed paperbacks are riven with alienation and animalism and our theatre is as obsessed with cruelty and perversion as it was in Paris in 1830.

The same old Romantic themes are there, too, all as if they had been dictated by the collaborating ghosts of Rousseau, Byron, Blake and de Sade in some leaky Paris dungeon: The Noble Savage (Rambo); freewheeling anarchism (the work of Henry Miller); the alienated violent man (the works of Colin Wilson and Norman Mailer); the empasis on the macabre (Stephen King and James Herbert); the dreams of perfecting the world by committing crimes (Bonnie and Clyde and James Bond films); the pictorial celebration of perversion (Francis Bacon); a virtual rewrite of de Sade's *130 Days of Sodom* (every book of pornography and many news stories in Rupert Murdoch's the *Sun* and the *News of the World*); the constant streams of blood (most adult videos and almost every American film made for television); and the fascination with violence and war (nearly every edition of television news).

Our modern cultural imagination, by which I merely mean

the working of our society's intellectual powers, demands that
many a situation smacks of the concentration camp or the street
riot; that nearly every image should be emblematic of shudder-
ing violence; that we should thus be made aware of the extreme
peril of our position. This philosophy or way of thinking,
particularly in the way the media selects and presents images,
tells us stridently that the world is irredeemably rotten and
insists the only reasonable conclusion is that God has fully
and finally abandoned the world, that He is, as that other
Romantic, Freidrich Nietzsche stated, dead.

Dr P. A. Sorokin, former sociology professor at Harvard, put
it this way:

> There has been a growing preoccupation of our writers with the
> social sewers, the broken homes of disloyal parents and unloved
> children, the bedroom of the prostitute, a brothel, a den of crimi-
> nals, a ward of the insane, a club of dishonest politicians, a street-
> corner gang of teenage delinquents, a hate-laden prison, a crime-
> ridden waterfront, the courtroom of a dishonest judge, the sex
> adventures of urbanised cavemen and rapists, the loves of adulter-
> ers and fornicators, of masochists, sadists, prostitutes, mistresses,
> playboys. Juicy loves, ids, orgasms and libidos are seductively
> prepared and served with all trimmings.

But this modern cultural imagination is not only anti-Christian
it is also anti-human and destructive of life itself – denying the
dignity of ordinary people and the validity of ordinary lives,
devaluing the function of sex and threatening the welfare of our
children. In the workings of this imagination the common, the
ordered and the familiar are the least trustworthy.

This imagination is steadily leading the whole world into
terror and darkness. It has all but managed to extinguish the
claims of a holy God, whose very first demand is that His people
become holy too, and all we can prophesy for certain is that,
thanks to satellite television, this imagination is going to become more and more powerful on every hearth and in every
home. T. S. Eliot forecast that civilisation will end in inter-
necine fighting. We shall all, he said, end up killing one another
on the streets.

3

Myths Which Enable Murder

In which we continue pursuing our literary quarry by inspecting the ideas of the fathers of modernism – Pay a visit to Norman Mailer in New York – Go to see Colin Wilson down in Cornwall – Travel back to the Moors Murders trial – End our literary pilgrimage by blaming the Man of Lawlessness for the death of John Lennon.

The Fathers of Modernism

Before moving to fresh fields let us stay awhile with literature and ask ourselves who provided the match for this all-engulfing fire? In the complex, interlacing avenues of modern literature you could point an accusing finger at almost every author and be nearly right. You could say almost anything at all about the fathers of modernism and be 'in the money'. You could drag almost any one of them into the dock and justly accuse them of being party to a conspiracy in provoking global lawlessness.

You might be tempted to start by heaping blame on the gloomy and alienated existentialism of Fyodor Dostoevsky, whose early characters address us 'from under the floorboards'. As a writer he was drawn to the extremes of poverty, crime and prostitution, while the hero of his most famous work, *Crime and Punishment*, Raskolnikov, murders an old money-lender with a hatchet and the rest of the book outlines the consequences of this act as the hero attempts to rationalise his motives. But each time he reaches an explanation he rejects it and continues to search for another. His brain is so filled with abstract theories that he has not only lost contact with reality he has lost contact with himself. 'A heart unhinged by theories,' says the prosecuting officer.[1]

You might then be tempted to point a finger at another of the fathers of modernism, Joseph Conrad, a solo adventurer without a country, who wrote sea stories and exotic romances set on ships or in the Far East. In *The Heart of Darkness*, Marlow journeys through all the circles of hell in the Congo, finally finding Kurtz and moral anarchy. Conrad's later works were all drawn to revolutionary anarchists. It would also be tempting to pick up James Joyce's *Ulysses* and start asking questions about Stephen Daedalus's journeys through the lavatory, the bar and brothel. Then there are the couplings, the masturbations and the sexual fantasies.

But if you were looking for the authentic voice of alienated man you could do no worse than Franz Kafka, with his haggard and haunted imagination: 'The Prophet of the Age of Anxiety'. He was possessed with notions of failed identity, persecution and sickness. In his famous black metaphysical fantasy, *The Trial*, we learn of Joseph K., who is arrested without charge and put on trial by a faceless state. As the story unfolds, dream is practically indistinguishable from reality and he is finally executed, like a dog. In *The Metamorphosis* a man wakes up and finds that he has been turned into a giant cockroach 'which has to be got rid of'.[2]

There are indeed broad and Romantic brush-strokes in the works of all these seminal writers – and they have made their contribution to our darkness, too – but there is a certain sense in which their very greatness transcended the criminal and darkly alien in which they chose to enmesh themselves. These were immense, subtle writers, masters of irony and ambiguity, who were struggling to come to terms with themselves and their age. Again and again we find in these works that noblest of all artistic struggles: the search to tap into the mind of God.

Dostoevsky becomes understandable – and even acceptable – in the context of his own society which was no more than a totalitarian state, riven with spies and exercising censorship over everything. He himself had been thrown into a Siberian prison-camp for entertaining 'liberal notions' and his heroes were always desperate to explore the extremities and dangers of this closed society. In his later books he was always asserting the need for faith, while his characters were always struggling to come to terms with Jesus. If *Crime and Punishment* is about anything at all, it is an examination of the nature of sin and redemption.

Similarly, Conrad was a writer of tremendous power who was concerned with the mechanics of betrayal – of one's country and one's self. Even his interest in anarchism was focused on the emotional contradictions that created such an idea. Also the mighty *Ulysses* is not so much a statement about revolution as a search for the random, the commonplace and the ordinary. Joyce is searching for meanings behind 'the irreducible modalities of the visible' and in Daedulus's journey we are again and again seeing new ways of looking at a complex world.

Even in the terrible and troubling words of Franz Kafka we find a great integrity since his work foresaw and foreshadowed the rise of Nazi Germany and the collapse of Western civilis- ation in the Second World War.[3]

No, what we are looking for are poor philosophers who stand fascinated by the destructive glitter of violence and nothing- ness, whose works do not stand on their own, but are essentially derivative of our Romantic legacy, outraging all laws of prob- ability and imitative form. And of them there is a whole shuffling legion, all clutching slim works which should all have been far, far slimmer.

For when the French gave the Romantic movement a burial date it is quite clear that this complex of attitudes never even got one foot in the grave and it is something to which we still all too blindly belong. In 1946 Henry Treece in his *How I See The Apocalypse* (Lindsay Drummond) wrote:

> This Romantic reaction, the scope of which is not yet even imagin- able, has taken various routes in making itself vocal. For instance there is the Paris movement (though it never gave itself such a name) of Perles, Henry Miller and Anais Nin; the Apocalyptic

Movement whose philosopher was J. F. Hendry; the Personalist attitude expounded by Stefan Schimanski ... the spasmodic epilepsy of Keidrych Rhys and the isolated Romanticism of such poets as Morwenna Donnelly, Vernon Watkins, W. R. Rodgers and John Heath-Stubbs, among many others.

The whole canon of the works of D. H. Lawrence, who invited us to think 'with the blood', belongs to that movement and it was certainly more than alive in the works of Jean-Paul Sartre and Samuel Beckett, in Ernest Hemingway and Thomas Wolfe, in Francis Bacon and Jackson Pollock, in Jean Genet and André Gide, in Ezra Pound and the whole theatre of cruelty.

But perhaps the saddest and most destructive outbreak of Romanticism was in the beatnik movement in the early 60s, which revived the key concepts of polymorphous sexuality and alienation. The Gospel was again that of hell garnished with a self-destructive vitality. The mainstay of the movement again took the form of a highly volatile protest against the assumption that art was no longer a registry of individual agony and exclusion. With the emergence of the hipster, the Romantic was no longer a drinker but a drunk and a whole generation reached out for mind-expanding drugs and a new freedom on the road which, in its turn, became a subtle enslavement. There were sloppy and stupid attacks on literary style, on poetic form, on defined genre boundaries. There were riots on the campuses. The pervading sin was narcissism by people whose significance was strictly internal. It became particularly insidious when it related the account of the individual to the needs of society. Its cry to society was ... Integrate me! ... its meaning was ... Surrender to me!

In America there emerged a whole new gang of 'holy barbarians' calling the young to revolt against unspecified conditions and, on that list, is quite the worst collection of purely poor thinkers (like Allen Ginsberg, William Burroughs, Henry Miller, Jack Kerouac, James Baldwin and Norman Mailer) who have ever actually inflicted damage on this, or any other, generation.[4]

Thus we had *Naked Lunch*; a wild narcissistic fantasy of perversion and death which might even have put the Marquis de Sade off his breakfast. We had Henry Miller invoking distinctly Byronic ethics when he said: 'Either you are crazy like the rest of civilised humanity, or you are sane and healthy. And if you are sane and healthy you are an anarchist and throw bombs.' Everywhere there was this unquenchable and obsessive love of violence – providing, of course, it was not in the artist's own backyard.

The Mailer Factor

But let us tarry a while with Norman Mailer. He is capable of recklessly brilliant bursts of good writing and, as we have seen in the past, those that write well, Byron for example, often exert the most influence, particularly on the immature imagination. Mailer has always been a potently influential writer and not only has he sought – and maintained to this day – an influence over the young, but he also exerts an influence on 'the intellectuals' of other arms of the media like television and the film industry. His openly acknowledged ideas actually celebrate and anoint notions of violence and murder and, if you read the body of his work, you would also begin to understand why the subjects of violence and murder are so strongly featured – and even legitimised – in most Hollywood films or on television. So what are his ideas?

His most famous essay is *The White Negro* which poeticises the glamour of madness and became the very text of the hipster. Mailer – this Rousseau from Brooklyn – recreated his own noble savage and he called his mythical hero 'a philosophical psychopath'. Half-beatnik, half-existentialist, all mind-expanding, his only code was 'to do what one feels whenever and wherever it is possible'. This hipster would 'return us to ourselves', to the 'affirmation of the barbarian', to 'a primitive passion about human nature'. 'Whether the life is criminal or not, the decision must be to encourage the psychopath in oneself.'[5]

Consider, he wrote, the actual case of two young men beating to death a sweetshop owner. Did it not have its beneficial aspect? 'One murders not only a weak, 50-year-old man, but an institution as well, one violates private property, one enters into a new relationship with the police and introduces a dangerous element into one's life.'

This is Romantic lunacy of the very highest order; all the more unforgivable since such ideas, if not exactly the language, have been freely derived from the European Romantics like Rousseau and de Sade. Yes, there really is nothing new under the sun. But this essay was far from a slight aberration in his work.

In his novel, *American Dream*, Mailer describes a man's murder of his wife as a positive act in the development of his personality, as a liberation, a catharsis. After the murder, the illness passes away from the murderer. This idea has a positive echo in the immensely successful film *Lethal Weapon* starring Mel Gibson. In the early parts of the film he is suffering from a mental disorder, but, after a long series of the most violent acts, he emerges smiling, purged, his sanity restored.

I caught up with Mailer in 1981 when, as a columnist for the *Observer*, I went to interview him in New York.[6] He was, at the time, typically, promoting his new work, *The Executioner's Song*. He turned out to be an engaging, immodest man; short and dumpy, almost as if he had been built out of circles, with tiny cold blue eyes, no neck to speak of, a bulging chest which made his arms hang out a little – almost as if to give him balance – and a thatch of thinning grey hair. He was clearly in good shape, working out every Saturday morning in the local gym where he really got down to it with his son and a former light-heavyweight champion.

I found early on he was quite likable, generous with his thoughts, and with a beguiling ability to send himself up. The urge to write had long left him, he said, but there was, ah, all this alimony to be found for his 'sweet, battling wives' and eight kids. Though, far from wearying with marriage, he added that he had a suspicion that he was going to marry sixteen times before he got through. 'I'm a sort of a bumbling masochist who will take ten shots to get one back in.'

Then, at 56, he had blown most of his money making three films and there was none left. His hand rubbed around his cheek and pulled at his nose as he talked. He had a very thick cough and occasionally smoothed the table in front of him with his hands – a very self-contained man, I thought, who had probably never experienced a moment of self-doubt. Of William Blake he said, 'He had a very fine mind and I feel very close to it.'

One subject cruised into another and we got on to his latest work, *The Executioner's Song*, about Gary Gilmore, who insisted on being executed for killing someone. Mailer said that he hoped the book would become a 'classic text in criminology' – which was the usual sort of publicity propaganda you expect from every writer – when he stopped me short and said something so startling that it actually made my brain jump. 'There is something saintly about murder.' I just wrote it down and looked at him. 'I know that you can spend the rest of your life explaining remarks like that. I am not in favour of murder, but I am saying that murder can give you feelings of life.'

He added that the notion of the psychopath continued to obsess him and that he had once thought of calling the Gilmore book *The Saint and the Psychopath*. His hands smoothed the table again and he was peering at it as if trying to find something hidden in the wood. 'Gary was an obvious psychopath with something saintly about him. I wanted to show that Gary was not insane. There was no record of him wavering.'

And there it was, as bold as brass; the Romanticising of murder – the wicked refusal to describe murder as the wanton, callous act of savagery that it, in reality, is. Mailer was not above using the knife himself, as he had once on his second wife, Adele Morales. According to her account in the *New York Daily Mirror* he, very drunk in 1960, took out a two and a half inch penknife and stabbed her in her upper abdomen and back. Later, in a bizarre television interview with Mike Wallace, he said, 'The knife to a juvenile delinquent is very meaningful. You see, it's his sword – his manhood.' He was arrested, but the case was dropped when Morales refused to sign a complaint against her husband.[7]

After I wrote my column about him in the *Observer*, he read it on his arrival in London and wanted to go straight back to New York. He described speaking to me as a very big mistake. 'In America they criticise you but in England they set out to destroy you,' he later moaned.

But Storming Norman, who once fought with a man in the street after that man called his poodle a queer, was far from destroyed and his ideas were to get him into more hot water. And lead to a murder in real life.

There was an American, a certain Jack Henry Abbott, locked up for murder, who began to write letters to Mailer. His letters described the conditions of life in the prison, though there is much in his language which suggests that prison was, indeed, the very best place for Mr Abbott. But the alarm bells of anyone might have started ringing on reading some of the following sentences in the Abbott letter:

'The judge sentenced me to the main penitentiary for the express purpose of having me raped by prisoners and reduced to a homosexual ... To the authorities, there is nothing seriously wrong with anyone getting raped in prison. On the contrary, the idea excites them, they *enjoy* it.'

Or there was: 'Here in prison the most respected and honoured men among us are those who have killed other men, particularly other prisoners. It is not merely fear but respect.

Or else he wrote of the 'scores of judges, of politicians, preachers and lawyers who have consciously conspired to crush me through the perpetration of intentional lies.'

Mailer was so impressed by these letters that he personally formed a like-minded group and managed to obtain parole for Abbott, celebrating the release with a dinner at Mailer's home. The letters were also published in book form, *In the Belly of the Beast* (Hutchinson), to which Mailer wrote a foreword in which we find the words: 'Crime is a positive experience for juvenile delinquents because it is more exciting, more meaningful, more mysterious, more transcendental, more religious than any other experience they have known.' He described Abbott as 'an intellectual, a radical, a potential leader.'

Within days of his release, after a row with a waiter in a New York restaurant, this potential leader took out his meaningful, mysterious, transcendental and religious knife to stab the waiter to death in an extremely brutal way. At the subsequent trial Mailer admitted to having 'blood on his hands', but never expressed any sympathy for Abbott's victim who, it has to be said, would still be alive had Mailer not got Abbott out. But Abbott is now back inside again.

This all-pervading and destructive atmosphere of violence and hatred, the emergence of crazed notions such as the Sanctity of the Polymorphous Perverse and the Necessary Murder Syndrome, have taken an unimaginable toll on life in America. Perhaps the saddest example of a waste of a good writer is supplied in the story of James Baldwin who, on the evidence of his earlier work, might have been judged the finest writer that America had ever produced. The stepson of a preacher, he wrote with the most glorious sensibility in a majestic prose that had clear echoes of the King James Bible on which he was reared.

Yet, as we watched his career develop, we also watched it becoming marred and fatally flawed by the fashionable rage and hate of his times. His novel, *Another Country*, was set squarely on the margins of society with the relationships of the main characters collapsing as they took up extreme, alienated positions. Every conceivable delinquency and perversion was thrown into this novel and by the 1960s, in the atmosphere largely generated by Mailer's *White Negro*, it was almost inevitable that Baldwin would formally abandon all his earlier ideas of love and racial reconciliation in favour of an extreme black nationalism. In *The Fire Next Time* his polemical stand was that of a black fascist – now he would sooner spend his time with a white racist than a white liberal – and he further argued that the use of violence was a legitimate right for those who were in any way 'victims'.[8]

Baldwin's rejection of the ways of love and non-violence were particularly tragic since his ideas are still persistently nourished by young blacks. But it is doubly tragic since, had he kept away from the Romantic hemlock of violence and alienation, he had more than enough talent actually to lead the young into a new world where they could have worked with one another. As for himself, Baldwin became a sad man, constantly sipping on a glass of whisky in all his waking moments, until he finally died in embittered exile in the South of France.

It is probably true that ideas – and particularly bad ideas – whizz around American society more freely than they do in Britain, precisely because it is a much freer society – and long may it remain so. Certainly the poisoned and poisoning Romantic tide is flowing as strongly as ever in its current literature and you have to look no further than the elaborate grotesqueries of John Barth; Truman Capote's fascination with madness and murder, not forgetting the ever-popular Gothic morbidities of Edgar Allan Poe.

In Britain this spirit is not quite so obvious in our serious literature, but the stains of this terminal illness are there nevertheless; in the dense, almost impenetrable mysticism of Lawrence Durrell; in the Joycean fantasy and moral anarchy of J. P. Donleavy; in practically the whole canon of Colin Wilson and in the punk alienation of Martin Amis. The real wonder is that such writers invariably claim to be giving us an insight into the present when their imaginations are so powerfully wedded to the corrupt literary sensibilities of the past.

But Baudelaire's flowers of evil are flourishing everywhere in our paperback industry when practically the first question a would-be publisher asks about a book is, 'What's the VR?' The violence ratio.

One 1988 report by the seventeen-nation Coalition Against Violent Entertainment found that modern American readers of popular fiction were entertaining themselves with more hate-filled, sadistic and gruesome material than any previous generation of human beings in world history. This trend had also come to Britain where publishers were setting an international pace in 'intense violence' in children's books. One Puffin paperback carried pages of vivid descriptions of the painful ways that people can die, including being eaten alive, stabbed and poisoned, crushed, buried alive, dismembered and unsouled. For example: 'Something thumps you on the back of the head, looking down you see the bloody head of a harpoon protruding from your stomach, your hands clutch at the gaping wound to try to stop your entrails spilling into the slime of the sewer.'

On a points system the report put Robert Ludlum and Frederick Forsyth at the top of the rogues' gallery, followed by Mario Puzo, James Clavell, Helen MacInnes, John le Carré, Stephen King, Rafael Sabatini, Leon Uris, Harold Robbins, Frank Yerby, Ken Follett, Sydney Sheldon, Jacqueline Susann and Zane Grey.

Colin Wilson and *The Outsider*

But there remains one little flourishing outpost of literary Romanticism down in Cornwall; Colin Wilson, who wrote his famous study of alienation, *The Outsider*, in a sleeping-bag on Hampstead Heath in 1956. Since then he has churned out a whole stream of books cataloguing crimes and perversions, examining brutal murders and grisly deaths, detailing stories of spooks and the occult, hauntings and possessions. All these aberrations are wrapped up in a gooey mysticism and much talk of The Truth.

Wilson is not a philosopher, bereft of any rigour or discipline, but perhaps his only importance lies as a populariser of Romantic ideas since *The Outsider* is a handy compendium of the basic notions of the alienated artist.[9] Certainly many eminent critics like Philip Toynbee went down on their knees when the book first came out, though they were quickly to jump up again when he produced his second. Since then, in his own words, he has largely been 'hatcheted or ignored'.

The Outsider is a survey of the 'hole-in-the-wall' man: he who stands outside society and 'sees too deep and too much'. What he sees is chaos. He is fatally caught between 'being and nothingness' and returns to his room like a spider, living alone, trying to avoid people. *The Outsider* finds misery and death moulded into the very stuff of the world. He sees himself surrounded by triviality and shallow thinkers. His recurring cry is, 'Nothing is worth doing' hence the result is a sort of spiritual syphilis as he feels endless disillusion until his end comes either in insanity or suicide.

From these initial expository ideas Wilson takes us on a canter around the lives and ideas of such as Henri Barbusse, Albert Camus, Ernest Hemingway, Hermann Hesse, T. E. Lawrence, Van Gogh, Nijinsky, Nietzsche, and Dostoevsky. Throughout these lives, often punctuated by long periods of madness and pain, the one abiding consistency is their rejection of God, often in favour of a lot of quasi-mystical searches which, as in Dr Lisle Adams's *Axel*, takes the form of the hero in his castle studying the Kabbalah and hermetic philosophies.

Nietzsche – 'the pagan philosopher with a hammer' – actually became God; he is the superman who 'looks down on suffering humanity like a hillman on the plains.' Nietzsche stood completely alone, 'the only healthy man in a sick universe', though, as it turned out, the only healthy man in a sick universe died racked with the twin perils of despair and syphilis.[10]

Throughout the accounts of these lives we are struck again and again by their invincible narcissism; by their individualistic simple-minded postures in the face of the incredible complexities of civilisation. This confusion was perhaps best summed up by T. E. Hulme, who was a real philosopher, in an essay on Romanticism and Classicism, in which he wrote:

> The Romantic, because he thinks man infinite, must always be talking about the infinite ... [He] is always flying, flying over abysses, flying up into eternal gases. The word Infinite is in every other line ... Here is the root of all Romanticism: that man, the individual, is an infinite reservoir of possibilities; and if you can so rearrange society by the destruction of the oppressive order then these possibilities will have a chance, and you will get Progress ... One can define the Classical quite clearly as the exact opposite of this. Man is an extraordinarily fixed and limited animal whose nature is absolutely constant. It is only by tradition and organisation that anything decent can be got out of him.[11]

The other striking feature of the lives of these outsiders is the quite astonishing messes in which they largely lived. The truly extraordinary feature of the Christian body of ideas is that it actually works – they enable us to live our lives more abundantly – but all the ideas of these great artists ever seemed to produce was a life of despair and pain with ears lopped off and children abandoned, periods in prison and endless nasty diseases, often culminating in madness and an early death of an unusually horrific kind.

It is also perhaps important to note that – in terms of analysis, rigour and the ability to draw an argument from a first premise to a final conclusion in clear, simple thought – not one of these outsiders would qualify for – let alone get through Part One – of a philosophy degree. They may have been fine artists in their own particular fields, but trained thinkers they were not. Had Nijinsky written 'God is a fire in the brain' for my old philosophy professor he would have been firmly advised to stick to dancing and shown the study door.

There is one dazzling exception, however, T. S. Eliot, who is often quoted in *The Outsider* even if that old Anglican was hardly one of them. Almost alone in terms of refinement, education and sheer intellectual power, T. S. Eliot stands out like the very sun above the tiny guttering candles of this lot. His mind, in the sheer urbanity of its prose, in its brilliance at destructive definition and its sense of the hard fact is not something that one normally associates with the religious sensibility. But he had the profoundest love of God and little but contempt for many of the artists of this time especially that wild man with no 'social or intellectual control', D. H. Lawrence.

I went down to see Colin Wilson in the winter of 1980, again for the *Observer* and, in a house stuffed to the gunnels with books and quite the largest collection of records I have ever seen, met an easy and sunny man, generous with his drink and spilling over with vivid, high-energy philosophical chatter. He was a dedicated wine drinker and very keen on food.[12]

My impressions of him kept multiplying and changing, but the abiding one was of his quite staggering candour. Writers almost never talk about their earnings – largely because many of them rarely make more than a few quid – but, unsolicited, he told me just about what all his fifty books had made and how he was just then wrestling with an overdraft. It just wasn't worth his being a tax exile, he said, because he didn't earn enough. His bestseller on the occult made a lot, but, spread over the years, that wasn't a lot at all and so, unlike other writers who had hit the jackpot, he still had to supplement his income from journalism.

For someone who had protected his privacy with such ferocity he could get into a fair few scrapes. The police called on him wondering what he was doing on the night of October 29th, 1975. It was the night the Yorkshire Ripper had made his first attack and part of one of Wilson's books sounded like one of the Ripper's letters. Wilson consulted his diaries and told them exactly. He wasn't attacking women in Yorkshire, but locked in his own lavatory in Mevagissey, Cornwall.

After *The Outsider* had appeared he faded into obscurity for ten years until 1966 when he picked up his first good review. He never thought of jacking it all in though. 'What would I do?' So he sustained himself through the bad years with the conviction that he had something important to say; that he was, well, a genius. He's had his fair share of fame, of course. 'But what can you do with fame? You can't eat it.'

With an eye perhaps on history he had set out almost every dot and line of his thoughts and doings in his journals which, just then, added up to thirteen fat, bound copies. 'I'm planning on not being forgotten,' he said with a wry smile. He had been working also for an incredible twenty-three years on one huge novel, *Lulu*, about a girl who destroys all the men she comes into contact with. He just couldn't seem to finish it, though parts of it might soon surface in a television series.

Just then he'd got two books out: *The New Existentialism*, dealing with such as Husserl and Wittgenstein, and *Franken-stein's Castle*, exploring his new theory which, he said, would overturn Freud. He explained this theory to me at some length – twice – but I didn't understand it at all and sat in his armchair feeling very thick indeed.

He didn't believe in God, of course, actually snorting when I asked him, as if it had been the most stupid question put to him all year. Romantics actually become their own gods, of course; they believe in the ability and power of the individual human mind to reshape society *on its own terms*.

The Moors Murders Trial Revisited

Despairing outsiders, who live in a hole in the wall, should, in truth, be blocked in that hole with three feet of reinforced concrete. They are not real people any more than Frankenstein in his castle is a real person in a real place. Their philosophies are life-denying in the sense that they refuse to confront reality and, in literature, a moment of reality is also a moment of truth. In almost everything the Romantic writes he denies the ordin-ary, valid claims of ordinary, valid people. Everything must be as bizarre and unlikely as possible.

But the serious evil of Romanticism is that, in its perverted and morbid preoccupations, it legitimises the claims of pornography. If Romanticism is in the very basement of human thought, fomenting disorder and lawlessness of every kind, then there is its natural bastard child, which dwells in the sewer: the deadly snails of naked pornography, unsullied by any philosophic ideals or pretensions to art, whose sadistic and perverted ideas, when released into the human mind, immediately feed on and distort that mind, bringing darkness where there was light, presenting horror where there was calm, destroying all values of right and wrong while creating – just as simply and surely as a carpenter fashions a chair – some of the most vicious and sadistic killers in our history.

As killers there was none more vicious and sadistic than the Moors Murderers, Ian Brady and Myra Hindley, who were charged in 1966 in Chester, England, with murdering a 17-year-old boy and two small children. The boy, it is perhaps necessary to recall, was hit by seventeen blows with an axe and strangled. The two small children were mutilated and tortured before being buried on Saddleworth Moor.

It emerged at the trial that the two killers owned fifty volumes of sado-masochistic pornography and read nothing else. Hindley, we learned, prior to meeting Brady had an impeccable background with no criminal record at all. That changed when she met Brady and, on their first date, he took her to see a film of the Nuremberg rallies.

Thereon they both systematically immersed themselves in such books as *The History of Corporal Punishment*, *The History of Torture through the Ages*, *Orgies of Torture and Brutality*, *The Pleasures of Torture Through the Ages*, *Sex Crimes and Sex Criminals*, *Sexual Anomalies and Perversions*, *Satin Heels and Stilettos*, *The Kiss of the Whip*, *Nuremberg Diary* and *Mein Kampf*.

'The flood of sadistic pornography which is making the Western world so hideous was conducive to such madness as may have been in them and is conducive to a madness of the whole of our society,' wrote Pamela Hansford Johnson in her book *On Iniquity*, an account of the trial.

Unsurprisingly, the hero of the Brady household turned out to be our old friend the Marquis de Sade. One famous passage from his *Juliette* was read out to the court:

Is murder a crime in the eyes of Nature? Doubtless we will humiliate man's pride in reducing him to the ranks of other productions of nature, but nevertheless he is merely an animal like any other, and in the eyes of Nature his death is no more important than that of a fly or an ox . . . Destruction is Nature's method of progress, and she prompts the murderer to destruction, so that his action shall be the same as plague or famine . . . in a word, murder is a horror, but a horror often necessary, never criminal and essential to tolerate in a republic.

Brady thought a lot about this passage, the court was told, and it may well have become the rationale for his killings. The jury also heard of another of de Sade's lines: 'God is a disease, a plague, a weight around a man's neck.'

Who Shot John Lennon?

The fact file is very thin on the life of Jerome David Salinger – the Greta Garbo of American letters – as Ian Hamilton found when he set out to write a biography of him, *In Search of J. D. Salinger* (Heinemann, 1988). Hamilton was thwarted almost every step of the way but, rightly or wrongly, he did manage to strip away some of the famous recluse's secrecy and sketched a life which was, well, lost almost beyond recall in the Romantic fog.

Born in 1919, J. D. Salinger was expelled from various prep schools and is supposed to have had a nervous breakdown during his war service. He was always ambitious to be a writer himself, while his own favourite writers included Kafka, Dostoevsky, Proust, Rimbaud, Coleridge and Blake. Although he had already written many well-received short stories for *The New Yorker*, he came finally into prominence in 1951 with the publication of his most famous work, *The Catcher in the Rye*, the story of Holden Caulfield, an alienated adolescent, trying to make his way 'in a world of phonies'. The book stirred immediate interest and, by 1968, it was declared one of America's twenty-five bestsellers since 1895. It still sells a quarter of a million copies a year and remains the most-banned book in America.

In 1953 Salinger settled in a cottage with ninety acres in the town of Cornish, Vermont – 'a kind of home-made house . . . no furnace, no electricity, no running water,' according to the vendors. Here he chopped his own wood and carried water from the spring. He grew his own vegetables. There was no telephone. 'He seemed to have a city boy's Romantic ideas about life in the country,' the vendors added. In Cornish he indulged his love of space, silence and secrecy, locked away behind a six-and-a-half-feet-high fence and working long hours on his typewriter.[13]

'When he's not pounding the typewriter, he's contemplating the Infinite,' said the chief editor at Hamish Hamilton, Roger Machell, who later observed that Salinger was 'perhaps the most brilliant but certainly the nuttiest author I have ever known'.

Salinger also developed a keen interest in Oriental mysticism in general and Zen Buddhism in particular. Sometimes he spoke of the twelve stages of enlightenment or would say that world travel was pointless. 'Inner travel is all that matters.' He also practised yoga and claimed that he would go into trances and meet his first wife, even though they were miles apart. They met telepathically. It is probably true – but pointless to try and quantify how true – that Salinger's personal interest in Zen did much to promote its popularity in America, particularly in the subsequent hippy flower-power movements.[14]

In 1954 the teen revolution came to America – editorialists wrote of the youthquake – and, not for the first, or last, time adolescent alienation had become a formidable commercial force. The big box-office hits in the cinema were Marlon Brando's *The Wild One*; James Dean's *Rebel Without A Cause* and Bill Hailey's *Rock Around The Clock*. '*The Catcher in the Rye* was the book every brooding adolescent had to buy,' wrote Ian Hamilton. 'It offered a college-boy version of Marlon Brando's leather jacket.' Salinger had become the guru for the young, even though this particular guru seemed not too keen on talking too much about anything at all.[15]

Critics were generally favourable towards *The Catcher in the Rye* on its publication, if not downright enthusiastic. But there were dissenting voices. George Steiner, in *The Nation* in 1959, wrote:

The young like to read about the young. Salinger writes *briefly* . . .
He demands of his readers nothing in the way of literacy or political
interest . . . Salinger flatters the very ignorance and moral shallow-
ness of his young readers. He suggests to them that formal ignorance, political apathy and a vague tristesse are positive virtues.
This is where his cunning and somewhat shoddy use of Zen comes
in. Zen is a fashion. People who lack even the rudiments of
knowledge needed to read Dante, or the nerve required by
Schopenhauer, snatch up the latest paperback on Zen.

Alfred Kazin in *Atlantic Monthly* acknowledged Salinger's gifts,
but accused him of encouraging a cosy, self-regarding pose of
alienation in his bored and affluent young readers:

Salinger's vast public, I am convinced, is based not merely on the
vast number of young people who recognise their emotional problems in his fiction and their frustrated rebellions in the sophisticated language he manipulates so skilfully. It is based even more on
the vast numbers who have been released by our society to think of
themselves as endlessly sensitive, spiritually alone, gifted, and
whose suffering lies in the narrowing of their consciousness to
themselves, in the withdrawal of their curiosity from a society
which they think they understand all too well, in the drying up of
their hope, their trust and their wonder in the great world itself.

The Times Literary Supplement took exception to the 'endless
stream of blasphemy and obscenity'. *The Catholic World* denounced the book for its 'formidably excessive use of amateur
swearing and coarse language'. William Poster wrote in *Com-
mentary*: 'The ennui, heartburn and weary revulsion of *The
Catcher in the Rye* are the inevitable actions, not of an adolescent,
however disenchanted, but of a well-paid satirist with a highly
developed technique, no point of view and no target to aim at
but himself.'

Mary McCarthy wrote of the seven faces of Salinger all
gazing into a terrifying narcissus pool. 'Salinger's world contains nothing but Salinger . . .' Ernest Jones, Freud's pupil and
biographer, wrote in *The Nation* that Salinger had merely
recorded 'what every 16-year-old Rousseau had ever felt.'[16]

The Catcher in the Rye has one of the most idiosyncratic and
arresting first sentences in modern literature: 'If you really

want to hear about it, the first thing you'll probably want to know is where I was born, and what my lousy childhood was like, and how my parents were occupied and all before they had me, all that David Copperfield kind of crap, but I don't feel like going into it.'[17]

So a nihilistic, rebellious note is struck and soon we start learning of the weight and shape of the ideas of this arch-adolescent and phoney-slayer, Holden Caulfield, as well as his movements around the previous Christmas. We learn of his brother D.B., a famous writer in Hollywood and the difficulties which led Caulfield to be expelled from his school, Pencey Prep. He is a heavy smoker who was unsettled there, deciding that it was full of crooks. One day, towards the end of term, he decides to take a train to New York where he asks the taxi-driver what happens to the ducks in Central Park when the lake is frozen over in winter. Did they just fly away or were they taken to the zoo? It is a repeated question to which he can never get a satisfactory answer. He hates most of all adults, dismissing them as phoneys. But all children are lovely, looking particularly beautiful when they are asleep. He is wedded to *the idea* of childhood.

Later, he checks in at the Edmont Hotel where, through a window, he watches a transvestite parading in his room and, in another, two people are spitting drink at one another. 'The trouble is that sort of junk is sort of fascinating to watch, even if you don't want it to be.' He hovers around the New York bars trying, but failing, to pick up women. He is dismissive of God and all religion. The disciples 'annoyed the hell' out of him and one Saturday night he drank a pint of Scotch in a chapel. Indeed, the only sign of any religious feeling at all comes when he regrets blowing cigarette smoke over a couple of nuns.

After a cruise around a jazz club in Greenwich Village – 'full of phoneys and jerks' – he goes back to the hotel where an elevator man, Maurice, finds him a prostitute. But, when she comes up, Caulfield does not want to do anything, claiming he's just had a mysterious operation. He gives her five dollars but, later, she comes back with Maurice who takes another five forcibly. In his fantasy Caulfield goes after him with a gun.

Caulfield tries to develop a relationship with a Sally Hayes and he takes her ice-skating. He suggests that they run away together and live in a log cabin. They would get married and he would chop wood in the winter. But Sally turns him down. Another night he goes to the Winter Bar where he gets drunk with an old friend who leaves him there. He is so drunk he starts acting as if he's got a bullet in his belly. 'I was the only guy in the bar with a bullet in their guts. I kept putting my hand under my jacket, on my stomach and all, to keep the blood from dripping all over the place.' Rocky's mob had got him. Later, soberish, he is in Central Park looking for those ducks and goes to see his sister, Phoebe.

'You don't like anything that's happening,' says Phoebe. 'You don't like any schools. You don't like a million things.'

He tells her he keeps picturing all these little kids playing a game in a field of rye. There are thousands of children and he is the only big one there. 'I'm standing on the edge of some crazy cliff. What I have to do, I have to catch everybody if they start to go over the cliff – I mean if they're running and don't look where they're going I have to come out from somewhere and *catch* them. That's all I'd do all day. I'd just be the catcher in the rye and all.'

Later, after an unsavoury encounter with his old teacher, he escapes back to New York where, more depressed than at any time in his life, he spends the night at Grand Central Station. He is utterly alone and decides to try and hitch-hike somewhere in America and become a petrol-pump attendant. He writes a farewell note to Phoebe which he delivers to her school. He arranges to meet her in a museum. She wants to run away with him, but he refuses. Instead, he claims that he's changed his mind and takes her to Central Park where he buys her a ticket for the carousel. He is afraid that she might fall off while fooling around on it, but says nothing. 'You . . . must not say anything . . . (to children) . . . it's bad if you say anything.' He feels a strange surge of happiness as he watches Phoebe go around and around on the carousel, finding, in the end, a form of grace in all that smiling innocence.

So we find that an eccentrically Romantic author has written an eccentrically Romantic creation. The very real artistic triumph of *The Catcher in the Rye* is its marvellous sense of artlessness. But, in total, it is a very old posture, albeit wrapped in a newish form since *The Catcher in the Rye* is nothing if not a summary of most key Romantic notions: the adolescent yearnings that reality can never satisfy; the fascination with the perverted; the fantasies of violence; the narcissistic dwelling on self and extravagant dismissal of everyone else; the impatient rejection of any ordered religious sensibility; the shuffling introversion of an alienated young man who does not like *anything* that is happening; the insistence on the innocence of all youth and the corresponding corruption of all adults.

The Catcher in the Rye is one long celebration of immaturity and, from what we do know of Salinger's life, we are also left with the uneasiest feeling that he actually approves of the ideas of his young Rousseau, though, on that point as on many others, he has always, perhaps wisely, stayed silent.

Certainly there is abundant evidence of his influence on the young and not-so-young. And there must be a hundred Holden Caulfields in as many films, of which Dustin Hoffman's *The Graduate* might be the most famous. Salinger is bound to exert an influence whether he intends to or not. T. S. Eliot again: 'An artist always exerts an influence over us whether he wants to or not and we are always influenced whether we want to be or not.'

But there was one on whom the influence of *The Catcher in the Rye* was murderous; one in whose imagination the story literally became a murder weapon and, ten years later, there are a lot of people still crying about it.

Mark David Chapman was a Southern boy from Texas who was raised near Atlanta in Georgia by a 'cold' ex-Army sergeant and a former nurse. He had an unremarkable youth and, in 1964, the Beatles had arrived in America provoking furies and riots everywhere they appeared. Two years later John Lennon started a huge storm when he said that the Beatles were more popular than Jesus. 'The disciples were thick and ordinary.' Lennon later apologised for his remarks, but he had already begun to drift away from the rest of the group, believing that he had some solo Messianic purpose; that, perhaps, *he* was the new Messiah.

By now Chapman, a podgy bespectacled youth, had a Beatle haircut and played the guitar. In his school, Columbia High, he took so many drugs he was called 'Garbage-head'. Rebellious and hostile, he ran away at the age of 15 but, at his lowest point, he began to hear the sound of another wind – the Jesus Revolution. In 1971 the charismatic Californian preacher, Arthur Blessit, who wanders the world shouldering a life-size wooden cross, brought Chapman to Christ. 'Arthur was not at all keen on drugs and told us to flush them down the john,' said Chapman. 'I had an encounter with Christ. I asked him to come into my life and he came. I read the Bible and worked in Atlanta.'[18]

After his conversion he met a girl, Judy Williams. 'He had high morals, high standards. He had his own way of feeling about things. He was a kind, *very* gentle person.' He also spoke in tongues and danced in the spirit. Chapman read *The Catcher in the Rye* for the first time at the age of 16, the same age as Holden Caulfield. He began to spend a lot of time with children at a YMCA camp. He was on a Pied Piper programme and they liked to follow him around, calling him Captain Nemo. 'He was very good with children and never spoke to them as children,' said the assistant camp director. 'He had grand passions which came and went. *The Catcher in the Rye* was one of his passions. I thought that next week he would have another.'

In 1975 he was helping Vietnamese children and gave a lot of himself, but he was becoming moody, distressed and guilt-ridden. He had his first sexual experience and announced that he was 'disappointed' with people. He had failed at college, denouncing it as a 'nest of phonies'; one of Caulfield's favourite phrases. He also broke off his engagement, perhaps imitating Caulfield's broken engagement.

In June 1977 he went to Hawaii where, when the money ran out, he tried to kill himself in his car, connecting the hose to the exhaust, only to be saved by a passing fisherman. He was taken to Castle Memorial Hospital where he was treated for 'severe neurotic depressive reaction'. But he came to see the failure of his suicide plan as a message from God so he then resolved to take hold of his life. He began working at a medical centre in Hawaii, married a Japanese travel agent in 1979, spending her money freely on his new love, collecting art. But by the next year he had become a tortured young man, sick and tired of everything, locked in endless cycles of depression. One local recalled that he would walk back and forth in front of their church, kicking pebbles and muttering threats.

He had also reread *The Catcher in the Rye* and saw Caulfield as an absolute mirror of his condition.

At that time Laurence Shames published an article about John Lennon in *Esquire*. The title was 'Lennon where are you?' It was sub-titled: 'In Search of the Beatle Who Spent Two Decades Seeking True Love and Cranial Bliss only to Discover Cows, Daytime Television and Palm Beach Real Estate.' On his own account Shames had gone out in search of a man whose appalling honesty had become the emblem and conscience of the age. But all he found was a 40-year-old millionaire, spending his time watching television, doting on his son and doing nothing. 'He had stopped making errors and stopped making music.'

Then 25, Chapman read the article and decided that Lennon was the ultimate phoney. 'The [Amsterdam Hilton] bed-ins were phoney. Everything was phoney. The man was a complete phoney.' He took to sitting in his bedroom in a lotus position chanting, 'John Lennon, I'm going to kill you, you phoney bastard.'

On October 23rd Chapman signed himself out of his work, writing the name John Lennon in the register and crossing it out many times. He bought a .38-calibre Saturday Night Special gun in downtown Honolulu and went looking for Lennon in New York. He signed into the YMCA and went to the lagoon in Central Park, asking the taxi-drivers 'where the ducks went in the winter', mirroring the behaviour and questions of Caulfield. He watched the children riding on the carousel. He found the Museum of Natural History where Caulfield had met his beloved Phoebe.

Unable to find Lennon he went back to Atlanta on November 8th. Here he had some target practice and picked up five hollow-nosed bullets that fly to pieces on impact, tearing their target to bits.

That month Lennon was actually beginning to emerge from his long isolation, bursting with new plans and preparing to launch his new record *Double Fantasy* with his wife, Yoko. They had both been in the recording studios and Lennon was giving interviews to all and sundry to promote the record. On

December 7th, a Sunday, Chapman was back in town and standing outside the Dakota building, the home of the Lennons. At the end of the morning Chapman left the Dakota and went to change hotels, signing into Room 2730 of the Sheraton Centre where he laid out his clothes and possessions before sending for a prostitute. He treated her exactly as did his literary hero, paying her twice the rate, doing nothing and sending her away. Now he had his gun and he was ready for the revenge slaying of 'Maurice', the elevator attendant that Caulfield imagines murdering. 'As soon as old Maurice opened the doors, he'd see me with the automatic in my hand and he'd start screaming at me, in this very high-pitched voice, to leave him alone. But I'd plug him anyway.' Only that was to come the next night.

The next morning he bought a new copy of *The Catcher in the Rye*. 'To Holden Caulfield from Holden Caulfield,' he wrote in it. 'This is my statement.' He planned to stay silent after the murder and let the book speak for him.

Later that day Lennon autographed an album for Chapman on his way out of the Dakota building and that night, in the recording studio, he told Jack Douglas prophetically that he knew that his days were numbered. 'I'm living on borrowed time.' By 10.50 p.m. they had come back to the Dakota and Chapman approached Lennon. 'No emotion, no anger, no nothing,' Chapman later recalled. 'There was a dead silence in my brain. He walked up and he looked at me. Then I heard in my head – do it, do it, do it. So I took out the gun and pulled the trigger five times.'

Lennon had two shots in the back, two in the shoulder and one went astray. 'John's been shot!' Yoko cried out. The alarm button was pressed. The doorman shouted at Chapman, 'You shot a man like that!'

'Don't worry,' said Chapman dropping his empty weapon like Holden Caulfield. When the police did arrive they found a youth standing in the yellow phosphorescence of the gate lantern, without a coat and reading his favourite paperback.

Chapman was to say later from Attica prison where he is now confined for life after pleading guilty:

It was all against phoniness. Anyone who had read the book would understand what I had done. Anyone who understood literature would understand that something extraordinary has happened from this extraordinary book which holds many answers. The reason I killed Lennon was to gain prominence, to promote the reading of *The Catcher in the Rye*. If you read this book you would see that I am The Catcher in the Rye of this generation.

The Many Faces of the Man of Lawlessness

So already we are beginning to see – in the broadest and darkest brush-strokes – something of the picture of our Man of Lawlessness as his evil spirit broods over and actually attacks the world. What is worth noting about him almost immediately is that we are dealing with the very shadow of shadows and a master of the darkest riddles since the extent of his deception is quite staggering.

One of his faces is clearly ugly and repellent as when he appears in the form of violent and sadistic pornography in murder trials. (It is perhaps worth noting that he has made an appearance in just about every major murder trial of this century, from the Moors Murders trial to that of the Cambridge rapist.) But he can also present a fey, humorous face – as in *The Catcher in the Rye* – even if, once you scrape away the seductive veneer, his spirit is there, active and real enough.

In the same way our Man of Lawlessness can come on as a lively and useful intellectual, anxious to promote such concepts as the realisation of 'inner selves' or the betterment of mankind, when, in reality, the raw energy behind the flow of his ideas is anti-intellectual and anti-life. He makes idealistic declarations, but his principal interest is only ever a perversion, violence and murder, no matter how he dresses it up. He also talks freely about religion, but has no feeling for – or any particular faith in – God, largely because he is rather more attracted to other more exotic religions.

It is precisely this chameleonic spirit which has meant that no one has ever been able to stop him because no one has yet ever worked out quite what he looks like. Whenever they did try and point a finger they pointed in the wrong direction. Wherever they looked they looked in the wrong place. Whenever they asked any questions they were the wrong questions.

Politicians and church leaders, in particular, have been notably unable to finger him for anything. Yes, our Man of Lawlessness has come a long, long way from that writing-desk in the Charenton asylum. Not content with controlling most of our leading writers, he has also been quietly taking over the cinema and video industries. He has also invaded virtually every corner of our television service.

But, having just claimed the life of perhaps the most famous pop singer in the world, our Romantic Assassin was clearly just warming up. Soon he was going to be rolling yet more balls of violence and terror all over the face of the land. Within months he was going to make an attempt on the life of the President of America. Within the same decade he was going to stage the biggest-ever peacetime massacre in Britain.

4

The Rambo Syndrome

In which an immature, directionless drop-out from Denver meets a violent, alienated man driving a New York taxi-cab – We travel to the steps of the Washington Hilton and learn the truth about the attempted assassination of Ronald Reagan – Examine the intellectual womb which gave birth to the most violent man in the world – And go to Hungerford where, after the biggest peacetime massacre in Britain, we find a charred video recorder.

A Taxi-driver and a Denver Drop-out

On Sunday December 14th, 1980, the world paid its final tribute to John Winston Ono Lennon. Some 100,000 people gathered in New York's Central Park where Lennon's favourite anthem, 'Give Peace a Chance', was played through the loud-speakers. There followed a ten-minute silent vigil which, at the widow's request, was to be observed all over the world. The vigil ended that chill winter afternoon with the sounds of Bach.

There was something quite raw and fatally beautiful in Lennon's music which had stirred all my generation and I still cannot listen to 'Woman' from the 'Double Fantasy' album without the saddest tears. But in that Central Park, where Caulfield and Chapman had walked before him, there was another young man who was as devastated as the rest of us; another young man central to our exposure of the Man of Lawlessness. He was John Hinckley, aged 25, from Denver, unshaven and red-eyed from bitter tears. Lennon had become an important part of his life, too. We had all grown up with Lennon and it was as if a member of our own family had been blown away by Chapman's Saturday Night Special.

Two days later, Hinckley, always a wanderer, rang up his parents telling them of his deep depression. He was in deep mourning. 'I want to come home, Mom.' When he returned to his Denver home, just before Christmas, he was listless and withdrawn, perhaps, his parents decided, suffering from the effects of an addiction to Valium. Earlier in the year he had been seeing a psychiatrist, but had run away again before anything had been accomplished. John had spent a lot of his young life on the move but, this Christmas, the family were being very considerate towards his grief, according to the account of his parents, Jack and Jo Ann Hinckley, *Breaking Points* (Hodder and Stoughton).[1]

'In the chandelier's glow I got a sudden look at John, crouched absolutely motionless over his plate, head on his chest, a portrait of despair,' said his mother of their Christmas dinner.

On New Year's Eve Hinckley sat alone in his bedroom, playing Beatle tapes on his cassette player and drinking peach brandy. He had been very insistent that his mother buy him only peach brandy that day. In the bedroom cupboard there was a gun and a black ski mask with holes for eyes. He had books on the Nazis, Ronald Reagan and Lee Harvey Oswald. There was also a pair of black pull-on boots and an Army jacket. As he sipped his peach brandy he recorded some words into his tape-recorder: 'Anything that I might do in 1981 would be solely for Jodie Foster's sake. I want to tell the world in some way that I worship her.'

But this young man's problems and destiny were not being fashioned by a book, as was the case of Mark Chapman. Hinckley was suffering from a destructive relationship with a film and, as we shall see, the mother and father of this film was also the great Romantic Perverter: none other than our Man of Lawlessness whose deadly and corrupting influence had

reached out and found himself another confused and unwitting
disciple.

John Hinckley was born in Oklahoma in 1955, but grew up in
Evergreen, 30 miles west of Denver. One of three children of
solid, respectable church-goers he had gone to junior high
school showing no special problems. He was an above-average
student, a good athlete, shy with girls, worried about his
pimples and addicted to rock music. From his early teenage
days he practised his first fumbling chords on a guitar.

In 1973 he entered Texas Tech in Dallas for a business
advisor major, but he showed no aptitude for it. He was clearly
a directionless, immature man, but not unintelligent, writing
some passable poetry and even the odd good line. Of his
high-school days he wrote: 'I stayed by myself in my apartment
and dreamed of future glory in some undefined field.'
His parents found him an attentive son, never violent and
particularly fond of their two cats which he pampered and
nursed.

In 1974 he dropped out of Texas Tech and went off to Los
Angeles to try his luck as a composer in Hollywood. After some
setbacks he wrote to his parents describing his 'success' as a
composer. Later he telephoned his parents, excitedly telling
them of his relationship with a young actress, 'Lynn Collins'.
There had been meetings in Malibu, meals in her apartment,
eating ice-cream while shopping. There were promises of recording sessions, too. Soon he was going to get $100,000 in
royalties and a mansion in Beverly Hills.

But everything went quickly and mysteriously wrong in
Hollywood and he came home in the autumn of 1976 when, to
his mother's horror, he began wearing sunglasses, a green army
fatigue jacket and a pair of black pull-on boots. His mother
thought it an outlandish get-up. He was also very particular
that he drank nothing but peach brandy. He also upset his
mother by making racialist remarks. That same winter he
asked her if she had ever seen the film *Taxi Driver*. She said no
and thought no more about it.

As the months went by his parents became more and more
worried about him, even sending him to a psychiatrist for
treatment for depression. He was suffering from an increasing

number of ills, including insomnia, swellings in his throat, pains in his arms, chest and legs. He also had this 'rocking feeling' in his head.

On March 1st, 1977, he flew back to Los Angeles to try his luck again, but within two weeks he had returned home. It was, said his mother, the cry of a child who had lost his way. But he then announced that he was going to re-enrol in college and they hoped that their child had finally grown up.

But he had not. He went back to Texas, but soon wrote saying that he was not going to continue with his course since he had revived his affair with Lynn Collins and they were both going to live together in Los Angeles. 'It is an absolute miracle from heaven that Lynn is still single and cares for me! I'm supposed to tell her to keep her eyes closed for a year in Hollywood while I diligently earn my degree a thousand miles away.'

No sooner had he gone than the affair with Lynn Collins seemed to have collapsed again and he bobbed up in New York announcing to his parents that he had written a novel which an agent was sending around the publishers. He was also starting a mail-order business and needed money for that. Finally, he wanted to join a writing seminar in Yale, but no sooner had he got there than, with all his money gone, he had headed back home again. Just what was their John up to?

Devastated by the death of John Lennon, Hinckley spent one last Christmas with his parents then on March 1st, 1981, the prodigal took off again to 'exorcise some demons'. His parents were not to see him free again.

President Ronald Reagan and his entourage were gunned down by six bullets outside the Washington Hilton on March 31st, 1981. The president was shot and a bullet passed through an aide's brain. The parents learned that the would-be assassin was their son John. They rushed to be with him and soon, largely through FBI sources, began learning the whole truth about the fantasy life of Hinckley Junior.

There had been no career as a composer. There had never been a wealthy Californian girlfriend named Lynn Collins. There had been no book agent in New York and no book. There had been no mail-order business and he had not signed into a writing seminar in Yale. Worse, six months earlier, he had been arrested in Nashville and fined sixty dollars for carrying three hand-guns while boarding a plane heading for a Jimmy Carter convention in Dayton, Ohio.

He had been to Yale though not for a writing seminar but to hang around the dormitory of Jodie Foster to whom he had kept sending letters. Just before shooting Reagan he sent her a letter which began: 'There is a definite possibility that I will be killed in my attempt to get Reagan. It is for this reason that I am writing you this letter now. As you well know I love you very much.' The letter ended with the final paragraph: 'Jodie I'm asking you to please look into your heart and give me the chance with this historical deed to gain your respect and love.' He later referred to the assassination attempt as an act of love.

But still the parents anguished about their son's motives, particularly as examining doctors had found none except that Hinckley had clearly developed an obsession for Jodie Foster. A fictitious story went around the media that he had been expelled from the Nazi party for having too-violent ideas.

One day, well into the preparation of Hinckley's defence, his mother mentioned two words to the defence lawyer, Greg Craig: peach brandy. 'I knew it!' the lawyer shouted, scattering paper in all directions as the revelation broke in his mind. 'It *had* to be peach brandy. That's what Travis Bickle drank. He became Travis Bickle. He *was* Travis.' But her John knew the difference between fiction and real life, didn't he?

Travis Bickle is the hero of *Taxi Driver*, a film directed by Martin Scorsese and written by Paul Schrader. The film starts hypnotically with shots of eyes everywhere and lone figures moving around unfriendly New York pavements. We meet Bickle, played by Robert de Niro, driving his taxi around the alien streets. He is an ex-marine and clearly a misfit, given to headaches and morbid introspection. He hates blacks and mutters racist slurs. He drags through his meaningless days on a diet of cereal topped with sugar and peach brandy. He is addicted to pornographic films and worries about his mind: 'I've got some really bad ideas inside my head.'

He sends his parents glowing accounts of the successful life he is living in his fantasies. 'I've been dating a girl for seven months,' he writes from his solitary room. 'I know you would be proud to see her.' Later he does indeed meet a girl, Betsy, a well-connected political compaign worker who appears to him like an angel. He becomes obsessed by her. 'You are the most beautiful woman that I have ever seen.' He pursues her persistently, sending her flowers and trying several times to call her.

But she rejects him after he takes her to a pornographic movie and he becomes even more hurt and dejected. But his life takes on a focus when he acquires an arsenal of guns – a hand-gun, a revolver, a Colt automatic and a .380 Walther. There is a change in his days 'which were indistinguishable from the rest'. He begins to get into shape with fifty press-ups every morning. 'Every muscle must be tight. The idea has been growing for some time – use force, all the king's men cannot put it back together again.' He also says: 'Listen, you screwheads, here's a man who would not take it any more.'

He starts stalking the presidential candidate for whom Betsy works. He wears the accessories of his new militancy – sunglasses, an olive-drab field jacket, black ankle-high pull-on boots. Now a 12-year-old prostitute called Iris, played by Jodie Foster, enters the story. She is being abused by her pimp and Travis just wants to talk to her. He wants to help and protect her. He wants to give her money to get away from her pimp.

'Now I see things clearly. I see that now. There has never been any choice for me.'

Later, fully armed, he becomes a primitive and stalks the presidential candidate, but runs away when he is spotted by the secret service. Now the film blazes into truly awesome violence when he storms the pimp's stronghold, guns blazing, blood and limbs flying everywhere as he shoots the pimp and landlord, but gets shot himself. Now Travis holds a bloodstained finger to his temple in a smiling gesture of triumph. He has sacrificed his life to save hers.

From now on this haunting and powerful film becomes magic fantasy, making very little sense. Travis recovers to become a local hero, transformed by this bloody act of violence from a nobody to an important person. Betsy is eager to be with him and he picks her up to give her a free ride in his taxi. Iris goes back to school. Pathetic failure has become a great celebrity, loved and applauded by all.

John Hinckley, it later emerged at his trial, had seen *Taxi Driver* sixteen times while in Los Angeles in 1976. 'The guns John bought were the same guns Travis bought,' the defence lawyer told the jury. 'He stalked political figures because Travis did. He shot people for the love of Jodie Foster because that's what happened in the film.'

Jodie Foster, also in evidence at the trial, confirmed that she had received the letters from Hinckley, including another note which said 'I will rescue you very soon': the same note Travis had sent Iris in *his* rescue letter. The parents also found the tape their son had recorded on New Year's Eve when, alone with his peach brandy, he said that anything he might do in 1981 would be solely for Jodie Foster's sake.

Professor Carpenter, of the Maryland School of Medicine, spent 45 hours with Hinckley, explaining process schizo-phrenia to the court and how one in a hundred Americans suffer from it. Such schizophrenics often lack conviction about their own identity, he said, and, in this terrifying predicament, snatch fragments of personality from books and films. The more Hinckley saw *Taxi Driver* the more he became like Travis Bickle, the professor continued. He wore the same clothes, ate the same junk food, bought the same guns. He probably invented Lynn Collins because Travis wrote to *his* parents about a rich and beautiful girlfriend. When *Newsweek* asked Hinckley why he bought so many guns, he replied: 'I bought so many guns because Travis bought so many. Ask him, not me.'

Like Travis, Hinckley engaged in target practice at a rifle-range. Like Travis he had gone to New York's Times Square looking for a child prostitute to save from degradation. Like Travis, Hinckley stalked presidential figures, pursuing Jimmy Carter in Washington in December 1980. He read and reread the book on which *Taxi Driver* was based. He bought the sound-track of the film and played it constantly. At a motel he signed the guest register J. Travis. 'The shock of Lennon's death compounded the chaos in his brain,' said Professor Carpenter.

Professor Carpenter believed that he was going on one last attempt to 'save' Jodie Foster when, in Washington, he saw the schedule of the president's movements the following day.

Incredibly, no one stopped him and he saw the president waving. And that hail of bullets began.

As it turned out, *Taxi Driver* was shown to the jury at the conclusion of the trial and was instrumental in Hinckley's being found not guilty by reason of insanity. But there was to be no magic fantasy end for Hinckley. He is still in a secure home where, hated and reviled by all except his parents, he has continued to declare his love for Jodie Foster and several times tried to kill himself.

But throughout this tragic story there is one overriding and all-too-real figure: the violent, alienated man living in his lonely room, given to morbidity and introspection when he is not indulging in a love of pornography and fulfilling his fantasies through violence. The film was actually based on the diaries of a would-be assassin, Arthur Bremer. This outsider is a protector of the 'innocent' who makes a revolutionary stand by arming himself and stalking a political leader. He finally commits acts of violence to make the world a better place. He is with us still: addressing us from beneath the floorboards, seeing misery and filth all around – the outsider whose fraudulent poses are so central to the Romantic fallacy.

Perhaps inevitably these ideas are reflected in the ideas of Martin Scorsese himself. 'I think most urban society is breaking down,' he said. 'The cities are getting old, things are not working, the bridges need repairing, the subway needs repairing, the plumbing needs repairing, the water pipes in the streets are breaking . . . Who's going to take care of it? What's going to happen? The complete decay of a city is a constant.'[2]

Of his film *Taxi Driver* he said:

> The whole key to the picture is that there's a difference to having a feeling and acting it out . . . Acting it out is not the way to go . . . It wasn't meant to have a reaction where the audience would say, Yeah, let's go out and kill. The idea was, if at all possible, to create an incredibly violent catharsis for the audience so they'd find themselves saying, 'Yes, do it – kill', and then afterwards thinking, 'My God, it's almost like a strange therapy session.'[3]

But Hinckley did not find it a strange therapy session. He said, Yeah, let's go out and kill. He found in the film a will to act and

had hardly begun even to guess what had got hold of him since
the Man of Lawlessness had firmly imprisoned him until he had
found his own violent escape which was so satisfyingly sweet to
the dark Romantic mind of the evil personage we are seeking to
reveal.

A Celebration of Death

The total colonisation of the modern cinema has arguably been
one of the most successful of all the Man of Lawlessness's
campaigns. There have been many brilliant films which have
said yes to life but, with him firmly in control, the cinema
industry has largely become a poisoned and poisoning hulk
whose vast and powerful outlets are leaching evil into every
corner of the world. For this cinema industry is nothing less
than the champion of exploding heads and diabolical babies; a
home for teenage werewolves and flesh-eating zombies; a place
for brains to be splattered on gravestones and mothers to be
eaten alive; the patron saint of teenage suicide, vampirism and
chainsaw massacres; the resident war counsellor of the 'crack'
wars in America; an unspeakably vile standard-bearer of evil
which is nothing more than a naked and continual celebration
of perversion, murder and death.

The word *death* figures in more film titles than any other word
in the language. The Devil appears in more film titles than
anyone else. And that is a fair mirror of the activities in which
this industry is engaged. It does not take too long to work out
that there are several distinctive tidal patterns in the modern
cinema even if they are governed by the same moon.

There are the Devil films in which he has virtually created a
public relations industry of his own from such as *The Sorrows of
Satan* (1925) to Jack Nicholson's 'Horny li'l devil' in *Witches of
Eastwick* (1987). Undoubtedly his big break-through came in
Rosemary's Baby (1968) with its big theme of Old Nick wants
your body. But his best career move came in *The Exorcist* (1973),
which became the largest grossing supernatural horror film of
all time, largely thanks to young Linda Blair's ability to scream
obscenities, vomit up green mud and masturbate with a
crucifix.[4]

Commercial success always spawns a stream of imitations in the cinema – where films are so busy feeding off one another they virtually become the same shoal of piranha fish – and *The Exorcist* was followed by *The Omen* (1976) with Adrian the Antichrist born into the New York middle classes and David Warner spectacularly beheaded by a sheet of flying glass. In *Cataclysm* (1980) Satan runs around as a nasty New York ballet critic and gives a grant to an atheist philosopher hard at work on a thesis which disproves the existence of God.

Another strong tidal pattern is that of the psycho killer, the star of so many slash and splatter films of which perhaps the most distinctive was *The Texas Chainsaw Massacre* (1974) when, in a straightforward story of unrelieved violence, a man had his head smashed in with a sledge-hammer, a girl was hung on a meat-hook and another was severed by a chainsaw. The sole surviving girl was then pursued in a nightmare chase by the chainsaw maniac until, amid much further blood and swivelling eyeballs, she escaped, with the final long shot being of the enraged maniac waving his chainsaw in the sunset. 'Never forget the sequel, best beloved.'

Other notables of this genre were *I Spit On Your Grave* (1980), which contained a rape scene lasting 45 minutes; *Targets* (1968) about an apparently normal young man who used his rifle on his wife and parents before picking off passers-by; *First Blood* (1982) about a traumatised ex-veteran who conducted a one-man war of revenge on a community who rejected him (of which a lot more later); *Death Wish* (1972) about how an upset vigilante went around bumping off muggers and *Driller Killer* (1980) in which the hero stalked the streets with a power drill and, at one stage, drilled a sleeping wino's forehead while riding the kicking corpse as if it were a bucking bronco.

From this we see how *Taxi Driver* is almost a compendium of psycho themes, according to Kim Newman in *Nightmare Movies* (Bloomsbury 1984). 'Travis Bickle is at once the unhealthy gun fanatic of *Targets*, the insane Vietnam veteran of *First Blood*, the unhinged city dweller of *The Driller Killer* and the maddened vigilante of *Death Wish*. He's also the rejected suitor of a princess and damn nearly a Lee Harvey Oswald type assassin until he finally emerges as an urban hero.'

But, of course, we also see in this example how films feed on –

and other films feed off – one another until in the end, they are all suffering from much the same virus and are hence much the same. Scorsese said that he had spent his formative years in the cinema and described himself as a cine-literate.

In 1988 film producers gathered for an international trade fair in Milan, MIFED, to sell their produce to cinema and video distributors. They also advertised in *Variety* to the extent of some 1,000 films. All but a handful had titles such as these: *Maniac Cop, Lethal Pursuit, Messenger of Death, Death Wish 4, Rage to Kill, Burning Vengeance, Born to Kill, Deadly Prey, Mankiller, I Was a Teenage Zombie, Doom Asylum, Shallow Grave, Edge of the Axe, Murder Lust, The Survivalist, Outlaw Force, Killer Instinct* and *Slaughterhouse Rock*.

As a majority art the cinema – as much and perhaps more than any other medium – supplies society with ideas and, in one film alone, there will be a mass of ideas, either spoken or buried in images, which are bound in some way to be influential on someone. But the kind of mind – the philosophy, if you will – that provides the sort of films on sale in Milan and peddles them through the corrupt and rotten end of the video industry is a mind which is obsessed by murder, perversion and 'forbidden' sado-eroticism. It is possessed by a sense of chaos lurking under the physical reality of things, which given the opportunity, it might be able to put right.

In its emphasis on the primacy of the imagination; in its celebration of sadism; in its rejection of the ordered claims of a religious sensibility and its insistence on the sick and the ugly; in its inversion of all normal values and inability to tell right from wrong; in its persistent pursuit of the bizarre, shocking and violent; in its key concepts of terror, vengeance and death this mind is nothing if it is not Romantic.

It is in this Romantic cul-de-sac which the British film industry, with some outstanding exceptions, has found itself irredeemably stuck, almost ever since it began making the Hammer horror films back in the 1950s. The industry then produced a string of mad oddities like *The Abominable Dr Phibes* (1972), in which a vengeance-crazed organist disposed of his enemies in accordance with the ten plagues of Egypt; *House of Whipcord* (1974), a sadistic bit of nonsense about a mad judge called Old Bailey, who kidnaps and tortures minor offenders because he thought the courts let them off too lightly; *Frightmare* (1974) about a cannibal old lady who makes a nasty use of her power drill; *House of Mortal Sin* (1975), in which a homicidal priest poisons one parishioner and beats another to death with a censer; Ken Russell's ludicrous *Gothic* (1986) and *Hellraiser* (1987) which featured such as sewn-shut eyelids, a throat wound held open by a surgical clamp and geometric traceries of pins hammered into a face.[5]

Almost all the other British films feature persistent and squalid preoccupations with the violence of East End gangsters . . . *Mona Lisa* (1986), *Buster* (1988); and a planned feature on the Krays. But we have also some arty film-makers whose works are almost parodies of the evil which is the subject of this enquiry.

Jubilee (1977), by Derek Jarman, is a tour of post-breakdown London and includes scenes of pram-burning and barbed-wire tightrope walking; a man eating a cockroach; Adolf Hitler alive and well in Devon and Toyah Wilcox castrating a man from the Special Branch. His *Sebastiane* (1975) is a religious epic with Latin dialogue and homosexual sex. And there is his *The Last of England* (1987) which, with no discernible story, variously shows such images as a man lying in a puddle and appearing to be masturbating on to a picture of the Mona Lisa. A young man is buggered by an SAS soldier on a Union Jack – or it might be the other way around. Here – or thereabouts – our 'story' ends.[6]

But these little people, with their determinedly little films, are but the dregs and drips of the tributaries of the main river the source of which we want to explore just now. No serious person would argue that the works of Derek Jarman constitute much of a threat to anyone – except perhaps to a few nutty art students – but there are much bigger and more dangerous fish in this river; multimillion-pound films which are as fantastically successful as they are influential. And many of them spring from one key Romantic concept which we have not yet introduced: the Nietzschean superman.

The Fabulous Narcissist

Of all the key Romantic thinkers we have so far considered, Friedrich Nietzsche was perhaps the most complete and committed outsider of them all. He has influenced most German novelists, poets and philosophers, taking a place in the German pantheon of philosophy next to Hegel and Kant. His clarion call that 'God is dead' has echoed down through to our own times while, throughout his work, he sculptured the role of the individual on a giant scale. For him God was dead precisely because *he* was God. In his mind narcissism reached truly fabulous proportions. It does not take a great leap of the imagination to understand Nazism when you have first understood the writings of Nietzsche.

He was born in Saxony in 1844, reading a great deal in his youth, writing poetry and his autobiography at the age of 13. Later, at school, he began dramatising himself as a Romantic hero. He had picked up the concept that every man was a potential genius and he began questioning his youthful Christianity. By the age of 28 he was standing alone against the world, dogmatically self-assertive, dismissing all Western philosophers – even the supremely rational Kant – as 'fools, prisoners, cheapeners of life'.[7]

We can find the beginning of this anti-rationality in his first book, *The Birth of Tragedy*, in which he argued that tragedy was born of a fusion of literature and art but was being killed by rationalism. He outlined his own ideas on the birth and death of Greek tragedy, talking of the rebirth of tragedy in his friend Richard Wagner's music. In tragedy one could face up to the horrors of existence and affirm life. Towards the end of the book he canvassed the possibility of an artistic Socrates; a philosopher with a passion for poetry and music as well as an intellectual conscience. This metaphor of the superman was to become an exact and illuminating image of the way he conceived his own spirit.

He became an academic but resigned from university in 1879, pleading poor health. Perhaps his most important book was *Thus Spake Zarathustra*, a rhapsodic and aphoristic attempt to present his whole philosophy. The times judged it most daring in form as well as in its ideas about morals and psychology. Throughout it the faith and morals of Western man were subject to merciless questioning. Always the posture was that of moral horror; Nietzsche was alienated from the whole of this man.

His key ideas were based on the concept of Pure Will, untrammelled by the demands of reason. There was also the

Will to Power: 'The strongest and highest will to life does not lie in the puny struggle to exist, but in the Will to War, the Will to Power . . .'

In *Thus Spake Zarathustra* he refined these concepts, giving them life and form, coming up with the superman – super-prophet, super-hero, super-warrior – who would freely exercise the demands of his own will and only develop the greatness in himself. So Zarathustra, a preacher of extremes, extolled people to be either saints or sinners: to do anything at all except be mediocre.

'Where is the lightning to lick you with its tongues? Where is the frenzy with which you must be infected?

'Behold, I teach you the Superman; he is the lightning, he is this frenzy . . .'

So the superman stood alone; the perfect and greatest embodiment of the individual whose lightning, whose frenzy were going to reshape the world by whatever means available. He was the only healthy man in a sick universe who, if necessary, would die alone.

'My Will clings to man; with chains I bind myself to man, because I am drawn upwards towards the Superman; thither tends my other Will.'

The trouble was that Nietzsche, the only healthy man in a sick universe, was already suffering quite badly from tertiary syphilis and had become silly putty for the last eleven years of his life. The chapters of his last book had titles such as 'Why I Am So Clever' and 'Why I Write Such Excellent Books'. He signed his letters Caesar and The King of Naples until he finally died in Weimar on August 25th, 1900. But his superman did not die with him.

The Spaghetti Superman

If we were looking for a precise date for the emergence of the Nietzschean superman on our cinema screens, we could do no worse than pick on 1962 when Ursula Andress wandered out of the Caribbean and into the arms of Sean Connery when, in *Dr No*, the whole improbable fantasy of James Bond began.

In a phenomenally successful series which the producers were to describe as 'sex and sadism for the *whole* family' (my italics) we then began following the fortunes of this snobby, invincible public-school hero as he killed people and blew smoke off his gun, casually and callously seduced beautiful women, wandered through society with 'a licence to kill', responsible only to M and his desires. When not bedding women or drinking vodka martinis, 'shaken not stirred', this superstud assassin was destroying another of Blofeld's hi-tech armies or blowing up SPECTRE's headquarters. 'He moves with a tensile grace that excitingly suggests the violence bottled in Bond,' dribbled *Time* magazine.

The films were blatant and overblown daydreams, reflecting the new affluence of the times in which, in the fast-moving excitement, all sense of right and wrong were diffused. Sex and violence were deployed purely for cinematic effect; he murdered for no other reason than that it looked good. Women were introduced into the story only as decorative sex objects; they were just there as units of pleasure. When Bond made love or war he always had a full-scale orchestra blazing away at his elbow.

This Bond superman became the first of the Anglo-American heroes, changing the whole idea of the English hero. He presided over the eclipse of the gentlemanly ethic, including the ideals of service and courtesy to women. He was to herald a whole new movement in the cinema, which was increasingly to glorify cold-blooded killing, vicious and thoughtless, the only aim of which was self-gratification.

But there was a sense in which the whole Bond canon slightly redeemed itself by its audacity and wit. Bond was always parodic, uncomplicated and flamboyantly heroic. But, in other hands, this notion of a wise-cracking superman was soon to change.

America's greatest and most enduring contribution to the cinema and the world was the Western in which, in the 'forties and 'fifties, we always found fixed-value systems. They were almost always morality tales involving a clear-cut struggle between good and evil. The end always came with the good guys in white hats pumping a few richly-deserved bullets into the bad guys with black hats.

Directors like John Ford, who made *My Darling Clementine*,

Wagon Master and *Rio Grande* spoke of old-fashioned values; of how it was good for a country to have heroes to look up to. Virtually free of any sort of sexuality, the emphasis was always on the primacy of the family, the importance of chivalry and virtue and the maintenance of law 'n' order.

But around the time of the emergence of James Bond all this was to change and we began to witness the spiralling growth of violence on our screens, the gleeful degradation of women and the promotion of a new kind of manhood, the psychopathic outsider who stands outside society and spits on its rules; the lawless superman riding the range with a gun in his hand and murder in his heart. Yes, 'them days is over' and the Western was consigned to an honourable grave.

If we were to button one single film for this premature burial we might try *Bonnie and Clyde*, the story of two perverted Robin Hood killers – 'They're young, they're in love and they kill people' – which, in the year Martin Luther King was assassinated, won an Oscar. These perpetual adolescents with no family and recognising no authority raced around killing people for money, running and running until they died. Where cowboys rode horses these two were always in cars and so the Western turned into the modern gangster film.

Bonnie and Clyde launched a whole new wave of films including *Butch Cassidy and the Sundance Kid* and *Easy Rider* in which America and its values were also seen from the outlaw's point of view and therefore rejected. Sam Peckinpah's *The Wild Bunch* was released at this time with its degradation of women and slow-motion ballets of orgiastic violence. Peckinpah was to blood capsules what Hitchcock was to suspense and, in defence of his work, he came up with the hairy old line that it was necessary to show violence in order to condemn it, a line with which directors persist to this day. This argument was given a novel twist in the film *Videodrome*, in which an announcer justified the hard-core pornography on the screen by saying that it was 'better on television than on the streets'.

But, perhaps more significantly, Sergio Leone made his *Dollars* trilogy of Italian Westerns in the mid-sixties and in them a relatively unknown actor, Clint Eastwood, started his rise to become a key icon in American culture. In these films he was a lone bounty hunter with no name, cigar in mouth and perpetually squinting into the sunlight. Everyone was blown away in great bursts of operatic violence and this creation of the invincible superman became its most studied in *High Plains Drifter* (1972).[8]

In this film Eastwood is the stranger – the dirty, unkempt, cigar-chewing man with no name – who rides in from the dusty plains to a small mining town. He kills three men for no apparent reason before casually raping two cheeky females. The suggestion is that they were so mouthy they probably deserved it. He is then deputed to protect the town from an approaching gang so he appoints a dwarf as the sheriff, casually dynamites the hotel and arranges for the whole town to be painted red and renamed Hell. When the gang does show up he allows them to fire and slaughter everyone before he puts paid to them. There is barely any talk and he shows no emotion or motive for his savage killings. With the whole town but a smouldering rubble he rides off over the plains again.

Everyone in the film, apart from the dwarf, is seen as contemptible. The rapes are seen as a way of reducing women to their true roles as the sex objects of the superman. The caped avenger is photographed from low angles to make him seem powerful and indestructible. This is the lawless Superman come with his deadly gun to sort out the world, the unsmiling outsider responsible only to his destructive instincts and desires.

The Spaghetti Westerns were followed by Eastwood's remarkably influential *Dirty Harry* (1971) in which we meet the lone Inspector Callahan, scripting solo dreams of power and revenge, particularly on street punks: 'Being this is a .44 Magnum, the most powerful handgun in the world, which could blow your head clean off – you've got to ask yourself one question: "Do I feel lucky?" Well, *do you, punk?*'

Michael Winner's brutal and unlovely *Death Wish* series started in 1976 in which Charles Bronson as yet another vigilante hunts and kills muggers in revenge for the murder of his wife. The same year produced *Taxi Driver*.

All these vigilante films produced hundreds of imitations; all came dealing sudden death and violence in order to make the world a better place to live in . . . *Robo-Cop*, *Predator*, *Die Hard*, *Dressed to Kill*, *Scarface*, *Dillinger* . . . everywhere these mighty

figures were wandering through our dreams and waking fantasies. We dressed and swaggered like them and, soon, there
were a few of us who were going to kill like them.

Arthur Penn, the dirctor of *Bonnie and Clyde*, said: 'We have a
violent society. It's not Greece, it's not Athens, it's not the
Renaissance – it's the American society and I would personify it
by saying that it's a violent one. So why not make films about
it?'[9] It was a very rare film that broke any new ground so, within
this Romantic cocoon of mirrored distortions and false
emphasis, the Man of Lawlessness finally begat one of his most
perfect creations: Rambo, 'the most violent man in the world'.

The Dragon's Teeth of Violence

The character of John Rambo first appeared from the pen of
David Morrell, an Iowa English professor, in his novel *First
Blood* in 1972. In it we meet Rambo, an ex-Vietnam veteran,
former Green Beret and winner of the Congressional Medal of
Honour. He first appears as a lone drifter wandering the back
roads of small-town America. In a small town he is moved on by
the sheriff. But he wants to eat and refuses to get on his way, so
the sheriff throws him into gaol. After a violent fight he breaks
out and is chased into the mountains where he is able to survive
since he is an expert in forest survival following his military
training. People die and are badly injured pursuing him.
Finally, fully armed, Rambo returns to the town where he
extracts the bloodiest revenge before he is shot just when he was
on the point of killing himself.

First Blood was turned into a film of the same name, directed
by Ted Kotcheff and starring Sylvester Stallone. The main
difference between the film and the book was that in the film
Rambo lives at the end and is consequently free to make the
equally successful sequel, *First Blood Part II*, which was sub-
titled: *The most violent man in the world is unleashed*. In this Rambo is
released from his American prison to penetrate the jungles of
Vietnam and to bring back the missing Americans who have
been tortured there. Again fully armed, he does so and kills
literally hundreds of Vietnamese.[10]

In *Rambo III* we find John Rambo in a Buddhist monastery in
Thailand where he has gone to find 'inner peace'. They want

him to go into Afghanistan to verify evidence of Russian atrocities and while at first he refuses he finally agrees when he learns that Colonel Trautman, his former commanding officer in Vietnam, has been captured by Russians and is imprisoned there. So, again armed with his knife and a compound high-tech bow, he goes into that country with a team of Afghans, destroys many Soviet gunships, tanks, armoured carriers and more than a hundred men, attacks a fort, destroys it and finally rescues Colonel Trautman. The film contains 245 acts of violence in 109 minutes.

From these barest of details we can see from the first episode that we have begun with a disappointed and friendless outsider, wandering the roads of America. Alienated from the start, he is progressively driven farther and farther to the edge until he has become a lawless superman given to extreme violence, fighting off all attempts to imprison him. As he moves into the mountains he becomes the Noble Savage, skilled in primitive warfare and forest survival.

In the second episode he is even more superhuman and the combined might of the Vietnamese army fails to make even a dent in him. He literally fashions his own destiny with relentless and savage acts of continual violence. Even his dress and appearance are primitive in the extreme, with exaggerated muscles and a lot of animal-like grunting. Rambo is never very big on talking; his very name has become a new byword for inarticulate violence.

In the third episode this huge fantasy of violence and destruction becomes even greater as he tears the Soviet army apart almost single-handedly. We also discover that he is half-Italian and half-Navajo, but had studied the Buddhist religion of a Montagnard guide who nursed him after he had been ambushed in North Vietnam. When he is not actually killing anyone he is meditating on nirvana and such. Well, such a positively Romantic creation could hardly be a normal Christian could he? That wouldn't fit into the Romantic loom at all.

This Rambo series has generated a billion dollars for its creators and it made Sylvester Stallone the second highest earner in America in 1988. He is due to receive $25 million from *Rambo 4*. There have been Rambo toys, Rambo survival kits, Rambo school bags, Rambo computer games, models of 'enemies' of Rambo, Rambo comics, Rambo diaries and Rambo knives. There have also been Rambo dues.

In July 1984 James Huberty, aged 41, walked into the Mc-Donald's in San Ysidro, Southern California, wearing a Rambo kit of black T-shirt and camouflage gear and proceeded to shoot dead twenty people and wound twenty more. Huberty himself was an outsider, growing up in the Amish religion, but not among the Amish people. He was difficult and highly-strung as a child, graduating fifty-first of seventy-seven at school.

For amusement he went shooting at groundhogs and inanimate targets. Later this developed into an obsession with martial arts, self-defence and weaponry. He married and had two daughters, but home life was stormy. Seven months before the massacre he lost his job as a welder in Ohio and moved to California. There he lost another job as a condominium guard.

The day he was sacked he took his family to the zoo, lunched at a different McDonald's, then went home, put on his Rambo kit and walked into the McDonald's in San Ysidro with a semi-automatic rifle, a shotgun and a hand-gun. When he was killed by a police marksman he still had a bag full of armour-piercing bullets.

In August 1987 Julian Knight, a 19-year-old from Melbourne, Australia, crouched beside the road in his suburban neighbourhood, picking off pedestrians and motorists as they passed by. Six people were killed and eighteen injured before he ran out of ammunition and was arrested, dressed in full military gear and armed with a pump-action shotgun and two semi-automatic rifles.

Knight's life was similarly characterised by failure. He was a drop-out from the Australian equivalent of Sandhurst, the Royal Military College at Duntroon, where his army officer father had been trained. Before he left he underwent basic special-weapons training. At school Knight's nickname was 'Sof' for soldier of fortune because he always wore army fatigues. Slightly built, he was always teased as a wimp.

Another dragon's tooth of violence sprang out of the ground on January 17th, 1989, in Stockton, California. Here James Purdy, aged 26, attacked Cleveland Elementary School while wearing a bullet-proof flak jacket, a bandolier of ammunition, a camouflage vest and earplugs. He was carrying two hand-guns and used a Russian AK 47 semi-automatic Kalashnikov complete with a banana clip of ammunition and a bayonet attached to it.

First he set fire to his car by shooting at three cans of petrol in it then he went into the school playground – where 70 per cent of the children were Vietnamese – killed five pupils and wounded a further thirty others before shooting himself in the head with his own hand-gun.

In his hotel room the police later found miniature plastic military figures and models of military vehicles. There was also a broken .22-calibre rifle, a small quantity of ammunition and a selection of camouflage-type clothing. Further police enquiries revealed that he was a drifter with a history of crimes dating back to 1980 in California, including a 1983 arrest and conviction in Los Angeles for the 'possession, manufacture or sale of dangerous weapons'. He was placed on probation. He was also convicted of being an accessory to a robbery in Woodland, California, in 1984, and was arrested in Los Angeles for soliciting sex, cultivation of marijuana and the possession of stolen property. His attack on the school was the fifth time in three years that a gunman had attacked children in US schools.[11]

So could any of these killings have anything to do with the Rambo films?

Well yes, said Dr David Hill, a clinical psychologist with Mind, the mental health charity. It must be more than a coincidence that the men dressed exactly like Rambo and carried his kind of weapons. There was a copy-cat element in the link. The films give people the props and methods for their outrages.

Well, no, say the creators. Sylvester Stallone is particularly miffed at any suggestion that these films might lead to real-life violence. Rambo does not exist, he insists. He's only a mythical comic-book character. This is just *movies*. They do not have a bad influence on people. They are made to entertain.

It is so unfair when Rambo gets blamed for every lunatic who lets loose with a gun. It is the height of irresponsibility to link Rambo with real-life maniacs. If Rambo was a real person he could have a field-day in court suing for libel. He has never gone on an unprovoked rampage against innocent citizens and he has never been shown to be mentally deranged. Sure he is isolated and depressed, but he is *not* psychotic. He is just an angry war veteran. Nothing more. There has never been any proven link between my films and these acts of violence.[12]

The Hungerford Massacre

In August 1987 the town of Hungerford was the scene of Britain's worst-ever peacetime massacre when Michael Ryan, aged 26, used a variety of weaponry to kill fifteen people and injure a further fifteen. The official inquest found no motive for Ryan's actions but, within the context of *First Blood*, there is a very clear motive. I want to show that there is a link between the film and that terrible massacre. But, first, it is necessary to explain, in some detail, what the film is all about.

First Blood opens with shots of John Rambo wandering the roads of small-town America. He is an unkempt loner with a thin beard and a sleeping-bag over his shoulder. He wears jeans turned up high, high-laced army boots and a khaki combat-jacket emblazoned with US insignia. He soon discovers that his only friend has recently died of cancer which he had brought back 'from that orange stuff in 'Nam'. Arriving at the small hick town of Hope in the middle of nowhere, he is moved on by the sheriff. Rambo is a former Green Beret with many decorations, who has done nothing, but gets locked up anyway.

During a search the sheriff finds a hunting-knife in Rambo's trousers. This knife is a key symbol in the film since, as we learn later, it contains aids for hunting and forest survival, including waterproof matches, a compass and a needle and thread for stitching wounds. Its long blade is also razor sharp with a serrated edge on the other side.

Rambo is besieged by memories of being tortured in Vietnam and, after being abused in the police-station cells, he breaks out after a violent fight with the police, one of whom is thrown through a window. He manages to retrieve his knife, pulls

someone off a motor-bike and heads for the safety and solitude
of the forest. There, alone, he can become strong and survive
since he knows all about forest survival.

He is pursued by a police gunman in a helicopter and
Doberman dogs. He acquires a length of twine and cuts up
some sacking for clothing. At one stage, trapped on top of a cliff,
he bays like a wounded animal. He manages to kill the gunman
in the helicopter by throwing a rock at it, making the gunman
fall out. Covered by leaves and with his face camouflaged with
mud he manages to stab one of his pursuers in the leg. He jumps
another from a tree. Another is shot by mistake. Another is
caught by a mantrap fashioned from small staves. Another is
tied to a tree.

This man is an expert in guerrilla warfare. He is trained to
live off the land. 'He will eat things that'll make a billy-goat
puke.' He kills a deer with a stave fashioned with his knife.
'You're in a war you can't win,' he warns his pursuers. 'Don't
push me or I'll give you a war you won't believe. Let it go. All I
wanted was something to eat. They drew first blood.'

The police and rookie state troopers close in on Rambo, but
he continues to wreak mayhem. Colonel Trautman turns up to
give advice. He warns them: 'Get in a good supply of body
bags.' Rambo shoots everyone, but exempts a child in his
bloody rampage.

Rambo disappears down a mineshaft where, underground,
he manages to light a torch to find his way through the water.
He is attacked by rats, but finally manages to escape when he
finds an airshaft. On the road he jumps a lorry and manages to
capture an MI6 carbine. He is pursued by a police-car which
collides with another and bursts into a ball of flame.

He is now wearing a black bandana with a bandolier of
ammunition slung around his shoulder. In his hijacked lorry he
manages to burst through a roadblock and begins his revenge
attack, according to one policeman, by setting fire to the 'petrol
station on the other side of town'. There are huge explosions of
flames. Everywhere the petrol tanks of cars are bursting into
flames.

Finally he lets off volley after volley of his MI6 carbine, going
into a shop and scattering gunpowder all over the floor before
firing it with his gun. Then, towards the end, he goes on to a roof

and fires at everything in sight. He shoots up the police-station and the policeman who had upset him at the beginning of the film. In the final scenes his pursuers and the helicopters close in on him. Alone with Colonel Trautman, he makes a long speech of whining self-pity. 'Where is everybody? Who are my friends? Back here there's nothing.' He is taken away to the lock-up.

We have now, following the Hungerford inquest, been able to build up a fairly clear picture of the kind of man that Michael Ryan was. He was a muscular six-footer with a thin growth of designer stubble, who lived in a small back street of Hungerford with his doting mother, Dorothy, and black Labrador dog. He had been a bitter disappointment to his father, who had died of cancer and, without any real friends, he spent his time in a world of fantasy. He often talked of his friend, 'a rich colonel', who was going to supply him with a string of exotic cars. He boasted about how he was going to visit the 95-year-old Colonel's tea plantation in India, even hinting that his elderly friend was going to pay for his flying lessons.

Police investigations discovered that there were no cars, no visits to India and no colonel.

He also fantasised about a military past, telling local children that he was a Red Beret paratrooper. A combat-jacket was always placed visibly in the back of his car, to remind everyone that he was a tough guy. He often carried a gun in his belt.

Another of his fantasies was that he was married to an Irish girl and had a furnished cottage and a child. But the marriage had not worked out 'because his wife had failed to buy a birthday present for his mother'. He had also said that he had found his wife in bed with an elderly uncle of his. He later spoke, falsely, of his engagement to another girl. At times his mother entered into Ryan's fantasies, speaking of Ryan's engagements and the grand plans that he had. She once said that her son had paid for her to take a trip to Venice on the Orient Express – but she had to cancel it because she could not afford to take time off work.

A post-mortem examination of Ryan's liver showed fatty changes 'consistent with – but not diagnostic of – a period of alcohol abuse.' He also worried about his health, going to a doctor sixteen times for a series of minor ailments brought on by stress. One of these visits was because he was worried about his thinning hair.

Isolated from the world of his neighbours, he often spoke to the local children about video and television films. One child recalled to me, when I went to investigate the aftermath of the massacre, that he had been talking about *The Godfather*, which had been shown on television just prior to the day of the massacre. Doubt has often been expressed about whether he owned a video. But he did. Two days after the massacre, in the presence of another writer, Robert Peart, I found the recorder in the charred ruins of his home.[13]

But, if we now go back to the actual events on August 19th, 1987, we find that Ryan began his murderous rampage one morning in the 4,500-acre isolation of Savernake Forest just outside Hungerford. It is a tangle of pine, beech and oak, criss-crossed by a network of unmarked lanes.

On that morning he had driven there in his Vauxhall Astra car, wearing summer clothes – a white shirt and light-blue trousers. In the boot was a complete forest survival kit which included a waterproof jacket, shoulder-holster, rucksack, Balaclava mask, drinking flask, respirator mask, waterproof trousers, kit-bag, NATO poncho adaptable as a groundsheet, pouch with first-aid kit and underpants, ear mufflers and battledress trousers.

Just near where Mrs Susan Godfrey and her two children were having a picnic, there was, Mr Peart and I found, two days later, a crudely-made hut of branches, surrounding a tree, invisible from the road. Whether or not it had anything to do with Ryan we do not know, but we do know that, just as Mrs Godfrey was clearing up the picnic, Ryan shot her sixteen times, but spared the two children, aged 2 and 4, leaving them to walk hand in hand for help.

After Ryan drove out of the woods, he called at the Golden Arrow filling station at Froxfield on the main road to Hungerford. First, he filled a gallon tank of petrol then put £15-worth in his tank. The Asian cashier, Mrs Kakaub Dean, noticed that, as always, he used pump number two. He was a regular customer, calling every two days. Ryan then fumbled in the boot of his car 'for ages', said the cashier, straightened and faced her through a partition of reinforced glass, firing one shot which went straight through. He then walked into the service station and fired a further burst at her until his gun jammed. The cashier was on the floor, pleading for her life. While we talked, Mr Peart noted that the video *First Blood* was on the shelves among an array of other violent and soft-porn videos, including *The Terminator* and *Daughter of Emmanuelle*.

Mrs Dean told me that she had no record of whether Ryan had been a member of their video club. However, within half an hour of our questioning, all violent films had been cleared from the shelves, as a photographer, Judah Passow – whom we asked to go and get a picture of them – later reported.

As Ryan headed for the town of his birth, Mrs Godfrey's children had been found. Then came the 999 call from the besieged garage. A rural police force, more used to dealing with Saturday-night drunks, was about to launch a huge manhunt.

Ryan went to his house in South View and went upstairs to change. In his bedroom he put on a bandolier of ammunition, a black bandana and a combat-jacket complete with a US insignia emblazoned on it, neither of which he had ever worn in public before, according to one of the local children. He did often wear a bandana and he was known locally as Rambo, but these were clearly special clothes for a special day and he was about to start a savage massacre.

He killed his mother with four shots from his Kalashnikov, two from a distance in front of her and as she fell face down two shots were fired into her back from a distance of less than four inches. He also killed his black Labrador. He then scattered the petrol that he had bought at Froxfield over the floor of his living-room and fired it by blasting the television set, setting the whole house ablaze. Next he pumped ten bullets into the petrol-tank of his Vauxhall Astra, clearly trying – but failing – to set it ablaze.

Then he went down the line of small terraced houses in South View, pumping bullet after bullet towards his neighbours' television sets, according to one witness. The bullets punched out holes the size of fists in the brickwork around the windows.

He next strode out on to the common, unleashing round after round. Another witness said he jogged back down South View as if he were a policeman or a guard. Lisa Mildenhall, aged 14, heard a cracking sound 'like a capgun'.

> I could see that he was carrying a great big rifle under his arm as if he was going to fire it. I stopped by the front door and the man stopped jogging as well. He was in the centre of our drive. I immediately recognised him as Michael Ryan. I looked straight at his face and he smiled at me. He fixed his eyes on mine then he crouched down and aimed the rifle at me. I just froze by the door. He fired the gun.

Lisa survived the four shots, but others were not so lucky. He killed a total of fifteen people, injuring a further fifteen. He had let loose a total of 119 shots, according to a ballistics expert. Eighty-four were fired from the Kalashnikov and all but one of the remainder from the Beretta. One shot was fired at a building from a 30-calibre MI semi-automatic carbine.

Finally he made for his old school, crouching with gun in hand combat-style, being shadowed by a police helicopter. In the distance were his beloved woods. The police closed in and surrounded the school. He went to the top classroom, tied a white handkerchief to the end of the barrel of his Kalashnikov before throwing it out of the window. He repeatedly asked Sergeant Brightwell, who was outside trying to communicate with him, what had happened to his mother. 'I didn't mean to kill her, it was a mistake,' he shouted. 'I wish I'd stayed in bed.' He also asked the sergeant to give his dog a decent burial.

Minutes later there was a muffled shot from the school and Ryan died of his own hand from a single shot of a Beretta tied to his wrist.

The inquest jury returned a verdict of unlawful killing on each of the fifteen people. Ryan's motives remained a mystery. The police said they were no further forward and the reasons may never be known.

The gravamen of my charge is that there are many parallels between the Ryan and Hinckley cases, albeit with different individuals working out a different relationship with two different films. They were both similar types of men, loners and given to fantasy, who in the absence of any real sense of their own identities forged a new one by absorbing the content of a favourite film. They even created friends out of their chosen films. Ryan conjured up a fantasy of a rich colonel, just as there was a colonel who was the chief supporting character in *First Blood*. Hinckley claimed to his parents that characters in *Taxi Driver* were his real friends – the wealthy 'Lynn', otherwise the rich campaign worker, was his 'real' friend.

The Hungerford inquest found no motive for the massacre, but how different might its verdict have been if, similarly to the case of Hinckley's trial, the jury had been shown *First Blood*?

Ryan's actions become fully explicable in the context of the film and the main points of contact are:

★ Forest survival techniques: both Ryan and Rambo were experts in forest survival. Had Ryan made it to Savernake forest there is no telling how long he might have survived there. Certainly his elaborate survival equipment suggests he had long been preparing for this. Significantly he began his murderous rampage in a forest and throughout the massacre there were clear echoes of the imagery of the film.

★ The dress: just like Hinckley, Ryan liked to walk around in military gear. Ryan had been photographed wearing an army camouflage hat. On the day I found the video-recorder in the ashes of his home there was also a Second World War helmet. Both wore thin beards. Both wore the same jackets. There is some dispute about the bandana, but the teenager I spoke to seemed to be a reliable witness.

★ The weaponry: as in the Hinckley case both used the same weaponry – both had similar carbines, though Ryan clearly found his Chinese-made Kalashnikov better equipped for his murderous purposes. Both had bandoliers of ammunition slung over their shoulders.

★ The attacks: Ryan attacked a petrol station just as Rambo had in the film. (It is a small detail, but one of the policemen in the film said that Rambo began his attack on 'a petrol station on the other side of town' – for Ryan, Froxfield was a small petrol station on the other side of town.) Both Rambo and Ryan spared children. Again and again, Ryan was going for petrol tanks of cars, clearly hoping to explode them into balls of fire. (Explosions of fired petrol are the favourite images in Rambo films.) Ryan launched a ferocious attack on his own car and the police later concluded that he was just trying to set it alight. Ryan fired his own home in a similar way to the one used by Rambo to fire the shop. (We may also note that Purdy attacked his own car in the same way before attacking the children in the school in Stockton. We might also note that Purdy supplied a savage new twist to these imitative murders since he slaughtered Vietnamese indiscriminately as Rambo had done in *First Blood, Part Two*.)

★ The motives: Rambo's attack was revenge against the hick town which had rejected him. Ryan had no real friends in Hungerford, often going round the town armed, warning people of dire consequences if they tried to tease him. He, too, felt rejected. Both believed that the world had given them a bad deal; both were collectors of 'injustice'.

★ Even the final scenes are bizarrely similar, both near the roof, both surrounded by police, both shadowed by helicopters. But, in the book, which Ryan is likely to have read, Rambo was on the point of blowing himself up when he was shot in the head. Ryan died at his own hand. In the film Rambo was led away to make his creators many millions of dollars with sequels.

(Kirk Douglas was, at one time, going to take the part of Colonel Trautman in the film *First Blood*, but he disagreed with Stallone about how the film should end. 'Merely, I thought it would be better, dramatically, if my character realises what a Frankenstein monster, amoral killer and menace to society he has created, and kills Stallone,' said Douglas. 'If they had listened to me there would have been no Rambos. They would have lost a billion dollars, but it would have been right.')[14]

There is just too much confirming detail in both these stories for it to be the coincidence that the creators of Rambo would like to claim. It is true that no one ever actually saw Ryan watch *First Blood*, but the overwhelming body of evidence suggests that he watched it again and again; that his imagination had entered as deeply into this film as Hinckley's had into *Taxi Driver*. I believe that Ryan became Rambo just as certainly as Hinckley became Travis Bickle. Both their imaginations had become embedded in two violent films which had fatally shaped their ideas and world views.

But the triumph of our Man of Lawlessness with these particular films was not to end there.

The Pattern Repeats

We move on now from Hungerford to the events at Higham Ferrers, a small village in Northamptonshire on January 6th, 1988.

This attack was rather small beer compared to the attempted assassination of the American president and the Hungerford massacre, but people were seriously injured and, as we shall see, there is the same set of fingerprints on this case, as I discovered when I went there to investigate it.

The bare facts of the incident are these: Darren Fowler, aged 16, had been expelled from the Higham Ferrers school. At 8.30 a.m. on the day in question he had walked to the school with his best friend, Simon Bates, as he had often done before, leaving him at the school gates. Bates said that his mood was 'normal' and he could offer no explanation for what was to happen later in the day.

Fowler returned home and, during the morning, was interviewed by a worker from the support unit in near-by Rushden, which had helped him since his expulsion the previous October. At 12.30 p.m. he again seemed normal, according to Simon Bates, as they chatted and went back to watch a video on television. This film was *Critters*, a rather bloodthirsty and, at times, frightening story of a group of small monsters, a little like hedgehogs with huge teeth, who arrive in a space-ship and proceed to attack a family in their home. Amid the grisly carnage a young boy finally takes his father's shotgun and manages to kill most of them.[15]

By 3.15 p.m. Fowler had changed, putting on a donkey jacket with a wolf's tail hanging from it, taken up a single-barrel shotgun which belonged to his father, slung a cartridge belt bandolier-style across his shoulder and strapped a knife to his thigh. He also took with him a second hunting-knife and a length of nylon rope. For trapping rabbits if he had to take to the forest, he later explained.

At 3.25 p.m. he entered the school-yard. Some pupils were

terrified by the sight of this armed invader, while many took no notice. Others cheered him on since he had become something of a legend before his expulsion, for ever threatening to 'grease' someone. Seconds later the first shot rang out – aimed at the window of the staffroom where, just moments earlier, teacher Jane Cousins had been looking out. She ducked, but was showered with glass as the window imploded inches above her. Now Fowler started shooting wildly at the buildings, peppering woodwork and brick with shots before making towards the science block. Inside he made a search of the building, although it did not become clear who or what he was looking for.

At 3.30 p.m., just after the bell rang for the end of school, deputy headmaster Michael Cousins and a mass of pupils were also entering the quadrangle as Fowler came out of the science block. Seconds later Fowler fired again and Mr Cousins was hit in the face, neck and chest. He was off school for five months as a result of his injuries. Two pupils, 12-year-olds Simon Druce and Ronald Sherratt, were also wounded in the face though no one is sure if it was another shot or the same one which wounded Mr Cousins.

Meanwhile Paul Greenall, head of boys' PE at the school, had started stalking the armed youth, waiting until the gun had been discharged before hitting him from behind with a rugby tackle and bringing him to the ground.

We have now, following Fowler's trial at Oxford Crown Court and my own enquiries in Higham Ferrers, been able to build up a picture of the kind of youth that he was. He was not a complete loner since he spent a lot of his time with another youth, Cliff Phillips, and his best friend, Simon Bates, with whom he shared a common interest in weaponry, military and forest survival magazines like *Nam* and watching violent videos. Although I could not trace exactly where Fowler got his videos I did discover that Simon Bates was a registered member of the Video Box in Rushden. 'Simon only liked films by two stars,' the manageress recalled to me. 'One was Sylvester Stallone and the other was Arnold Schwarzenegger.'

In the window of Video Box there was a poster advertising the film *War Zone*. The copy read: 'It doesn't matter who you kill . . . as long as you kill someone.'

In the school Fowler was a rejected and despised youth. Weedy, with long mousy hair and a sardonic smile often on his lips, the other pupils used to call him 'Smelly' or 'The Gypsy'. One recalled to me that he was often in the playground on his own, walking around and around muttering to himself, believing that everyone had it in for him. He had already been expelled once but, following the intervention of social workers, had been reinstated only to be expelled again.

He knew almost every detail of the Hungerford massacre, it emerged at his trial where he was ordered to be detained for life. 'It seems that the events in the earlier part of last year in Berkshire had assumed a position in his mind which caused him from time to time to quote from them and indicate that he had in mind to do something similar in the area of his school or his home town,' the court was told.

He had left a simple will scrawled in an exercise book in his bedroom on the day of the shooting, indicating that he did not intend to return. But, nevertheless, he was not fully convinced that he was going to kill himself, Michael Ryan-style, since he had also taken the nylon rope with him for snaring rabbits and sheath knives for survival. 'Just in case I changed my mind about killing myself.'

He had also developed an obsession for a 16-year-old girl Karen Arnold. Fowler began pestering her after she broke up with Simon Bates, but she firmly rejected him saying that there was no way that she would go out with him. He often waited near her home late at night in appalling weather. 'He had become a dreadful pest,' said Karen's father. 'I had to see him off repeatedly.' Fowler once pulled a knife on the father who took it from him. Fowler had also often threatened to 'take out' Karen's new boyfriend, Jason.

Most boys develop obsessions with girls at some time in their lives, but even when he was in custody he wrote to her asking her to buy an engagement ring. 'We can start again where we left off. I'll be out in ten years.' Fowler was no Hinckley, but again we have evidence of the same poor grasp of reality; the same lack of understanding that he was getting nowhere. (Hinckley continued to write to Jodie Foster after he was locked away, still declaring his love for her.)

Fowler is so inarticulate that we shall probably never know

exactly what was in his mind on that day. But what we do know is that he watched the Rambo films and that, in the manner of his dress and his interest in forest survival, he was also clearly trying to emulate his hero. There was also the common element of revenge against those who had rejected him. We also know that there was a storm of violent imagery fresh in his mind on the day of the attack since *Critters* is a very violent video. On Simon Bates's account Fowler became increasingly agitated as the film progressed, constantly turning and winking at him.

His parents refused to speak to me, as did the school, but the deputy headmaster was later to refer to young people being subjected to a whole range of frequently negative and violent images. Fowler's solicitor did speak to me, but was not at all sure if the Rambo films were an influence. But she added that she had not seen one. This is important since, if you have not seen one of these films, the pictorial symbolism – as it has come to live and work in such immature imaginations – is not apparent. It should perhaps be noted that it took a long time after the Hinckley shooting for the lawyers and psychiatrists to tease out the real story.

It is also perhaps worth noting the comment on *First Blood* in Leslie Halliwell's *Film Guide*: 'This film is socially irresponsible. There are enough nuts out there without giving them someone to cheer on.'[16]

There was also another shooting at Walsall on September 11th, 1988, when Anthony Haskett, aged 18, a former Territorial Army cadet, rampaged through the streets of Walsall in the West Midlands after a nightclub drinking session. Armed with a 12-bore shotgun and wearing a bandolier of seventy-six cartridges, Haskett returned to the centre of the city as revellers spilled out of the nightclubs and discos. He shot three black youths and threatened others. As the police moved in he put the gun to his chin and pulled the trigger, killing himself.

Senior police described the shooting as a 'mini-Hungerford' and Superintendent Martin Burton, of the West Midlands force, said, 'I think that he was trying to be Rambo.' The police also revealed the contents of his bedroom, which included a cross-bow, airguns, knives, a machete, a Balaclava, a starting pistol and camouflage paste. There were also two military books, *Military Small Arms* and *Assault Weapons*. On the walls were pictures of Rambo. The camouflage paste crops up a lot in the Rambo stories.[17] In *Rambo III* there is a can of leopard grease mixed with lamp-black for that purpose. Indeed, as we look at the stories we find that these youths seem to be familiar with even the tiniest details.

The inquest jury returned a verdict of accidental death on Haskett and I later sent my accounts of the shootings at Hungerford, Higham Ferrers and Walsall – as they have appeared in this chapter – to the police superintendents in charge of investigating them. I invited them to check my accounts for factual accuracy and wondered if they could supply any further illuminating detail. If my arguments had any merit, I said, then clearly other surface details such as what the youngsters wore at the time of the incidents, assumed a new importance. Only the Walsall police responded.

'We took your report on board during our enquiries into the Haskett case, but the results were inconclusive,' the sergeant concerned with the investigation told me. 'The Haskett family did not own a video though young Anthony may have seen the film elsewhere with friends. It is likely he had since his bedroom walls were absolutely festooned with Rambo photographs.'

However the sergeant added that he was in complete agreement with my ideas on the role of the films in these massacres. He had noticed a rise in fearful weaponry over the previous year, particularly among the Asian community, who had begun using petrol bombs. He believed that most of these crimes were video-related though, of course, it was difficult to prove. There was a massive problem in pirating and illegal tapes. The young girls liked love stories which had led to a lot of family problems, while the young boys loved ultra-macho heroes and freely identified with them.

These continuing stories of cinematic possession are beginning to pose the most ominous threats to all civilised society, and the only real certainty is that the Man of Lawlessness is even now busy hatching many more Travis Bickles and John Rambos on their living-room carpets. The Man of Lawlessness will then see to it that they somehow get their hands on some real weaponry, but, in the meantime, they have got hammers, knives, Stanley knives . . . and they fight rough.

So the high-gloss violence of the film industry is being distilled nightly into a severe kicking outside a pub; the continual violent fantasies of the disaffected outsider are being acted out on the soccer terraces every Saturday afternoon. All the cases we have looked at in this chapter have been famous cases which have generated an enormous amount of public interest. They are the highly visible tips of the iceberg and it does not now take a tremendous leap of the imagination to see why our soccer fans have turned into marauding psychopaths, to begin understanding the real roots of modern lawlessness. These boys have found a leader and they are following him willingly. They are *there*, right behind him.

Paul Scarrot, our most-convicted soccer thug, who has received thirteen jail sentences over as many years, said that he had seen *A Clockwork Orange* three times and had liked it a lot. He had thought it 'pure' which speaks volumes for Mr Scarrot's critical intelligence. 'If there was a modern-day Alex he would be chundering around Dusseldorf with a six-pack of lager,' he said.[18]

We might recall that *A Clockwork Orange* (1971) portrays a future Britain of desolation and violence. Alex, a young gangster, guilty of rape and murder, is released from prison after being experimentally brainwashed. He is interested in rape, ultra-violence and Beethoven, but finds society more violent than in his time.

A truly repulsive film with incoherent sounds and jazzed-up images, it was actually suppressed by its director, Stanley Kubrick – who also owned the rights – which is why it will never be seen again in the cinema or on video in Britain. Kubrick was horrified to see that young men were dressing up in bowler hats, like his fictional gangsters, then running around and beating up old people. In 1973 a 16-year-old boy beat up a tramp and was said to be copying characters in *A Clockwork Orange*. In another court case we learned that a youth had attacked another quite viciously and, when it was learned that he was again aping characters in *A Clockwork Orange*, the judge described the film as evil.

And so the case against the film and video industries

continues to mount; it starts to become a well-documented force which no one can deny. Films are more and more being mentioned in criminal trials. Again and again we are hearing evidence of how bloody-minded acts can spring out of the artist's bloody-minded visions.

A man was sentenced to three years in prison after crashing through a police road-block with a family of four inside his car. He was re-enacting the scene from the film *Vanishing Point*, Norwich Crown Court was told. *Vanishing Point* (1971) is a film about a racing driver, high on amphetamines, who is chased by the police through the Nevada desert.

The night before serial killer Theodore 'Ted' Bundy was electrocuted in Florida on January 25th, 1989, he confessed to killing almost two dozen women and said that he believed that his addiction to pornographic videos had fuelled his sadistic fantasies. He added that society had a right to protect itself from his 'weakness'.[19]

On January 30th, 1989, Valerio 'Gigi' Viccei, an Italian armed robber wanted in connection with at least fifty-seven serious crimes and said to be one of the most dangerous men in Europe, was given a 22-year prison sentence in London for his part in Britain's biggest armed robbery. He had already served various prison sentences for armed robbery and drug and arms dealing in Italy, had lived on the fringes of political terrorist groups and was known as a braggart with a taste for carrying guns and living off women. He had jumped bail in his native country, facing a seven-year sentence. He ran around London in a black Ferrari, wore designer clothes and was almost permanently high on cocaine.[20]

It emerged at his trial in the Old Bailey that Viccei had seen Brian de Palma's *Scarface* no less than sixty times. *Scarface* (1987) is the story of a cocaine-snorting gangster with a liking for a fancy life style and abusing women, who is also an emigré, though from Cuba. The film is absurdly brutal with a super-abundance of bad language, according to Leslie Halliwell in his *Film Guide*.

The film and video industries make much of the fact that their films are certificated in advance of release and are therefore 'fit' for consumption by those of the right age. But it is now clear

that, confronted by the resolute advance of the Man of Lawlessness within both these booming industries, this system of
certification, particularly with regard to videos, is no more than
the tiniest obstacle to him.

Hinckley was 26, the same age as Ryan. Fowler was 16 and
Haskett 18. The Rambo killers in America were 41 and 26. The
Melbourne killer was 19. Bundy was 42 and Viccei was 34. The
Rambo films all had a 15 certificate while *Taxi Driver* was an 18.
Apart from the fact that age is clearly no protection from the
Romantic evil enshrined in these films, there can hardly be said
to be any control over who sees what.

My local video-shop man said that young people can get
almost anything they want just as they can obtain alcohol if
they want. He will not knowingly give a tape to anyone under
age, but, if an elderly person wants it – or even a parent – there
is nothing he can do about it. The person is then free to invite
the whole street in if he wants. And such safeguards as there are
will clearly collapse even further when satellite television moves
into full swing. Soft porn is already available throughout the
day via satellite in France. At least in the heyday of the cinema
you had to *look* 18 to get in to see an X film.

Taxi Driver is still widely available in most video shops, but
after Hinckley's widely-publicised trial, the British Video Association should have known of the vital role that it played in
the attack on President Reagan. Why is it still available? Did
they not see that there was a reasonable risk that it might
capture yet another immature or schizophrenic imagination?
Even the screenwriter of *Taxi Driver*, Paul Schrader, publicly
acknowledged the connection between the film and the shooting of Reagan, but added that he himself had not created the
hero. Just after Hinckley's attempt on the life of the president
there were five further copy-cat attacks in America.

The tempting conclusion is that such films, together with
their enormous merchandising possibilities, are still only available because of the vast sums of money they generate. It is
becoming clear that the acquisition of money is one of the Man
of Lawlessness's most basic instincts.

5

A Theatre for Terrorism

In which we march with IRA supporters up the Falls Road in Belfast – Wonder at the never-ending drama of terror – Meet a beguiling mouthpiece for the IRA killers – Examine Sartre's existentialist heresy – Urge the throwing away of the blue pencil, the scissors and the bonfire – And catch sight of the Man of Lawlessness eating popcorn in his favourite theatre.

Belfast Rhetoric

It was a grey, moisty day in Belfast on Sunday, August 14th, 1988. Every half an hour or so a cold shower of rain came spitting down on the sprawling city ringed by high hills and sitting on a sea lough. It was, as they say here, raining shoemakers' knives. Down on the banks of the lough were the giant crucifix shapes of the Harland and Wolff shipyard.

We had come to the Falls Road and, in one side-street, a pipe and drum band of children no older than 11 were practising. They were wearing black tams and sunglasses. Their uniforms were decked out in the white, green and orange of the Republican movement. Others were coming through the rain unfurling huge, gaudy banners as those drums rolled savagely again and again.

This was the Republican's annual anti-internment march

along Falls Road, a wide highway which twists through the
heart of Catholic West Belfast. There were ugly swathes of
barbed wire and chunks of glass atop the walls all along the
road. All the shop windows had metal shutters. A few houses
had been completely gutted with some walls blackened by huge
smudges from petrol-bomb attacks. Closed-circuit television
cameras were mounted above the entrances of the shops and
one small off-licence actually looked like a mini-fortress, surrounded by wire fencing, a huge football-type turnstile and a
camera to check you before you were let in to buy a bottle. The
social-security office was similarly wired, grilled and videoed.
Some end-of-terrace walls were painted with bright military
murals: TO BEAR ARMS IS A LEGITIMATE RIGHT, said
one, over 'heroic' silhouettes holding aloft Armalites.

Milltown cemetery was about halfway down the road with its
Republican plot for the IRA men 'killed on active service'.
Bobby Sands, the hunger-striker, lay there as did the Gibraltar
bombers. Earlier that summer the cemetery had been the scene
of a famous attack when a Loyalist began shooting and throwing mortar-bombs during one of the huge IRA funerals.

As more marchers gathered at the top of Falls Road, the
Royal Ulster Constabulary and the army were moving about in
force, walking watchfully next to line after line of armoured
Land-rovers. The police trained their gun sights on the
marchers and the surrounding roof-tops, looking through their
telescopic sights for any sign of trouble. Disconcertingly they
trained their guns at your head, too, and you wondered what
would happen if your hand made a sudden move to your inside
pocket. Small groups of army men kept moving around covering one another's backs. Those Republican drums were still
pounding with a frenzied insistence.

But there was another large element to this march, too, and
as the marchers all took off into the cold teeth of yet another
shower of rain, they kept circling around in sizable packs: the
members of the national and international media, with their
cameras and notebooks. They kept surging around twitchily,
waiting for the trouble which had been forecast on the
grapevine. Many of them clearly thought that they *were* in a war
since they were dressed for violent action: combat-jackets,
denim trousers, training shoes, Cambodian liberation shawls,

chests and shoulders bulging with cameras. You also, quite soon, began to see how they were thinking since, as the march approached the heavily-fortified Andersonstown police-station, many of the photographers were busy trying to frame the swaying banners against the grim silhouette of the police-station. This was, after all, a war. Still those drums kept pounding.

On this day in 1988 we were well into one of the IRA's most savage summer campaigns ever. Six soldiers had been killed on a charity fun run the previous July; a homebound soldier had been gunned down at the traffic-lights at Ostend; workmen had been riddled by bullets in Belleek; a coach had been blown up in Ballygawley, killing eight soldiers; a car went up in flames in the Belfast rush hour; the house of a senior civil servant had been blown up while he had been sleeping with his family . . .

The publicity these attacks received had been spectacular by any standards, particularly when you consider that there are more practising Buddhists in Ireland than there are gunmen. The army estimates that there are no more than sixty men on what the IRA calls 'active service', but behind this vanguard there are thought to be about 200 who could join in terrorist attacks when needed. Yet, thanks to the media, which had breathlessly recorded every bomb and bullet, their terror had spread to every corner of the world.

These bombings had broken through the boredom gates at editorial conferences in cities as far apart as New York and Sydney.[1] Although not normally interested in the bewildering details of Northern Ireland politics, they gave the attacks extensive coverage. Margaret Thatcher, at the time in Australia, had to struggle past small crowds of hostile IRA sympathisers. Inevitably she was asked if it was time for the British troops to be pulled out. Focus was again put on the time-to-go movement. Then another bomb went off and there was a public debate on whether it was safe for the Prime Minister to go on a walkabout in Sydney. Again and again Australian interviewers had asked her about the IRA . . . all grist to the Provisionals' propaganda machine.

'Kill one and frighten 10,000,' Sun Tsu, a Chinese philos-opher, wrote more than 2,000 years ago. A lot of bridges have passed under the water since he coined that neat aphorism.

Now, as the IRA have been quick to understand, thanks to the media, you can kill one and frighten practically the whole world.

As the march progressed up the Falls Road, this rainy Sunday afternoon, there were two small incidents. Four women, who had been collecting money in buckets for those locked up in Long Kesh, had their buckets confiscated by the army and several small children had sneaked up through the side-streets to throw stones at the march.

It is the way that small children have been sucked into this conflict of sectarian hatred which is one of its most sickening features. I had been walking up to the Falls Road earlier that afternoon when I had spotted two small toddlers swaying on the edge of the pavement. I dashed forward fearing that they were going to wander on to the busy road, but, as it turned out, they were there throwing bits of a broken flowerpot at the passing army vans. 'We're only throwing at the pigs,' one said as he wandered back to his pile of broken pot to find another suitable bit. He might not have been 5 years old. Even the dogs in Catholic areas are trained to chase after army patrols.

As the march came to an end near a row of shops at the other end of Falls Road everyone gathered in front of the fortified Republican headquarters where the Sinn Fein top brass were standing in a raised garden to address the crowd. Sinn Fein is the political wing of the IRA. The mood was quiet and tense, with eyes darting around. A few young stewards ran towards something, which turned out to be nothing, and a marshal on a loudspeaker appealed for calm. There was a distant siren. 'Just an ambulance,' a man from the Irish press whispered into his tape-recorder. Television cameras from as far apart as Holland and France had crowded into the raised garden next to the main speakers. Media are always allowed privileged entry at such events. A photographer in a Cambodian liberation scarf, possibly Italian, was standing on the end of the garden wall, camera in hand and gazing out at the crowds, waiting to record the action which we had been promised would come.

Sinn Fein had, in the past, used this rally to put on a show for the benefit of the media – a display of weapons, perhaps, or the sudden appearance of an IRA fugitive who said a few words, gave a quick wave for the cameras and then vanished again like a ghost at dawn.

The RUC and army watched the proceedings from the other side of the road and there was little doubt in anyone's mind that they would go in, plastic bullets flying, if one particular terrorist did show his face. They, too, were being very jumpy with one RUC man, worried that he had been photographed, turning on a photographer, David Mansell, and trying to confiscate his film. That fear seemed to have seeped into every corner of Northern Ireland. There were some times when it seemed so real you felt that you could reach out and actually touch it.

We learned from the chief marshal that representatives of the Basque Liberation Movement, Noraid (the American supporters of the IRA) and the Troops-out Movement had joined us 'for this great day'. This was the seventeenth anniversary march to mark the original internment and on this very spot one of their men had been 'murdered' by the RUC, the chief marshal said. They were also looking for contributions for a sponsored run around the exercise-yard of Long Kesh, the IRA internment camp. There was a message from the prisoners delivered by Patricia McCauley: 'We are witnessing a risen people showing their strength. For the last twenty years Britain has used every weapon to break us. Our people are not defeated and confident of victory.'

Other rhetorical batons were taken up by a Basque separatist; a large bearded American from Noraid; and then Martin McGuinness of Sinn Fein, a baby-faced man with an angelic mop of curls, wherein all likeness to an angel ends. He praised IRA violence as the 'only voice that the British understand'. He added that internment was the biggest mistake of their lives and it didn't solve any problems.

> We stood up and have never sat down. The British have used every weapon to defeat us . . . murder, assassination and internment. The reintroduction of internment will not defeat the Republican movement. We see the IRA as freedom fighters and they will bring about the British defeat. There will be no condemnation of the IRA from us. They are our blood and our tears and we will never let those people down.

The next to take the microphone was Gerry Adams, the president of Sinn Fein. 'The Republicans have always been prepared to negotiate,' he began. 'The only terrorists are in British uniform. We say that the IRA has a right to armed struggle. The British have declared war on Northern Ireland.'

We were treated to the usual IRA rhetoric, but as the threats mounted and, more insidiously, some journalists were named and denounced as liars, you began to wonder at the extraordinary attention that every word was receiving from the massed armies of the media. It would be difficult to think of any political demonstration anywhere in the world where empty rhetoric could receive such rapt and widespread attention.

Certainly if any other group in Ireland – or, indeed, anywhere else – had a march they would be very lucky to attract the attention of one cameraman – unless they began threatening to throw bombs, or actually did throw bombs. Then the media would doubtless become putty in their hands just as the media are now putty in the IRA hands. For that was the only compelling conclusion that rainy afternoon in Belfast. The media were here in the Falls Road in West Belfast, in such force, because there had been the promise of violence. But, apart from violent words, there was none.

The speeches came to an end and the chief marshal asked everyone to go home quietly. But he did invite the press inside the headquarters. Weapons? An appearance by a wanted terrorist? We all surged inside the wire gates, waving our press cards in the air. But all the chief marshal wanted to do was to complain about the way the army had taken the collecting buckets from those three women.

Everyone milled around in the garden for a while before returning to the city. Martin McGuinness and Gerry Adams gave little press conferences of their own, answering all questions politely and wishing the journalists 'good luck' when they had finished their questioning. Gerry Adams is a past master at handling the media. If he ever gets trapped by any tricky questions in front of a television camera he often starts effing and blinding, knowing that it would not be transmitted.

As we trudged down to our hotel the general opinion of journalists seemed to be that it had not been much good, a disappointment even. Some news-desks, like the *Daily Tele-*

graph's, decided that there was nothing in it.[2] *The Independent* gave it a front-page splash complete with a photograph of Martin McGuinness looking angelic and framed by some trees. I LOVE WEST BELFAST, said a button on his pullover, prompting one to wonder why he so wholeheartedly approved of all the bombs that were tearing the city apart. Other newspapers gave it a few paragraphs, concentrating on the children's stone-throwing and the confiscation of the collecting buckets. The march did, however, make all the local television news-bulletins.

Another day in covering the war in Northern Ireland.

The Vietnam Syndrome

If there were about a hundred of you, both actors and actresses, who wanted to put on a play to explain to the public what you believed in then you would first have to find a theatre. Having located this theatre you would then need someone to take the money in the box-office; someone to sell programmes and drinks; stage-hands to shift the scenery; sound and lighting systems; publicity to attract the public in; and, ideally, plenty of critics who would eagerly analyse your production and declare in public print if your play had any worth.

It just so happens that there are around 100 hard-core terrorists in the IRA who believe in a united Ireland. They are elected by no one and are responsible only to themselves – indeed, except for a few isolated areas, popular support for more than half a century has been measured in single-figure percentages.[3] But, to ensure the continuing exposure of their beliefs, they did indeed need a platform or theatre. As it turned out there was a ready-made theatre, which was ideal for their purposes and would give them the maximum exposure, providing, as they worked out for themselves, they could come up with an attractive production which the punters would find riveting. The IRA knew exactly what, in public terms, made for a good production.

So what they did was forget about any dramatic monologues in their production – and any other sort of speechifying which might make the public restless and bored – providing, instead, a fast-moving and continuous story line of spectacular and dramatic violence which ensured a permanent and perfect theatre for their 100 strolling players since, as we must by now have understood, if there is one thing both the media and public love above all else, it is a continuous flow of spectacular and dramatic violence.

As it stands now and has been for the past twenty years, every main production by the IRA – both successful and bungled – has been given a guaranteed, if short, run on the BBC's *Nine O'Clock Violence* or ITN's *GBH at Ten*. All the productions, however, get a much longer run locally, particularly in Ulster's local papers, hourly radio bulletins and television magazine programmes. Here we get every aspect of the smallest details of each and every IRA production down to every splinter, every shard of glass and every dried-up drop of blood on the pavement – all in close-up and glorious Technicolor.

If, during an interval, say, a member of the IRA cast did try and vary the terms of his contract by actually walking on to the stage and making a speech about what their latest production was about then a huge wooden hook would come from behind the curtains to drag him off by the neck, and the stage lights would mysteriously fail. But he would not be too concerned since he knew that the play was the message; that the clear aim was to inflict so much damage and cause so much violence that the great audience of British public opinion would, in the end, shocked by it all, demand the recall of British troops. British opinion polls – which have consistently shown a majority in favour of withdrawal – have already suggested that this 'Vietnam Syndrome' exists.

But the real trouble with this production is that it is extremely long and expensive. The war in Ulster has cost in excess of £10bn. More than 2,500 people have died in it with a further 24,000 maimed or injured. The security officers in the North, including the prison officers and the army, have lost nearly 1,000 men. The IRA has lost some 200 and has been responsible for some 1,500 deaths. There have been approaching 40,000 terrorist incidents and terrorists have been responsible for a thirty-fold rise in armed robbery in ten years. *And all for a stage production involving some 100 men!*

There is, however, no sign at all of this production's coming to an end and already the theatre's publicity people have been telling us, on the quiet, that the cast have plans to vary their hugely successful and attention-getting production. A more liberal use of Semtex explosive is envisaged to liven up the plot. To keep the nausea level high there will be more attacks on civilian homes.

Thrill to the new flame-throwers, courtesy of Colonel Gadaffi. Enjoy the very latest booby-traps and home-made Drogue bombs, canisters packed with explosives. Just wait until they produce their new SAM missiles.

But during my last visit to Belfast in the summer of 1988 there were already some very loud questions being asked about this theatre of terrorism. For the first time that I could remember people were openly wondering if it wasn't time to pull down the curtain on this particular act. They were asking these questions and wondering these thoughts because they were beginning to understand finally that the media were of the most paramount importance to all terrorist campaigns; that the terrorists were extremely few in number and that publicity was everything. They were beginning to understand that terrorists had become the great entertainers of our time.

Lord Annan wrote in his report about television:

Terrorism feeds off publicity: publicity is its main hope of intimidating government and the public: publicity gives it further chance for recruitment. The acts terrorists commit are each minor incidents in their general campaign to attract attention to their cause. No democracy can tolerate terrorism because it is a denial of the democratic assumption that injustice can, in time, be put right through discussion, peaceful persuasion and compromise. By killing and destroying, the terrorists are bound to extort publicity – and hence one of their ends – because such news will be reported.[4]

The week before my arrival in Belfast General Tony Farrar-Hockley, the first Commander of Land Forces in Northern Ireland wrote to *The Times*:

What gives the terrorists the principal reward is publicity for their crimes. Currently they receive plenty of it in front-page spreads which continue for days. This cannot be in the interests of a society seeking to combat terrorism. Doubtless news of outrages should be reported, but not on the front pages for days on end, or in highly coloured terms conveying the notion of a national crisis or grave error.[5]

In the following week, Barry White, a columnist for *The Belfast Telegraph*, also broke the normal journalistic silence and asked if the media were not devoting too much time to acts of terrorism. 'They have to be reported, but when a good part of their purpose is to spread terror, through the media, should we spend so much time contributing to their effectiveness?'[6]

White later told me that another feature of that present summer campaign of IRA violence was that there was always a necessity for people to issue comments, warning workmen and civil servants alike of the consequences of associating with the security forces.

> They did not get away with this in any previous campaigns. We should be practising more self-censorship. Journalists should begin by asking if they were helping or hindering. We are becoming more conscious of the way they are manipulating us. And the national and international media should think more of it, too. On this newspaper we are thinking of it all the time. We do what we can from day to day. Quite a lot of false stories are started by the foreign media and then we do what we can to put together the pieces.

Charles Fenyesi, an American journalist, who was briefly taken hostage by a group of terrorists in Washington in the late 'seventies, wrote an article in *The Quill*: 'Looking Into the Muzzle of Terrorists'. 'There is a gnawing suspicion that the news media awaken, legitimise and . . . stroke fantasies of violence which might otherwise lie dormant and that, on a deeper level than any court can probe, newsmen are responsible for a climate congenial to terrorism.'[7]

In the 'seventies in Quebec the so-called *Front de la Liberation Quebecois* murdered a minister and kidnapped a British trade commissioner. The FLQ were given constant exposure on television and treated as a species of opposition within the democratic system. Reporters interviewed FLQ spokesmen to find out their arguments. They were demanding an independent Quebec. One television interviewer asked how kidnapping and murder could help liberate Quebec. 'Well, you're here. I mean we've got that far.'

Academics in Aberdeen and Israel are also working on this notion of terrorism as theatre. The argument runs that the media and the terrorists have, albeit for entirely different motives, entered into a symbiotic relationship with one another and that they have become co-producers in terror.

It was the British Prime Minister, Mrs Margaret Thatcher, who first drew the world's attention to the relationship between the media and terrorism in the summer of 1985 after the TWA airliner hijack in Beirut. 'The time has come to consider the power of the media to influence the progress of terrorism,' she told the American Bar Association in London. 'There is an urgent need to starve the terrorist of the oxygen of publicity.'

At the time the world's media were jostling around the beleaguered plane on the tarmac of Beirut airport. The hijackers even offered American television networks tours of the captured aircraft for $1,000 and interviews with the hostages for $12,500. At one memorable press conference the hijackers abandoned it and sent the media home for misbehaving.

Time editorialist Charles Krauthammer interpreted events this way:

> During 17 days of astonishing symbiosis, television and terrorists co-produced – there is no better word for it – a hostage drama . . . There under laboratory conditions journalists met terror, in a pure culture, uncontaminated by civilisation. The results are not encouraging. Terror needed a partner in crime to give the event life. The media, television above all, obliged . . . Insensitivity to the families; exploitation of the hostages; absurd, degrading references to jailers; interference with diplomacy; giving over the airwaves to people whose claim on air-time is based entirely on the fact that they are forcibly holding innocent Americans.[8]

One American academic, Professor Yonah Alexander, saw clear parallels between the salesmanship of the market-place and the antics of the Romantic revolutionary. 'Like advertising terrorism increases the effectiveness of its messages by focusing on spectacular violent deeds and keeping the issues alive through repetition,' he said. Noel Koch, in charge of terrorism in the Pentagon, said: 'Terrorism is drama. It's got suspense, it's got grievance, it's got people at risk, it's got families that are crying – you can't duplicate that in fiction.'[9]

It has also got lots of violence.

A Media Mouthpiece

So what is the exact nature of the relationship between the terrorist groups in Northern Ireland and the media? Is the oxygen of publicity playing a vital role in the destruction of the Province? Could it really be possible that the media, however unwittingly, has set up a huge theatre of terrorism there so that the IRA can have a stage to act out its savage, violent fantasies and make its undemocratic demands before a global audience?

Let us at least take as a basic premise that the IRA are the most brilliant masters of publicity and propaganda which they value above all else. They know that they can keep show-boating their bombs in front of the media indefinitely and that, in the end, the only way in which they can win this war is by winning the all-important propaganda war. Danny Morrison, Sinn Fein's publicity director, replying to criticisms that IRA attacks on off-duty servicemen were cowardly, said, 'It's all propaganda.'

Intelligence reports estimate that the IRA needs at least £5m a year to keep going. Business fronts raise an estimated £2m each year. Building-site frauds bring in £1.5m, drinking clubs and gambling machines account for another £1m and taxis bring in £175,000. Armed robberies net the IRA a further £300,000 in Ulster, while larger robberies in the Republic make about £1.5m a year. They pay active members around £20 a week and a further £20 a week goes to the families of IRA prisoners. An unknown amount is spent on arms – explosives are supplied free by Libya – but one of their biggest expenses is supporting Sinn Fein and paying for publications and propaganda.[10]

Thus the IRA conduct seminars on how to deal with the media. Bombings and hijackings are often timed for maximum impact on the evening news: terrorist acts come at four o'clock in the afternoon – often in the rush hour – in time for the six o'clock news.[11] Shooting incidents are also timed for the news and one analysis of sixty bomb explosions in July 1974 showed that more than 80 per cent of them were timed to obtain maximum coverage on the news.[12]

For major statements they call press conferences or issue statements on a FAX machine from their headquarters in Falls Road. They are such cynical manipulators of the media that they even go so far as to print two versions of their *Republican News*: one for the home market which is often full of left-wing propaganda, and another for the American market, with the left-wing stuff taken out because 'the Americans do not like that kind of thing'.[13]

Experienced IRA-watchers say that they could easily have predicted this summer's campaign. News was slack and a bomb in London would have made a major impact. A few more in Europe, with the detonation of an army bus with many casualties – one body was horrifically wrapped around a tree – and they were back in business. Journalists from all over the world came streaming back to Belfast to update the state of the IRA. Anguished editorials were written wondering what we should do next. Significantly there were very few IRA bombs during the Falklands campaign, since the eyes of the media were elsewhere.

All terrorist groups in Northern Ireland have been issued by the media with their own code-words to authenticate any of their 'executions'. Thus a voice will call a newspaper or local radio station to say that such and such has been 'executed' using such and such weapons. A code-word will be given and the line go dead. There are sound journalistic reasons for this practice, but, on other occasions, three members of the media will be told to be in a certain place at a certain time. They will then be taken off and shown something – usually a display of arms. They never tip off the police – much to the police's annoyance – and while that is not the function of the press, we are again beginning to see evidence of a very real relationship between the media and the terrorists.

A Royal Ulster Constabulary spokesman also complained bitterly to me about what he saw as double standards. 'Why don't they ever cross-examine the Provos as they do us? I know that journalists are threatened and intimidated, but you never hear them challenge the Provos on what they have to say. They even issue contradictory statements about their murders and everything goes in. There is no feeling of remorse, no humanity.'

A visiting pressman can even meet a spokesman for the Provisionals merely by telephoning a Belfast number and making an appointment. By so doing, a few days later, I went down to their heavily-guarded offices in the Falls Road and spoke with Richard McAuley, an ex-Long-Kesh internee and director of publicity for Sinn Fein. A television security camera was mounted outside the door and a young man nervously monitored all visitors before opening the two metal gates. Inside people sat around in an airless and warm waiting-room since all the windows had been bricked in.

After waiting about half an hour I was shown upstairs to meet McAuley, an engaging young man with gold-rimmed spectacles, who spoke cheerfully about their relationship with the media, explaining that, to move with the times, they had dispensed with the old-fashioned telex machine to issue their statements, and moved on to FAX. They even sent statements to Protestant newspapers. A smile and slight wave of the hand. 'They do not use them, but we live in hope.'

We recognise the great importance of publicity, but, in terms of resources, we cannot hope to compete with the army or police. The British media tends to be difficult, though the home-grown press has become slightly more amenable. They see that they cannot ignore the Republicans or Sinn Fein.

Language is all-important and they keep calling us criminals or gangsters. The *Sunday Times* is always going on about our so-called racketeering and that reinforces people's views of the movement. Also the Press do their readers a considerable disservice with their talks of splits and factions within the movement. There were political differences – there have always been political differences in Sinn Fein – but their stories are always based on erroneous information. They come here with no new insights into the politics of the country.

Our responsibility is to get the Republican position across. We always try to make contact with journalists through press conferences and briefings. You have to do it if you are going to get your message across. Margaret Thatcher is a master of publicity and the British manipulate the media all the time. We have two people working here full time with several others across the North. We moved on to FAX because the telex was quite slow. News needs to get out with speed. We sometimes have to fight for our statements. The IRA will give us news of their shootings or sometimes the news will come out of Dublin. Downtown Radio here in Belfast is also very quick with the news. There are journalists we will not co-operate with since they are not sympathetic to the movement. They allow their hostility to get in the way of reality and what they write becomes black propaganda. But there is no real way around the problem and you have to tackle it as best you can. I think we have a reputation for not lying. We may avoid difficulty and might not give the full details of an incident, but we don't have any credibility if we are caught out lying.

So we have heard, in its fullest sense, the fluent language of the modern public-relations man: the humour, the gloss-over splits, the objection to pejorative language used against the client, the emphasis on integrity and truth. Even the glossiness of the handouts, with the stylish letterheads, is practically indistinguishable from that of a Mayfair public-relations consultant.

As the interview was coming to an end I asked – as it was clearly important to them to get their message across – wasn't violence counter-productive to that aim? He paused and smiled and paused again. Strangely, it was not a question that had been put to him before and it was the only time during the interview that his fluency had deserted him. 'Yes, violence does have its counter-productive aspects,' he said finally. 'Killing people is not nice. It affects how people see the movement. The BBC is only ever interested in showing a film of the latest bomb attack. Analysis does not come into it. But, if there were no bombings, people like you would not come here. Ireland would be another quiet graveyard, distant and forgotten about. We could not allow that.'

So we have one candid view on why the killings continue – to maintain an international media presence. As I was leaving the office a set of television equipment was being shouldered up the stairs.

Sartre's Existentialist Heresy

There has been an enduring and modish fascination with
terrorist violence – both for its own dramatic properties and as
an instrument for the few to gain freedom from the many – by
our intellectuals and perhaps none institutionalised it in our
actions and thoughts more than the French existentialist
philosopher, Jean-Paul Sartre (1905–80).[14]

A lonely child, he told us in his autobiography *Les Mots*, he
might go with his mother to the park in Paris when they went
from group to group in the vain hope of being accepted – only
finally to retreat to the sixth floor of their apartment 'on the
heights where [the] dreams dwell'. His mother kept him in frocks
and long hair but *les mots* – the words – saved the only child and
from thereon he began a truly prodigious writing career which
culminated in his being awarded the Nobel Prize for Literature
in 1964, which he declined.

As a student he read some 300 books a year and his main
passion was for the American novel. It was while teaching at Le
Havre that he published his first claim to fame, *La Nausée*
which, written in the form of a diary, shows his hero Roquentin
undergoing feelings of deep revulsion when confronted both by
the world and his own body. The tone is iconoclastic, the
manner surly, the outlook chaotic. So we are back again into the
world of the outsider, addressing us from beneath the floorboards and telling us how terrible everything is. *Oui Pierre*, there
really is nothing new under the sun.

In the next phase of his work he turned his attention to the
concept of social responsibility. A writer must show man as he
is. *Nowhere is a man more than when he is in action*. This was the
kernel of his existentialism which was, in essence, a personal
philosophy of action. A man's character and significance are
determined by his actions, not his views – by his deeds, not
words. 'Existentialism defines man by his actions,' said Sartre.
'It tells him that hope only lies in action, and that the only thing
that allows a man to live is action. So man commits himself to
his life and thereby draws his image, beyond which there is
nothing.' The new European was the new existentialist individual – 'alone without excuses'. This is what he meant when he
said we are condemned to be free. And the disillusioned young

found all this immensely attractive; it was rebellious, noble, committed and violent. Anyone could be an existentialist and soon Sartre was king of the *enragés* (angry ones). He openly dreamed of conquering the world with his theories. His world, he said, was 'travel, polygamy, transparency'.

Perhaps his most famous play was *Huis Clos* with its message 'Hell is other people', in which, again totally alienated, he expressed dislike and disgust with the whole of humanity. But we can see his real philosophical credentials most clearly in his 700-page book about the homosexual thief, Jean Genet, which was one long celebration of antinomianism, anarchy and sexual perversion. With this book he ceased to become a thinker and became an intellectual sensationalist. He emerged openly as what we had always suspected anyway: a fully paid-up, card-carrying Romantic.

After the Second World War – in which this great man of action did nothing but write – he took an interest in French political movements, becoming an outspoken admirer of Russia until the Soviet invasion of Budapest in 1956. Later he spent his time travelling the Third World, hobnobbing with various dictators and denouncing American 'war crimes' in Vietnam. He also became a patron of Frantz Fanon, the African ideologue who wrote, 'For a black man to shoot down a European is to kill two birds with one stone, to destroy an oppressor and the man he oppresses at the same time.'

We are clearly back to Mailer's self-liberation through murder, while Sartre himself perfected the technique of characterising the existing order as violent so that you are then justified in overthrowing it violently. This belief still lives in the Nelson Mandela school of fighting with violence those who violently oppress you. It is one of the Man of Lawlessness's most favourite and confusing lies. He, almost more than anyone, understands that when you come to violence, you can confuse almost anyone with anything.

The hideous crimes committed in Cambodia, involving the death of millions, were done by a group of Francophone middle-class intellectuals known as Angka Leu. Of its eight leaders, all had studied in France in the 1950s where they had absorbed Sartre's philosophy of philosophical activism and 'necessary violence'. Not only was he the godfather of modern terrorism but these mass murderers were his ideological children.[15]

Sartre spent his remaining years doddering around Paris, saluting the student barricades and specialising in little more than the underwear of young girls. 'Violence is the only thing remaining to the students who have not yet entered into their fathers' system,' he said. He also told the students: 'What is interesting about your action is that it puts the imagination in power.'

Finally, this addled Romantic, with his drunken fatuities, died on April 15th 1980, when some 25,000 turned up at Montparnasse to mourn at his funeral. But just *what* where they mourning?

It was late on a Sunday night and we were back in the Europa, the main hotel in Belfast, where the media rest up and exchange stories when they are not out scouring the city streets on the scent of trouble. As this summer campaign had hotted up they had been coming in from all over the world – gathering in groups at the bar, notebooks sticking out of pockets and their television equipment piled high around the plush armchairs of the lobby.

Some have found that they can actually cover the conflict without ever actually moving out of the safety of the hotel. Indeed, it is often a disadvantage to move out of the hotel since, here, they can make regular check calls to the army or police for any news of trouble. Some also have little portable television sets so that they can, over dinner perhaps, monitor what the television news is saying. Local newspapers are scoured avidly. Many of them also have tiny radios with earplugs so that, on the hour, they can listen to the news on Belfast's Downtown Radio. So, then, if one arm of the media gets it, they soon all get it – within minutes. Nothing is kept secret for long. News is not after all news unless it is published or broadcast. A visiting pressman can sound authoritative and well-informed without ever leaving the bar-stool of the Europa.

In the early days of the current wave of troubles this hotel was the most-bombed in Europe, but that has all changed. The army, police and para-military groups all fight hard for the ear of the media. Even the UVF (the loyalist paramilitaries) has its own press centre where you are assured of tea and muffins.[16] No journalist has ever been killed in this conflict.

I had been coming back and forth to the Europa for seventeen years, first coming here for the *Sunday Times* at the time of the last internment in 1971. Then a green horn, I had walked, unbelieving, around those hate-filled pavements with the colours of the Union Jack painted on one kerb and the colours of the Republican tricolour on the other side. I had heard shots ring out in the darkness, seen homes ransacked and burned, even stood consoling a woman one afternoon as she sobbed pitifully while neighbours of many years' standing swarmed into her house and pulled all her furniture out into her front garden. During those days I had stared squarely into the face of a new and terrifying hate.

But it has to be said that I was worse than useless at reporting the war, since I believed that what I believe now – that the media are at the root of it all – and, after a few visits, I was never sent back there by the *Sunday Times*. I did, however, go to Londonderry to spend some time with the army for the *Observer*, and kept coming back for a number of other reasons – working on a book about pilgrimage, promoting various books and to see friends. But now, this savage summer, I had come back specifically to look at the relationship between the media and the IRA.

The members of the media and their ideas had not changed much over the years, I found. They were still invigorating company – cheerful, cynical, boozy, with a rude story about everyone. But, apparently, the behaviour of continental photographers, particularly the French, has often been abominable. There have been reports of photographers paying young thugs to throw rocks and bottles at passing army crews. One American television crew recorded one such incident on film. In the Falls Road a crew was seen by the police inciting rioters to damage a building site. In another incident a crew was actually directing the rioters to create better picture sequences. Some dismiss such stories as media folklore, but the problem was seen as being sufficiently serious to provoke a meeting of all photographers here in the Europa when a statement was read out warning against such practices.[17]

The Bobby Sands funeral probably supplied the IRA with

their most spectacular *coup de théatre* when the IRA actually
built a grandstand for all the international photographers in
Milltown cemetery. Some 100,000 attended and the funeral
procession was led by a pipe-and-drum band with the coffin
flanked by a black-clad guard of honour. The whump-
whumping of the army helicopter overhead served to intensify
the emotions of the occasion and, just before interment, six
uniformed men materialised to fire a volley over the coffin to the
great cheers of the crowd.

One American columnist was exposed for totally fabricating
one story in the New York *Daily News*. He made up the name of
a soldier, got the patrol going in the wrong direction and
claimed that a pilot flying into Belfast said: 'We are now going
into Belfast, turn your clocks back 800 years.'

But such stories are isolated and rare. Fantasists quickly
expose themselves since there are too many professionals
fishing the same pool who would never dream of such a thing.
Some do embroider a few stories with a few colourful 'facts', but
generally their accuracy is not in question. Neither is their
objectivity. Most reporters regard *all* sides in this conflict with a
huge dose of cynicism and proceed to report the war on that
basis. They see their role as purely descriptive rather than
analytical.

No, the lie at the heart of the troubles, in which they are all
unwittingly engaged, is far more subtle and intensely more
destructive than a few fabricated stories.

More people were filtering into the Europa late that night
and, in one group, there were representatives of *Reuters*, *Press
Association*, *The Times* and the *Daily Telegraph*. Television crews
whizzed in and out and, at the bar, I began talking to a man, not
a reporter, who fixed things for the BBC. Media people talk
among themselves obsessively about the troubles and, while
this man had no high position as such, I was struck by the cold
and knowing insight of what he had to say.

> We could see that this campaign was coming this summer. Mrs
> Thatcher had gone to Australia with the world's press and there-
> fore she was vulnerable. Out there she can't issue statements from
> Downing Street saying 'How terrible'. She has to face the press and

they ask her, 'What do you think about the IRA?' They just love it every time she mentions their name. The IRA has always thought internationally. They are always wondering where we are going to be looking next.

Of course we are here for the bombs. No one is interested in talk but, do remember, if we left, they would let off bigger bombs until we came back again. If we didn't come back, they would let off even bigger bombs. Like a bad marriage we are stuck with them. And they understand us. They understand everything about publicity. They know everything about news.

The IRA have had a good run just now, but what I'm worried about is that the UVF will decide that they are losing the publicity race so they'll doubtless be getting back into action soon. INLA – a bunch of Newry thugs – started shooting one another last year and we're waiting for them to start performing again soon. [INLA did indeed start bombing the following day.]

The way it works for the BBC is the Ulster television carries all the funerals and London takes what it fancies. There's been so much trouble just now, we've come from London as back-up. There's been a lot of internal worrying about all these funerals – the grieving widows, the lowering of coffins into holes, the displays of arms . . . There are new unofficial ground rules and the thinking is that people should be left with a nice feeling. Not too much agony, you know. But we *are* manipulated all the time. We know that and they know that. This could go on for another twenty years. There's no end in sight just now.

The next day I went to see the army in Lisburn and it has to be said that they take their propaganda every bit as seriously as the other combatants in this conflict. Every army officer has a buff-coloured restricted document entitled *Manual of Public Relations*. Under the heading 'Establishing Rapport' it says that reporters and photographers 'should always be treated as guests of officer status and hospitality should be offered to them on suitable occasions.'[18]

The welcome was indeed genial, beginning with a long and detailed briefing of the troubles. The IRA and INLA have generated 95 per cent of the violence against the security forces, I was told, with the Loyalist terrorist groups being the UVF, the UFF, the Protestant Action Force and the Red Hand Commandos.

The terrorists like to operate in their own patch, using local knowledge and often running South of the border. The Provisional IRA has some 100 to 300 men who would shoot a soldier, plant a bomb or take part in an attack. In addition to them there was a larger group who would always give help to a gunman. A substantial group would be Sinn Fein activists, believing in the ballot box and the Armalite. The IRA also knee-capped people accused of passing on information or anti-social behaviour.

The IRA are no longer a cowboy outfit, the army spokesman explained, having learned a lot by their mistakes. We hardly ever hear of car bombs now since they are indiscriminate weapons and it is uncertain when they will go off. The army once used to describe them mordantly as 'own goals' referring to the fact that they invariably exploded before the terrorist could retreat and would often kill innocent civilians. It also appeared that Gerry Adams had decided that they were bad for the image of Sinn Fein. A few years ago they were attacking commercial targets, but were now concentrating more and more on the security forces.

They do ring the changes, once using home-made Drogue bombs. They then had RDG-7 rocket launchers for attacking armoured vehicles. Three years ago they launched an attack on an army Land-rover, but missed, with the warhead going into a school where a nun was teaching twenty-seven children. 'It did not go off, but was seen as a massive public relations blunder.'

To give some idea of the way that the IRA has become more efficient: it took 191 attacks in 1979 to kill one policeman or soldier, but now it took about twenty attacks and they took a lot more care to ensure their getaway. 'Terrorists have all the advantages. Any problems and they have all the options.'

They also have all the advantages in terms of public relations. 'Unlike the government, the terrorist public-relations man is not accountable to anyone. He can state something as a fact when it is not. He is rarely challenged. They are not bound by the Queensberry Rules. But they are very skilful. They keep it simple. Brits Out.'

The IRA have always issued statements routinely though, as Barry White said, these statements were now being used more and more. Some are quite extensive and one in *The Times*, in an earlier campaign, went on for six paragraphs when the IRA was warning building contractors not to accept contracts with security services or they would be shot. 'Over the last four months our intelligence personnel have compiled accurate and extensive dossiers on all those involved in such work,' the statement said. 'As a result of this intelligence we are now in a position to take effective action if builders do not henceforth desist from playing an active role in support of the Crown forces.'

Indeed the IRA – who, it is again perhaps worth reminding ourselves, consist of only 100 hard-core members – now routinely issue statements to the media. They make statements saying that they have had a bad year, but then warn of a new terror. They still warn building contractors not to work for the police or army. They can say almost anything they like and it all gets reported.

They have always manipulated the media, the army spokesman said, particularly at terrorist funerals with someone giving the oration, the firing of shots, the masked gunmen – all staged for the television cameras. When Bishop Daley said that he was not going to allow this to happen, they fired shots at a place of their own choosing, inviting the media to go along there. Details of these invitations are never passed on to the security forces. The BBC had missed an invitation to a recent display of arms in connection with a funeral so they carried a still photograph. The Protestants do not have that kind of funeral. There are never any troubles at Protestant funerals.

Just last week the IRA issued a statement through the media asking people not to frequent certain areas. Otherwise the IRA would not be responsible. If you had to narrow it down to one thing: the media extends the same right of speech to the bad guys as the good guys. Section 31 in the Republic forbids terrorists from being allowed television time and giving Press conferences.

You can often get a dial-a-riot situation, by simply reporting that trouble has broken out; many run to the outbreak to join in. If one lot are throwing stones the other lot run in to throw stones, too. That week forty-two people had been arrested for street rioting. Street riots provide great media spectacles.

(Another aspect of dial-a-riot was once made to me by the Dean of Londonderry, the Very Reverend George Good. Sometimes television cameras would be set up in Londonderry and a riot followed in a few minutes, he said. When there were riots everyone longed for 6 p.m. to come. That was when the rampaging mobs went home to watch themselves on the television news. Then, reinvigorated, they would come pouring back on to the streets again.)[19]

Exactly how many of the killings take place in Northern Ireland for the sole purpose of publicity and propaganda is problematic and probably unknowable. At one stage in our interview the army spokesman suggested that 70 to 80 per cent of the attacks take place with one eye on the media. But, after I related this over a dinner with the Northern Ireland office, the same spokesman rang me back and denied that he had, in fact, said this.

But, in any event, we were again beginning to see further evidence of how the IRA had chosen the media as its main weapon of propaganda – and how the media submissively acquiesced to their deadly game. After a drink and a sandwich I left Lisburn simply wondering how the media had managed to get away with it for so long. There was in my journey, I fully admit, an element of having a theory for which I was seeking supporting evidence, yet on this visit I was not having to dig very hard anywhere. From almost every source evidence was deluging into my notebook that there was a huge lie at work in Ulster; one which had never been quite nailed.

Those who work in the media – it should again be strongly emphasised – are not aware that they are all joined in an embrace of savage and evil principles which are having savage and evil effects. They believe that anyone who challenges their work is an idiot who has been in the country for five minutes and understands nothing about its history. Newsmen might not be exactly helping the situation, but they are causing no harm either, they tell themselves. They are merely, at great personal risk and with enormous courage, gathering the news of the day. They abhor what is going on, in the same way as every other sane person. They are merely the mirrors of events over which they have no control.

But it is somewhere in the distorting reflections of these mirrors that the dark silhouette of the lie is taking shape.

I made an appointment to see John Conway, the BBC's editor of news and current affairs in Northern Ireland, and met a bright, personable man who had been on the *Belfast Telegraph* and had been doing this job for four and a half years. What he said about his job is a good and clear illustration of the thinking which informs the news.

Our guidelines are taken from the BBC Yellow Pages' case law dealing with violence and conflict. But they are only guidelines and are a starting-point for journalists on the ground. We are constantly updating them for our policy group. Major events like the prison sieges in Scotland are analysed and regional news editors travel to London for weekly meetings.

At a recent IRA funeral the ITN crew were present for the gun salute in a back street. We were not present, but we did use a still. It looked to the viewer as if it had been staged. Personally I do not like gun salutes, but they might be tolerable to show in the context of a funeral when all sides are making political points. If people were firing shots we should be negligent in not transmitting those shots.

Paramilitary groups supply videos, which are sometimes shown and sometimes not. We show them on their news' values. An IRA roadblock stopped the traffic for twenty minutes in Northern Ireland. We thought long and hard about it and showed some of it in the context of security. A local MP was making points. Here is a bunch of heavily-armed people taking over a road. We thought that it was in the public interest.

Our work is very difficult. A lot of the players have been at it for twenty years and have become quite sophisticated. They issue contradictory statements and 90 per cent of propaganda goes into the litter-bin. It is always very difficult to work out what comes first – the chicken or the egg. If I were a worker I should like to know if I was under any sort of threat and then I could take precautions. And we must remember that 78 per cent of all violence takes place away from the gaze of the media.

Would a withdrawal of the media have any effect?

No. It would be unworkable and unenforceable. The Republicans have their own newspaper. You would never get the Irish newspapers to comply nor the American or French, etc. In such a situation rumour would flourish and encourage terrorists to commit more spectacular crimes. People would be more prey to the paramilitaries. We do chase ambulances and this is all about dispelling rumour. In the present upsurge we have had to holler for more help from London. We are reasonably comfortable in what we are doing. The problems are not as bad as they were a few years back.

We cover all funerals – unless a family asks otherwise. The terrorists always have the first and last shout. Orations help to put the man in the context of his community. We are always aware that we operate in the full glare of a very critical populace. The point is that, if you kill people in a spectacular fashion, you are going to get a lot of publicity.

Do they deserve it?

You get back to news values. If you get killed quietly then you are done quietly. Spectacular deaths tend to generate a spectacular amount of publicity.

So here we have an insight into the way newsmen think about the news. We are back again to the centrality and overpowering importance of ideas in our culture, since these are the ideas which frame the way in which we are given our news. We have not only seen the way that the IRA has found an unwilling foster mother but, having been saddled with that role, the way that the foster mother then defends the way she is bringing up her violent and delinquent son. There is nothing at all wrong with the way we are bringing up this baby. Nothing.

If people were shooting guns they would be negligent in not showing that shooting. Paramilitary videos are shown on the basis of news values. If what is happening has 'a context' or 'it is in the public interest' then it should be shown. They themselves do not know if the chicken comes before the egg and, while the combined intelligence of the BBC cannot work that out, they continue to show the bloody results of violence. If they stopped showing the violence then everyone else would carry on doing so – so they have to continue. In fact, quite to the contrary, if they withdrew, the violence would get worse. The pursuit of ambulances is all about dispelling rumour. They had been at it for a long time and were reasonably comfortable in what they were doing. Orations about murderers put them in 'the context' of the community. Spectacular deaths deserve spectacular publicity.

Another extended justification for reporting violence was once given by Richard Francis, a former BBC Controller of Northern Ireland:

> It has been suggested that if there is trouble in the town we should not report it until it is over. One case quoted was when there was a riot going on in West Belfast during the course of which four Protestants were shot in East Belfast. It was suggested that we should have withheld broadcasting that information till after the riot in another part of the town was over. I don't accept that at all. In a town like Belfast, which is like a village, rumour can travel faster than radio. If we had not announced unequivocally that four Protestants had been shot, the rioting crowds would likely have made it four not fourteen, not shot but dead, and the riot could have been very much worse than it was.[20]

It looks as if you can justify almost every decision with the usual BBC-speak of 'context' or 'dispelling rumour'. There are then 'good reasons', enshrined in the BBC's Yellow Pages, for turning out the chaotic processions of sectarian killings, terrorist shootings, street riots and the endless funerals which form the basis of most Ulster news bulletins.

This is *news*, yet – whichever way you may look at it and whatever context you put it in and whatever rumours you may dispel or how many further riots you may have prevented – this news is nothing more than the *persistent pursuit of violence*. That is what this news is all about and it is these ideas which are leading to the inexorable brutalising of the community in which the television news has become as standard a feature of every home as a cup of tea. It is not the violence itself which is the real evil in Ulster. It is the relentless pursuit of that violence which is the real lie smouldering and burning in this province's dying heart. That dominance of that lie is the particular and peculiar triumph of the Man of Lawlessness in this desperate part of the world.

Even as the IRA has become so triumphant in exploiting this vicious lie then so, too, a whole host of other terrorist groups have also seized it knowing that all they have to do is practise or threaten violence. So then, early in 1989, there were the beginnings of other terrorist groups who at one stage seemed to be busy multiplying like wood-worm in an antique wardrobe, ranging from the Animal Liberation Front – who blew up part of Bristol University – to the Black Liberation Front in the West Midlands – who were threatening to shoot a chief constable unless he resigned – to Meibion Glyndwr, the Sons of Glyndwr who want Welsh independence and are reported to have napalm.

Just what should we miss if we never heard from these cranks? Just why do they get so much attention? Well, perhaps we are now beginning to understand why.

There are many who are beginning to ask why this news does not reflect the real lives of real people in a real world. St Paul urged us to think on whatsoever things are true, whatsoever things are just, whatsoever things are pure, whatsoever things are lovely, whatsoever things are of good report; if there be any virtue, and if there be any praise, think on these things (Phil. 4: 8–9). *Think on these things and know God.*

This line is also enshrined in the dedication panel of Broadcasting House, Portland Place, London.

This Temple of the Arts and Muses is dedicated to Almighty God by the first Governors of Broadcasting in the year 1931, Sir John Reith being Director-General. It is their prayer that good seed sown may bring forth a good harvest, that all things hostile to peace and purity may be banished from this house and that the people, inclining their ear to whatsoever things are beautiful and honest and of good report, may tread the path of wisdom and uprightness.

Yet such are our current news values, we publicise whatsoever is ugly, whatsoever is violent, whatsoever is perverted, whatsoever is of bad report. There is nothing of the spirit of God in our news and, in fact, it is destructive of His mind and surely causing the wildest grief in His heart. He knows that the bad seed sown is bringing home a bitter and dead harvest. He understands that the people, inclining their eyes to whatsoever things are brutal and criminal and of violent report, are treading the path of folly and hatred. He understands the way in which the Man of Lawlessness works.

On another visit to Ulster I remember the television news was being particularly apocalyptic and obnoxious – *about nothing at all*. A boy had gone missing for days, leading to

increasingly hysterical reports about his possible kid
by some group or other. He was finally found sleeping
had one fix of heroin too many, on a building site. Anot ....
a full item was given to the digging of a hole in a football pitch.
You don't always need a bomb, mad words and a telephone
number to make the news – sometimes a spade will do.

But try explaining any of this to the head of ITN or the
present Director-General of the BBC or the Controller for BBC
in Northern Ireland, Colin Morris, himself a minister of the
church. These men are among the most powerful apologists for
the media in the land.

In May 1988, Colin Morris gave the University of Ulster
Convocation Lecture, *Tip-toeing Through the Minefield*, the text of
which was notable for its complete and total defence of the BBC
and all its work. All decisions on the media coverage of
terrorism had been largely right. Words like impartiality,
balance, neutral, objectivity and fairly were printed in bold.

In a key section on the tiny band of terrorists, he said:

> Terrorism is sometimes mindless, motiveless and pathologically
> destructive; at other times it may be a suppurating sore, a revolting
> symptom that some part of the body politic is really hurting. And
> democracy has got to find out, it has got to scrutinise its life to see
> whether there are areas of rottenness which might harbour para-
> sitic organisms. To change the metaphor – society must be made
> aware of the nature of its enemies and what intellectual force their
> ideas possess. How can you fight an enemy whose strength you are
> unable or unwilling to assess?

In that process of examination Dr Morris continued, the media
have a central role – under carefully controlled conditions, just
as a surgeon may examine a cancer under carefully controlled
conditions, to ensure that the disease is not inadvertently
spread, so broadcasters must find mechanisms for scrutinising
dangerous and destructive ideas without exposing themselves
to manipulation and becoming dupes of those whom they seek
to expose.

> And we live in constant awareness of the dangers of manipulation.
> Everybody in Northern Ireland wishes to harness us to their war
> chariots – the Government, the politicians, the paramilitaries and a

fiercely sectarian public opinion. To pretend that we have never succumbed would be foolish; but over twenty years' experience of the Trouble, broadcasters and journalists have acquired a lot of experience in detecting the strategies of manipulation and side-stepping them. But, of course, we still sometimes get caught out.

Sometimes?
Later in his speech he began talking of the carbon monoxide of publicity.

Every piece of audience research done by the BBC has indicated revulsion on the part of the vast majority of viewers when they see violence, illegal acts and terrorist supporters on television and there is a marked increase in support for the police and security forces. Only when the human consequences of terrorism are seen in all their horror will there be dispelled some romantic notions of the freedom struggle tenaciously held in places remote from the blood-stained locus of action.

But this, I believe, shows the profoundest misunderstanding of the way in which even the terrorists themselves see their way forward. Their method is precisely so to sicken and revolt and weaken our will in Ulster that we shall, in the end, just be hurrying to pull out of Northern Ireland. And their principal medium is where it will have the most impact – on Dr Morris's beloved television. So when we see the blood-stained mat-tresses, the youths tarred and feathered, blood spattered on the pavement (a great favourite of television news this), the mangled bodies . . . when we see all this and we *are* revolted that is precisely what the IRA want us to see and why, in the end, we may well pull out.

On November 15th 1987, Mary Kenny wrote in the *Sunday Telegraph*: 'It is not particularly useful to shower abuse on the IRA – "scum", "swine", "bastards", etc. in the manner of the popular tabloids.'[21] It should be remembered that the IRA tactic is to sicken the British so thoroughly that people in this country come to feel that they want nothing more to do with Ireland. Thus the IRA and their sort *like* being denounced by the *Star*, the *Sun* and the *Daily Mirror* in big headlines: they believe it edges them nearer their goal. To be as repellent as possible is part of the plan.

Dr Colin Morris's real problem is that he loves television and, whenever he gets on the subject, there is no detectable cynicism at all in his thoughts or words. He wrote in his *God-in-a-Box* (Hodder and Stoughton, 1984):

> On television, good more or less triumphs over evil. Everything just about works out right in the end; complexities are, on balance, simplified and opposing opinions get fairly stated with none of them allowed to dominate. People tend to do the decent thing, and in the spectrum of mood which ranges from optimism to despair, the needle settles a little shakily on the sunny sector.
>
> No awful human calamity such as famine, earthquake or war is allowed to burn its searing images into the viewer's consciousness without being followed by the announcer's emollient comment, 'And now for something completely different . . .' By the end of the evening, black horror has paled into dull grey. And rightly so. A diet of unremitting woe is not only indigestible but ultimately counter-productive. When horror becomes insupportable, a merciful numbing sensation steals over the human soul.
>
> The strict truth is that the bigot, fanatic and extremist haven't got an outside chance of an uncontested run on national television in Britain. The liberal ideology of television may be misty and vague but it effortlessly rules the ether. The decency barrier, vapid as it is, has proved impenetrable to the shock waves of extremism.

Sir Ian Trethowan, the BBC Director-General, in *The Times* on June 4th, 1981, responded to suggestions that television cameras should be pulled out of Northern Ireland. 'But there was no television at Easter, 1916, nor in the years of the Troubles that followed, let alone in all the earlier periods of violence in Irish history,' he wrote.[22]

This is a favourite and recurring argument by all media apologists, so let us recall that from 1868 – when the Buffalo Express in New York state reported the violent death of John Lynch of Grace's Ohio Unit of Fenians – the press has always reported Ireland and Irish affairs largely in terms of its violence.[23]

The Easter rising of 1916 was reported in detail by newspapers, as were the sporadic and often bungled attacks on the British forces. In 1922 a British War Office record noted that in one department, namely publicity, Sinn Fein was unrivalled.

'This department was energetic, subtle and exceptionally skilful in mixing truth, falsehood and exaggeration and was
perhaps the most powerful and least fought arm of the Sinn
Fein forces.' The start of the real guerrilla war against the
British troops in Northern Ireland began in 1947 and these
attacks were always reported, followed then – as now – by
arrogant and often grandiloquent statements of responsibility
by the IRA.[24]

Acts of vandalism and downright buffoonery were always
launched for their 'headline-catching' qualities, but the IRA,
never more than 200 strong and never adding up to much, was
all but moribund by 1966. For fifty years both the press and the
infant television had ignored the very real problems of gerry-
mandering, the hated B Specials and the denial of Catholic
rights, but then there was violence. The civil-rights marches
started and heads were cracked.[25] And wherever two were
gathered in the name of violence then so, too, there was
television. More heads were cracked and more television
cameras turned up. After fifty years of silence the Irish problem
jumped out of its grave and back into the headlines. And then
came the start of the troubles whose career and intensity in the
Province almost exactly matches the career of television
there.

The civil-rights marches were attacked in Londonderry and,
within days, Belfast was engulfed in riots. Petrol bombs were
hurled, Catholic houses fired by Protestant mobs and vice
versa. The IRA dug up what they had hidden in the city, but
could manage no more than two Thompsons, a sten gun, one
Lee-Enfield and nine hand-guns.[26] But they could fire a few
symbolic bullets *and* they could make a few statements. And the
Man of Lawlessness promptly did the rest.

He seized on every flickering flame of sectarian violence and
poured rivers of gasoline over them. Anyone with a gun became
a silhouetted celebrity to be interviewed. He revived the dead
IRA and fomented mob riots by shovelling news of war and
rumours of war into every home. Threats of hatred became
amplified; acts of vandalism became declarations of war;
isolated street gangs became armies on the move. There were
single-shot snipings, and bombings followed by routine phone
calls claiming credit.

Such *seemed* the murderous and armed intentions of the
Catholic community; the Man of Lawlessness also managed to
spawn the Protestant murder gangs of the UDA. Blindly,
recklessly, hatefully he managed to get both sides to reach for
one another's throats. Homes were ransacked, gangsterism and
racketeering flourished, civilisation *appeared* to be falling apart
and every move was promoted and exaggerated beyond its true
importance in the deadly sunshine of publicity. The poison of
the few became the grief and terror of the many. Brigadier
Richard Clutterbuck, a trenchant commentator on these issues,
wrote in his *The Media and Political Violence*: 'There is good
reason to believe that the immense publicity given to the INLA
after the murder of Airey Neave MP was a major factor in the
IRA's decision to match it by murdering Earl Mountbatten. It
certainly brought them a matching publicity splash.'[27]

The Man of Lawlessness had seized and exploited his
opportunity avidly in the Province and has not, to this day, let
go.

But hold on there. You can't blame us. We are the BBC. We
are never, ever wrong about anything. We have got our Yellow
Pages. We have never made any mistakes and, if we had been
exploited, as you suggest, we should have been the very first to
have seen through it. We are *impartial*.

Future historians will hang that ironic word on the tombstone of the BBC when the real history of the troubles comes to
be written.

Even in my own experience I have encountered a total
unwillingness to entertain any opposing points of view in
Northern Ireland as when, in 1986, I made a film for Central
Television, *Visions of a Media Man*, when I gave the television
service there a bit of stick. Well, a lot of stick actually. The film
was networked throughout Britain, but never shown in
Northern Ireland where it had been scheduled to appear.

A few years later I was flown, at the expense of Ulster
Television, to Northern Ireland to talk about my new book,
Stained Glass Hours. There, next to the tomb of St Patrick, in
Downpatrick, I was filmed explaining that there was a new set
of demons at work in Northern Ireland which were every bit as
terrifying and destructive as the ones St Patrick had once found
here – except that the new demons were technological and they

lived in the media and we did not understand how they were
destroying us.

Even as I spoke those words in front of that television crew I
knew that the film would not be shown, and it was not. But all I
have ever truly understood in my stumble through life is that
you are what you live and believe and that there is never any
room for compromise. Opposition to these powerful people is
a very lonely business.

Video Visions

In 1983, in the first novel I ever wrote, *The Electric Harvest*, I sat
down and tried to envisage a Britain in the video age, if current
trends continued.[28] All football supporters would have been
banned from football grounds and the matches played only for
television. Official attempts to control the booming crime wave
would include secret labour camps in the North of England and
daily televised public floggings. Television helicopters and
armoured television vans would be scouring the city streets
looking for 'on-the-spot' crime. The black populations would
be forcibly confined to their own ghettos 'for their own safety'
and the cable and satellite systems would be overflowing
with sleaze and violence, including 'snuff' films. Keith
Richards – the only surviving member of the Rolling Stones –
was negotiating to buy Buckingham Palace.

We had finally lost our will in Ulster and pulled the troops
out, which had resulted in a civil war in which hundreds were
dying daily.

It was a deliberately grim and black picture which sought to
dramatise the argument that the media mafia actually creates
violence rather than, as it likes to suppose, merely reflects it. It
is with no satisfaction at all that, today, I see our country
moving steadily down that terrible road. Already football
matches have been played only for television behind locked
doors because of terrace violence and it should be remembered
that the horrific tragedy at the Hillsborough football stadium
on April 15th, 1989, in which 95 Liverpool fans were crushed to
death, would not have happened but for the perimeter fences
put up to control soccer hooligans. Then the soccer season

ended, as it had begun, with record numbers of fights amongst
rival fans – all dutifully recorded by television cameras and
shown to us repeatedly on the news.

But particularly during 1988 and particularly in the television news coverage of Northern Ireland, I have seen virtual
reruns of *The Electric Harvest*, especially in the murders of the
plain-clothes servicemen after an IRA funeral in Milltown
cemetery. Already the first signs of a dead harvest are there for
all to see.

It now seems time to cut through two decades of 'telemag-
newsspeak' to point out clearly and unequivocally that unless
our ideas about news change, and change immediately, the
whole province is going to slide into anarchy and destruction in
which *everyone is going to lose everything*. It is time to tell *all* those
who organise our news and provide us with our social information that, however unwittingly, they have got it all wrong; that
they have instigated a wholesale moral perversion in Ulster;
and that it is time that this evil pursuit of violence is stopped.

Nowhere in this book – or in my mind – is there an argument
– either covert or overt – for banning a film, burning a book or
the Government censorship of news. There have always been
too many who are all too ready with the scissors, the blue pencil
and the bonfire. Censorship always promotes what it seeks to
extinguish and one Third Reich was enough for any one world.

We are clearly going to have to come to terms with a news
media which has an important and useful role in analysing
events, finding the reasons why such events happened, recording rites of passage and showing us unrevealed aspects of the
real world. But anyone who cares for Northern Ireland and her
children should now stand up together and create a forum for
debate – away from the eyes of all the media – and decide on
their arguments, clarify their ideas and mobilise their anger.
Then they should send a deputation to all the media executives
in Ulster and expose their ideas to a whole hurricane of hard
questions and truth-telling.

And the very first question should be: Why are you so
powerfully and persistently obsessed with the violence of the
few?

And a few more questions might take the line of: In view of
the devastating consequences for *all* the community, why not

just ignore the actions of the men of violence? All right, so they will blow up bigger things to attract attention – that is a problem *you* created and not us. You provided terrorism with a home in the first place. But, if they continue bombing, then still ignore them until they are fully and finally convinced that there is no more profit to them with publicity if they continue down that road. You might find your news values sacred, but we find our children's safety, security and stability even more sacred. We do not want to be dragging the bodies of our children home through the fields of a dead harvest. We do not want to pay for your ideas with their lives – and neither shall we.

It is not that you sometimes get things wrong, but you have never, ever, since the troubles started, got anything right. We bear no malice towards you; we understand that you came to this country with all the received ideas on news and that you have only ever seen it as your difficult job, but you have fed off our misfortunes for twenty years now – you have filled up quite enough programmes and made quite enough films and sold quite enough newspapers – and now we just want you all to go home and leave the local media to get on with what T. S. Eliot defined as its proper job of reflecting the culture of the community.

In October 1988 the Government announced that in an effort to curb the oxygen of publicity to the terror groups there would be a direct television ban of the words of all leaders of such extremist groups as the IRA, the Protestant Red Hand, Sinn Fein and the Ulster Defence Association. 'The Government has decided that the time has now come to deny this easy platform to those who use it [television] to propagate terrorism,' Douglas Hurd, the Home Secretary, told the House of Commons.

This ban was, in my view, misconceived and yet another botch-up in tackling the problem of terrorists who *use violence*. No one has ever been interested in their arguments anyway – least of all television news – and, indeed, an interview with a terrorist had not been conducted on television for ages. But this news service always was – and still is – powerfully interested in terrorist violence and it is out of this fatal conjunction that most all terrorist power has sprung. All we have ever heard about is their violence and the net effect of the ban is that violence is all we are ever going to hear about in the future.

And perhaps equally predictably the powerful voices of the media mafia made outraged noises about this 'political inter-ference' immediately joining together and complaining about censorship.

But it is not government bans – particularly those inspired by Margaret Thatcher, who does not enjoy widespread affection in Ulster – that are needed here. What is needed is that the peoples of Ulster come together in common mind and tell the media to clean themselves up. Christians, in particular, should be looking to arouse the consciences of all good men in Northern Ireland who will just go to the media and tell them the truth, since the truth is the only really effective way of control-ling lies. Those who would censor lies to make way for the truth either do not understand the power of truth, or they do not believe in it. Serving up an unrelieved diet of violence is not the truth, no matter what justifications are found for doing it. Most news is little more than the bewitched and Romantic obsession with unreason.

But the truth will prevail one day. We just have to believe that or there is very little point in our ever getting out of bed again. The truth will set us free.

If the media executives did come to see any power or truth in such arguments; if they saw that they had managed to give a hundred men the power to ruin and destabilise the country; if they knew that they had set up a giant theatre of terrorism and given the murdering gangsters of the IRA a worldwide stage; if they accepted that they had helped the media to become the internal locomotive power of the troubles; if they understood that it was their daily shower of the black rain of violence and hatred on to every home that had broken and divided the communities . . . if they even started to acknowledge the truth of a fraction of these charges . . . then they would immediately pack it all up and it is likely that this civil war would come to an end.

But such a move is very unlikely even if it would only involve the truly terrible admission that there had been blood on their hands and that they had become an important, if unexposed, protagonist in this war. So this war will carry on.

What I am arguing is not that wars and natural disasters should not be reported, but that the violence of a small group of lunatics should be ignored by the media – but not by the judiciary. I do not believe that, in the short term, the violence will necessarily go away, but that it will assume its proper proportion. (I have been told by a documentary film-maker, but been unable to investigate for myself, that violence stopped in the South African townships following the Botha ban on television there in November 1985.) Furthermore, the reports on the violence in Northern Ireland would no longer have the serious destabilising effect on the province and their million and a half people, nor will they promote further violence as happened – as we shall see in the next chapter – during the racial riots in our own cities over the last few years. The root causes of violence in our society, it is becoming clear, are images of violence.

But for today anyway the truth is not making much progress in Northern Ireland and the television executives are bound to continue to refuse to believe that there is any truth in these arguments. They will continue to dismiss such arguments with their favourite word: *simplistic*. Violent films will continue to be made. Books about worried revolutionaries will continue to be written. Television news will continue to feature murder after murder. The situation will continue to worsen and the Romantic poison will continue to infect the community's very bloodstream.

On January 25th, 1989, the BBC screened a film, *Elephant*, directed by Alan Clarke, which was set in Belfast and just portrayed sectarian killing after sectarian killing. The murders were heavily stylised with no background music or dialogue. In its sensationalism and relentless savagery the film told us very clearly what a gung-ho Romantic Alan Clarke is – he also made the brutal *Scum*. 'Publicity is always given to the big bombings and shootings so I wanted to publicise the small murders,' he said the day after the screening on television.

Perhaps even more saddening was that yet another nail was hammered into the coffin of Northern Ireland; yet more commercial mileage had been made out of the escalating violence. This film was perhaps the most naked example yet of exactly the kind of film that the Man of Lawlessness loves the most.

In February 1989 Clarke was at it on the BBC again with a film called *The Firm*, which told the sorry story of Clive Bissell –

Bexy – a soccer hooligan who, with an arsenal of weapons, roams the country with his gang and fighting with other gangs. Cars went up in flames, fights were ferocious and cheeks were slashed with Stanley knives. Bexy's baby even cut herself badly while playing with his Stanley knife. The only explanation that he gave for his behaviour was that he needed a buzz. No mention, naturally, of the influence of films, television or the work of Alan Clarke.

But what was truly unforgivable about the film was not so much its content as its timing since it was shown during the week in which the BBC issued its new guidelines on violence. 'The consequences of violent acts should not be overlooked otherwise there is a danger of seeming to sanitise them,' the guidelines said. 'It is important to take particular care when dealing with weapons which might encourage imitation or methods which might suggest how violence can be made more effective.'

The very fact that *The Firm* was shown at all suggests that such guidelines were yet another species of the BBC's mealy-mouthed words which could be freely and totally ignored.

Today our Man of Lawlessness remains firmly in control and the cause of truth is struggling to get even so much as a toehold. In Ulster the people are crying out in those barbed-wire streets with barely any understanding of the real nature of the evil which has overtaken them. The Psalmist said that we become what we see and, thanks to almost all arms of the media, which feeds on a diet of hatred, bigotry and violence, this is surely what has happened.

At a private meeting Sir John Hermon, the head of the Royal Ulster Constabulary, put it another way:

> Is the freedom of terrorist organisations to disseminate their propaganda through the news media a price we must pay for the maintenance of democracy? Is it acceptable that the terrorist should have the freedom of radio, television and newspapers to justify murder, to threaten more murder, to intimidate, to poison people's minds and to spread fear, hatred and division? Or should the safeguarding of life and the protection of the quality of life place a limitation on the freedom of the media? Should the terrorist's abuse of this democratic freedom be denied him in the interests of the common good?

There will never be any peace in Ulster as long as the media keeps its current ideas on news with the activities of the men of terror inflamed, exaggerated and distorted until the whole frightened country finally comes to impale itself on its own violence and fear. For that is the real nature of evil, certainly as it is working in Ulster; the way in which it deceives everyone, including those who are promoting it. When you listen to media apologists you get the quite firm impression that they are gathering up all this street violence *for our own good* and, what is much worse than that dotty notion, these men with more letters after their names than a chiropodist, *actually believe it*. When evil comes it always comes with evil's undiluted power to deceive. That is the real secret at the heart of the mystery of lawlessness. As we shall see again later, even the very elect of God will be taken in.

A Libyan Flame-thrower

At the end of my Belfast visit in that fearful summer of 1988 I took a taxi from the Europa to the airport. The driver was a blond, softly-spoken man whose thoughts seemed to have a curious integrity about them, which is not what strikes you about many taxi-drivers. It turned out that he had been an active Republican who, many years ago, had been caught in possession of a Drogue bomb. He had been sent to prison, but during that time he'd had a religious experience, he said, and turned to the Lord. On his release he had gone into a Cistercian monastery, but found that the life there did not quite suit him so he had left to become a taxi-driver. Now, still faithful, he was a happy man or, at least, as happy as anyone could be in Belfast these days.

He still heard the gossip about the activities of his old cronies, of course, and added that, just now, 'the boys' had acquired new SAM missiles and flame-throwers, courtesy of Colonel Gaddafi. They had plans to use them on the British mainland. Did I think the flame-throwers would have much of an effect on Britain's stability?

I did not know, I said. All I was absolutely certain of was that when two Army cleaners were incinerated on their way home for tea in some London back lane, the worldwide publicity would be enormous. The sheer sense of theatre would be amazing.

Later, sitting on the plane I caught yet another glimpse, in my mind's eye, of the Man of Lawlessness and his cultural habits. In matters of art he always enjoyed the most bloody and barbaric tableaux, I decided. In matters of music it was always the sound of shootings and war or cries of pain which raised his emotions. But, in terms of the theatre, he loved plays with simple story lines and lots of straightforward killings.

I actually thought that I did get a glimpse of him sitting in his theatre of terrorism, laughing, with a bag of popcorn in his hand, as the curtain rose yet again on yet another act showing the demons of violence attacking the children of innocence. At the end of every act – which was always much the same as the previous act – he was rapturous with applause. He understood fully how the images and metaphors of violence destroyed our relationship with God and *that*, as far as he was concerned, was the real and proper function of all art.

6

Riots on the Village Green

*In which we inspect the ideas of Marshall McLuhan – Visit the
racial disorders in Brixton – Take a trip to sunny Miami and
violence-torn South Africa – Get hauled up before the Press
Council for making abusive remarks about the video industry –
And track down the caves of alienation where the soccer hooligan
was born.*

The Global Village

We do not understand television; we have never even started to
understand its power and the way it works in our society and on
our cultural imagination. It is The Force. But what is The
Force?

One man who did try to understand and explain The Force
was Marshall McLuhan, a Canadian educated at Cambridge.
Early in his career he began a journal, *Explorations*, which was
concerned with 'exploring the grammar of such languages as
print, newspapers and television' and with 'the revolutions in
the packaging and distribution of ideas and feelings'. He
believed that the clearest way to see through a culture was to
attend to its tools for conversation. These conversational tools
were widely deployed in our media which in its turn shaped our
culture. If we wanted to understand our society then all we had
to do was study our media. There everything would be

explained. The media brought us messages and shaped our environments. Parts of the media were 'hot' – low in audience participation – and others were 'cool' – requiring work to be done by the audience. The media was the message.

Everyone is being changed and reshaped on the electronic hearth, he argued. Television has become a landmark in the evolution of human consciousness. But it is not only the individual who is being changed by television but the world itself. Through The Force the world was beginning to acquire a new worldwide nervous system. The world was becoming one television global village – a new age of Pentecostal unity – in which international boundaries would disappear and we should all enter into one central communality, sharing our ideas, feelings and values in a seamless web of electronics.

McLuhan believed that this deconstruction of a widely complex world into a single village was a good and positive act; that the media would recreate and invigorate a collapsed culture. The scientific forces of the Renaissance had effectively destroyed religious belief and so, now, the scientific advances of the electronic media would unite world culture and revive its religious sensibility.

Many who believed that the world was falling apart found such ideas attractive, if controversial. The age of the media had found its first prophet and, for the first time, we had a new grammar and vocabulary with which to write about the media. We were excited about the notion of being one television global village. There was a real hope that this electronic Babel might create a lively and vital culture which would surround our lives with something new, forceful and brilliant. Academics began behaving like half-starved dogs who had just been thrown a huge and meaty bone, filling up acres of space about the metaphors of the media, its structuralist approach, the rhetoric of the image, the semiotics of this and the mechanical myths of that. We were heading into a Brave New World in which the academics had a lot of fun while we, the new villagers, flourished in our great new electronic environment. It was not to be.

Already alien forces, excited beyond measure by the prospect of worldwide domination, had quickly come into our village, offering their services. They came in their best suits and clutching the most brilliant degrees. They spoke about their anxiety to serve the community. But in reality, and unknown to themselves, they were already serving someone else. For it was not the ideals of love, truth and beauty that were now being promoted by the new village seers, rather the images of hatred, falsehood, ugliness and violence. The 'olde worlde' charm of the Morris dancers tip-tapping around a maypole in the village green were 'rescheduled' because people needed to know about a riot some 200 miles away. The miscreant plastered by a few cabbages in the village stocks was replaced by the mass murderer dying in a gas chamber. The ducks on the village pond became horrific monsters bursting out of people's chests and running amok, killing all and sundry. The parson in his pulpit became the ranting terrorist making his unreasonable and undemocratic demands. Was this the grammar and vocabulary of the new village that McLuhan believed was going to unite a disordered world and revive a new religion? Was he guilty of a facile optimism, or was he watching a different television set from the rest of us?

Faster than light, drifting between a series of mirrors, when only his coat-tails were occasionally spotted, the ideas and values of our Man of Lawlessness took over as the real village seer. Like Clint Eastwood's Man With No Name he had drifted in from nowhere and become both sheriff and landlord. And since his silent and virtually unnoticed takeover, he has been making repeated and powerful displays of his destructive talents with such deceptive guile that he has still not been identified.

As we have just seen, he has been working virtually unnoticed and unchallenged in Northern Ireland for the last twenty years. His power is both inexhaustible and inextinguishable. If anyone ever challenges the validity of any of his decisions or movements then a dozen brilliant men in sharkskin suits will leap forward and defend his interests powerfully and ferociously. Yes, the world clearly did have a new electronic nervous system and, once he had adjusted to it, the Man of Lawlessness had begun his work with relish. At long last he had found a perfect cosmos within which to work and, just like Luke Skywalker, was using The Force.

The Riots Spread

Some of his very best efforts with The Force have been made in the streets of Britain where, in the summer of 1981, on Friday, July 10th, there was a riot in Liverpool's Toxteth. The siren call of trouble soon had the television cameras hurrying down into the riot-torn streets and, within hours, the Man of Lawlessness had inflamed a fury of rioting activity throughout Britain. Almost every city came to the boil, and hundreds, if not thousands, were rising in mindless attack.

The very air in our streets was thick with tension and fear. I was walking down the main road of London's Stoke Newington the day after Toxteth – one of the few multiracial areas to escape rioting in London – when a man broke a window. Whether he had been watching the '*Six O'Clock Violence*' was not known, but everywhere there were screams with people running into shop doorways to hide. That night there was a huge riot in Brixton and riots in many other cities.

While the riots were going on in these largely working-class areas, there was another outbreak of agitated bodies in the middle-class areas when whole armies of 'experts' ran for buses and taxis to get to the radio stations and television studios where they let loose a hurricane of theories about the reasons for the rioting. There was much talk of overzealous policing, inner-city deprivation, drugs and lenient sentencing. Their favourite whipping-boy was our old friend Mr Unemployment, who gets the blame for just about everything these days.

One of the few who was not heaping the blame on the much-abused Mr Unemployment was Mary Whitehouse, who, while watching the television news, saw with horror, among other sequences, a youth kicking out a huge plate-glass window in Toxteth. The youth sprang back as the window hit the ground then stepped through the shattered frame and helped himself to some clothes. Mrs Whitehouse sent off two telegrams, one to Peter Woon, editor of BBC Television News, and one to David Nicholas, editor of Independent Television News. Both telegrams urged, 'Please consider whether the current massive television coverage of acts of vandalism and violence is contributing to the spread of the riots . . .'[1]

To her amazement both telegrams were read out without comment on both news channels.

In a party political broadcast during those riots Margaret Thatcher looked drawn and nervous. 'Nothing can condone the appalling level of violence that we have seen on television,' she said. 'We all know that violence will destroy everything we value. That is why the violence must be stopped. The law must be upheld. People must be protected. Then we can put these terrible events behind us, repair the damage and begin to rebuild confidence.' Even as she spoke rioting was spreading through the country. Even quiet places with low immigrant populations like Cirencester and Aldershot were hit by troubles. The Prime Minister spent eight hours on July 9th at Scotland Yard and Brixton police-stations. Four days later she paid a much-publicised visit to Toxteth, where she said:

We are now living with the first television generation. A generation of adults brought up for twenty-five years on continuous television – some of them watching it for four or more hours a day. Television images inevitably come to represent the norms and aspirations for the viewers. How could some young people, who had been brought up to watch television for several hours a day, do otherwise than absorb some of the values to which they were exposed by it? How could they fail to be affected in their attitudes and conduct by the attitudes and behaviour they saw portrayed on the screen?

You do of course have the duty to report the sort of events we have been witnessing recently. [She went on, looking directly at television reporters.] You have a duty to show the disfigurations of society as well as its more agreeable aspects. But may I put the point to you in the way it was put to me by one of your colleagues in television? If the television of the Western world uses its freedom continually to show all that is worst in our society, while the centrally-controlled television of the Communist world and the dictatorships show only what is judged advantageous to them and suppress everything else – how are the uncommitted to judge between us? How can they fail to misjudge us if they view matters only through a distorted mirror? Our democracy can only be damaged if we distort, whether by neglect or intent.[2]

But despite these words the television coverage continued and so, purely coincidentally it must be understood by all, did the riots. Everywhere from Toxteth to Wood Green youths were appearing with Balaclavas and bin liners over their heads. Cars were being overturned and set on fire. Petrol bombs were exploding against walls in cities hundreds of miles apart. Milk-floats were being commandeered. The village green had never been in such a mess and next thing they would be digging up the cricket pitch, by Jove. Lawlessness rules, OK? Yes, he most certainly did and still does.

Later David Nicholas admitted in a letter to Mary White-house that, 'Media coverage of the disturbance last week has probably had some copy-cat effect.' Peter Woon of the BBC also said that it would be 'foolish to pretend that there has been no copy-cat effect'. Nevertheless, the coverage of the riots continued and later that same month we found David Nicholas, speaking in the Edinburgh International Television Festival, in a far from contrite mood and boldly making some very familiar assertions.

> Television news must cover street violence as it happens, despite the danger that it might be copied by people seeing it on their screens. I am deeply concerned about young people copying violence they see in the news coverage on television. But television would do a public disservice by misrepresenting what was happening on the streets. I certainly think one has to face up to reality. There is certainly an element of documentation. The hallmarks of the Belfast street academy have been re-enacted on the streets of our cities in the past few weeks. But we should be misinterpreting an event if we did not tell it to the best of our ability as it happens. People want to know whether to steer clear of trouble or get their kids off the street.
>
> The public would not have been helped if ITN and other news organisations had shown a toned-down version of riots in Toxteth, Brixton, Liverpool and other places. Would the public have been able to make a sensible contribution to the subsequent debate or weigh those issues in their own minds if television had not told it as it was?

Richard Francis, who had become Head of News and Current Affairs at the BBC, also issued a statement after the riots asking if they 'were to deny the vast majority of the public information that they had a right to know, a picture they had a right to see, for fear of stimulating law-breakers on the fringe?' Again he

asserted that there was no conclusive evidence that television
had the effect that people like Mary Whitehouse claimed.[3]

So here we were back in that well-dug foxhole all over again;
back with the public's need to know; the television people's
sacred duty to report reality as they see it; their public-spirited
effort to warn people away from trouble areas; and their
enormous concern that the public sees the violence as it is so
that they can make a measured Aristotelian response.

The next summer there was a stormy protest in Brixton
about the demolition of homes in which three people received
minor injuries and five were arrested. 'Black Mob on the
Rampage', spluttered the *Sun*. 'Police Rout Brixton Mob',
reported the *Daily Mail*. The incidents were also covered by
both television channels. Yet the week before some 800 black
youngsters had staged a triumphant disco evening in aid of
charity in Brixton, but none of the media was anywhere to be
seen at this event, which went totally unreported as, of course,
there had been no violence at this disco. The public did not
need to know about this outbreak of peace, according to
'telemagnewspeak'. It was not necessary for them to know
when something had gone well so that they could frame their
response.

There were, of course, the most enormous and compelling
public reasons for one of the following news bulletins screened
by the BBC on November 2nd, 1984. It began with a commend-
able item on the Ethiopian crisis and was followed by an item
about three young thugs who broke into a house, cut off one of
the husband's toes and stuffed it into his mouth. This was
followed by an item about an Indian garage where a Sikh was
cornered by Hindus and burned alive. There was the battered
face of another Sikh who had been beaten up on a train. Next
there was an item about an assassinated Polish priest and his
funeral in a graveyard in Warsaw. Then came the Iraq–Iran
war and we were shown the dust, dirt and a cut-throat.
Rocket-launchers blasted away in the background. There was
an item about a grandmother who was executed in America by
injection after a protracted spell in Death Row, but we did not
actually watch the needle going into the skin since that might
have been upsetting.[4]

There is no peace or beauty, then, this summer evening in

our little village. The ducks have all died after their pond was polluted by acid rain. The village green is brown and dead following napalm defoliation. The blacksmith has beaten his ploughshares into swords and run off to join the IRA. The chapel is at violent war with the church – or perhaps it is vice versa. There are bloody riots in the Women's Institute and, as we suspected all along, the parson is a pervert who, in a fit of violent jealousy late last night, cut off one of the sexton's toes.

That's as near as McLuhan's global village is going to get to being reunited into one cultural body, with a revived faith, which is to say not very near at all. Yes, all of us are being changed on the electronic hearth, but with almost every video and with almost every news bulletin, all for the worse. There is no spirit of God at work anywhere in this village. This is a damned and doomed village which has been taken over by the Man of Lawlessness. T. S. Eliot's nightmare day when we are going to end up killing one another around the village green is clearly far closer than anyone has yet dared imagine.

But despite our infinite weariness and periodic complaints, riots have remained a staple and much-loved component of our news bulletins, though the one question that no one had actually managed to answer, in that battle-scarred summer of 1981, was why all those cities had become engulfed in riots at the same time since, apart from a bit of fringe copy-catting, television had nothing to do with it. Nothing at all. Did every would-be looter in the land, in widely distant cities, all decide independently that the night had come for a spot of lively pillaging? The answer soon came and was featured on both television news services.

On the account of David Cox, Head of Current Affairs at London Weekend Television, Stephen Hearst, controller of the BBC Future Policy Group – an executive charged with defending the industry's image – met Michael Tracey, head of the British Film Institute's new Broadcasting Research Unit who was 'looking for targets for probes of topicality and relevance'. They lunched, as these people are wont to do, and 'no sooner had the cheese-board arrived' than they had found a topical and relevant target. They would investigate the relationship between television and the riots.[5]

The report, financed by the BBC and the IBA to the tune of

some £1,000, and produced within days, rejected any possibility that television had any influence on the riots. 'It took no account whatever of the long-term conditioning effect of televised violence, nor of the cumulative effect of the coverage of the techniques of violent protest – the stoning, burning of cars, petrol bombs, etc – which have appeared on our television screens for many years,' said Mary Whitehouse.

Apparently the Institute's researchers had spoken to fifty teenagers and according to them fewer than 10 per cent had actually watched any kind of television news at all. The news of the rioting was, apparently, mostly carried from pub to pub or, if not that, by telephone. Their reports were put out in full on both ITN and the BBC, giving those great and pure organisations a full pardon for any contribution that they may have made to the disorders.

Later a voice of sanity did ring out when Lord Scarman finally delivered his report on the Brixton disorders.

> The media, particularly the broadcasting media, do in my view bear a responsibility for the escalation of the disorders (including the looting) in Brixton on Saturday, 11 April, and for their continuation the following day, and for their imitative element in the later disorders elsewhere . . . I do urge editors and producers . . . at all times to bear in mind that rioters, and others, in their exhibition of violence respond alarmingly to what they see (wrongly but understandably) as the encouraging presence of the TV camera and the reporter.

In his conclusion Lord Scarman emphasised particularly, and as a matter of urgency, the need for newspaper editors, television and radio producers and journalists to give continuous attention to the social implications of their awesome power to influence minds, the attitudes and the behaviour, not only of the reading, viewing and listening public, but also of those whose unlawful behaviour they report.

But, in this world, you believe only what you want to believe so the reporting of disorders has continued until we came to the summer of 1985 when, for virtually a whole month, our little village was again immersed in almost daily reports of rioting in South Africa. This summer in question the British public 'needed to know' all about the violence in South Africa and

night after night were presented with images of blacks assault-
ing heavily-defended police lines, with mobs killing one
another, some with burning necklaces of rubber tyres. We were
also shown people actually being hacked to death so that
'we could better understand the situation' and 'frame our
response'.

Devoid of any moral context, these reports gave the impression that such acts were understandable, even justifiable.
The clear message to young blacks in Britain was that if you did
not get what you perceived as your rights then you were entitled
to riot for them.

Every night the twin spirits of violence and unreason were
distorted and inflamed through our square-eyed monsters then
having their predictable effect in Britain since, towards the end
of that summer, Handsworth, a Birmingham suburb, went up
in flames as largely black youths went on an orgy of looting,
arson and violent assault. One in Rastafarian dreadlocks made
most of the front pages carrying a petrol bomb. The Man of
Lawlessness's faculty – having accomplished some exciting
research in South Africa, with some sound field research in the
Belfast Street Academy – had found hundreds of new potential
undergraduates.

Then, again predictably, since the immediate media invasion of Handsworth was almost as vigorous as the rioting,
parts of Liverpool went up again and so did Tottenham where a
gun was used and a policeman was hacked to death by three
young blacks.

It is always totally consistent with the work of the Man of
Lawlessness that he can always mobilise most effectively those
without any formal religious sense; in this case young blacks,
many of whom have lost their original culture and religious
values. Lawlessness finds it almost impossible to operate in the
presence of strong belief and unshakable conviction. The
biggest misreading of the Ulster crisis is to call it 'a religious
war' as it is almost only the activities of the churches on both
sides which have prevented it from becoming a bigger blood-
bath than it already is.

A Lesson from America

The same full-scale promotion of civil disorder happened in America when, after a riot in one city, they spread all over the country. Edmund Carpenter wrote in *Don Quixote*:

> Suppose a person, even an entire group is ignored by the media. Until recently America was full of invisibles. Blacks were ignored in literature. On radio they became Amos 'n' Andy played by two white men. On film they became comic servants. They were never shown as cowboys though in real life about a third of the post-Civil-War cowhands were black. Deadwood Dick was as black as coal, but on film he turned pink-cheeked and blue-eyed. Blacks made their first public appearance on TV when they turned to violence. Suddenly they were no longer invisible. For one brief moment they could be seen on TV. At which point they were also seen on the streets.[6]

So the key to a 'TV appearance' – as must have occurred to all – was to cause a lot of aggravation . . . murder, violence, vandalism, *anything* and *they would be noticed*. They would become pleasing to the Man of Lawlessness and he would anoint them by enabling them to bask in the sunshine of the warmest and most brilliant publicity.

The use of violence to attain publicity has long been understood in Britain. 'Suffragettes quite literally played with fire,' wrote J. B. Priestley. 'They set to work in all manner of buildings – they planted bombs in many famous churches, not even exempting Westminster Abbey and, determined to get publicity at all costs, they smashed a case of porcelain in the British Museum. It was all bold propaganda out of control.'[7]

In *Race Against Prime Time*, an American documentary examining television news coverage of race riots in Miami in 1980, the evidence was incontrovertible. Citizens in a Miami ghetto saw that only acts of lawlessness attracted the television crews. Media interest in black culture or injustice was nil so the citizens served up lots of trouble and got the attention which they felt they needed.

In the local newsroom it emerged that the journalists' prime source of information was the police radio frequencies. As a result, the television audience was offered an incoherent succession of violent images, which were stripped of their social and historical context as the broadcasting professionals unthinkingly complied with newsroom ethics. In times of stress the journalist, like the soldier, does not question commands. He just goes in and does it, trying not to think of the consequences.

Since the civil rights era of the late 'sixties, American television has set up guidelines for the coverage of civil strife. These vary from station to station, but usually include a ban on interviewing rioters, a ban on the use of identifiable cars and an injunction not to report violence while ignoring its cause. The last is evidently the hardest rule to keep.

Establishing the Link

Every research project ever conducted on the relationship between television and violence has shown a link between televised and social violence. And violence is violence whether it is on *Play for Today*, a Hollywood film or a news bulletin. There seems to be some unwritten rule, which never quite made it into the BBC's Yellow Pages, that violence stops being violence when it is on a news bulletin; that because it happened in reality, it is then allowable on our screens regardless of the riotous consequences. Ulster has paid in full for that unwritten rule.

In the autumn of 1984, at the height of the miners' strike, when scenes of picket-line violence were being shown continually on the news, a primary-school headmaster was startled to see similar scenes being re-enacted at his own school. During the mid-morning break he was in his study and happened to look out of the window and see the entire playground clear with one half of the children at one end and the other half at the other. On a given signal the two companies began to charge towards the middle of the playground with a crunch encounter resulting in the whole school fighting. He rushed out into the playground to break them up, grabbed one boy out of the mêlée and asked what on earth they were doing. The child replied: 'It's all right, sir. We're playing police and miners!'

A total of some 700 reports have established the link between aggressive behaviour in children and their exposure to 'aggression' of any kind. As far back as 1975, Dr Michael Rothenberg wrote in the *Journal of the American Medical Association*: 'One hundred and forty-six articles in behavioural science journals, representing 50 studies involving 10,000 children and adolescents from every conceivable background, all showed that viewing violence produced increased aggressive behaviour in the young and that immediate remedial action in terms of television programming is warranted.'[8]

President Johnson's Commission on the Causes and Prevention of Violence, 1969 – prompted by the assassinations of John and Robert Kennedy and Martin Luther King – concluded that: 'Violence on television encourages violent forms of behavior and fosters moral and social values about violence in family life, which are unacceptable in a civilized society.' Two years later the US Surgeon-General reported the same conclusion and three American television networks agreed that the case against television violence had been proven.

The 1976 Royal Commission on Violence in Ottawa concluded that, 'We believe that, while increased exploitation and depiction of violence in the media is only one of the many social factors contributing to crime, it is the largest single variable most amenable to rectification.' In 1982, after a ten-year study, the American National Institute of Mental Health found that 'in magnitude, TV is as strongly correlated with aggressive behaviour as any other behavioural variable that has been measured.' One of its authors, Dr D. Pearl, said, 'We have come to the unanimous conclusion that there is a causal relationship between television violence and real-life violence.'

In 1979 Dr William Belson published his massive seven-year study of 1,565 London boys, which concluded that the evidence proving a significant relationship between TV and adolescent violence is as scientifically valid as the evidence connecting smoking with lung cancer.

The report's main conclusions were fourfold:

1 Long-term exposure to television violence increases substantially the degree to which adolescent boys engage in serious violence themselves.

2 This effect is greater with respect to exposure to programmes that present violence in the context of close personal relationships, that show violence being done by 'good' guys or

in the maintenance of law and order, that are realistic in
presentation, that show gratuitous violence, that present
violent Westerns.

3   The serious violence that is increased by television tends to
be unskilled and spontaneous in character.

4   The increase in violent behaviour produced by exposure
to television is not accompanied by attitude changes at the
conscious level.

In a survey of fifty-eight paediatricians who had received
accounts from a parent/guardian about a violent video being
influential on his/her child's emotional behaviour, thirty-one
paediatricians said that the children's behaviour had worsened
following seeing the violent video; ten said that the behaviour
had remained the same, while not one paediatrician felt that the
child's behaviour had improved following seeing a violent
video.[9]

One doctor concluded, 'I am convinced in my mind that
watching ordinary violent films on television increases the
tendency to violence, depending on the home background and
the stability and security in the home and the parents'
attitudes.'

The video industry is still relatively new and little direct
research has been done on the question of whether watching
violence on video has a different effect from watching violence
on broadcast television. But this has now been remedied by
some decisive and pioneering work by Simon Armitage and
Peter Ainsworth, two psychologists based at the University of
Manchester. They conducted a survey of young male offenders
in a detention centre in the North of England and the results
were published in a Paper given to the British Psychological
Society's Annual Conference in Scotland on March 31st,
1989.

Their study, based on interviews with twenty-six young
offenders, identified a positive video subculture in which *all*
respondents admitted to having watched videos prior to their
current sentence, some watching about four videos a week and
a few watching their favourites as often as thirty times. The
study found that watching videos was an important aspect of
the behaviour among young offenders and that the youngsters

felt left out – and even lied – if they had not seen a particular video.

For the purposes of the study the offenders were split into two groups: Group A, who had all been sentenced for violent crimes, and Group B, who had been sentenced for non-violent crimes. The favourite films of the violent offenders were *Quadrophenia*, *The Warriors*, *Friday 13*, *Scarface* and *Poltergeist*. *Rambo – First Blood, Part Two* was the film that had been seen by most of them and Rambo headed their list of favourite characters. Violence was the persistent theme which ran through their preferences. All the respondents (or members of the family) were members of a video club and only *one* of them had ever been refused the hire of a film in a shop even though *all* of them had been under-age at the time of the hire.

Of the violent offenders, 54 per cent said that they believed that they had been excited by violence on video; 31 per cent believed that they had actually become violent through seeing violence on video and 31 per cent said that they had used weapons that they had seen on video, like knives, death stars, rice flails and razor blades. But an astonishing 69 per cent believed that they had thought about trying a certain style of fighting – like kung fu kicks or head-butting – after seeing it on video.

'There seems no control at all on what these youngsters can hire and that is extremely worrying,' Peter Ainsworth told me. 'Norms of behaviour are more likely to be formed during the early years. We also noted a marked degree of desensitisation in the violent groups to the extent that they no longer seemed worried about the damage that they were causing other people *or* to themselves.'

And so, after all these reports which speak with the same authoritative voice and come to the same inescapable conclusion, how do we stand as I write? In truth we have more violence on our screens than ever. All the authors and researchers involved in these reports may as well have not bothered for all the impact they have had.

And due to the colossal rise of the video-recorder, which was in 1.8 per cent of all households in 1981, 7.2 per cent in 1982, 17.6 per cent in 1983 and now stands in some 68 per cent of all households – second only to Japan – the video industry in particular has become a veritable Cain's nursery which has mounted the most serious menace ever made to all our children. The video industry has become the Man of Lawlessness's favourite tool with which he has managed to undermine the family, erode the moral claims of religion and glorify the breaking of the law while also managing some impeccably destructive and unlovely creations like the street gang and the soccer hooligan.

In September 1988 Prince Charles, while opening the new Museum of the Moving Image in London, condemned those responsible for 'the excessive menu of gratuitous violence on television and video.' Expressing his concern on behalf of 'all those of us who have children', he rejected the argument of those 'who defend their so-called art by claiming to portray the actuality of real life'. He was equally dismissive of those who maintained that the viewer could always switch the television set off.

He was particularly critical of the video industry and pointed out that all types of video were available to children.

> If you claim that a diet of violence is likely to have some effect on the way that some people behave then you are told that there is no proof that this has any effect. But this is palpable nonsense. It is a trick used by experts to confuse us and what we are seeing with our own eyes. It is high time someone told these experts that, like the emperor with his new clothes, they are wearing nothing at all.

What followed his remarks then was the same as preceded them. In the following week one report discovered that there were twenty-five killings on our television screens, including horrific scenes of IRA executions, bomb blasts and murders. Scores more killings were portrayed in a string of movies, including 'spaghetti Westerns' and the usual episodes of those cult series such as *Miami Vice* and *The Equaliser*.[10]

The Prince's widely-publicised intervention came at a good time for me as I was just about to be hauled up before the Press Council by the video industry, following an article I had written in the *Sunday Telegraph* in which I had described the video industry as 'rotten to the core' and 'pedlars of hatred'. The video people declared themselves most miffed by this description and reported me to that august body only to report me again when, in a further article again in the *Sunday Telegraph*, congratulating Prince Charles on his remarks, I compounded my 'crime' by calling them 'corrupt and rotten'.

The Hearing

The Press Council on December 6th, 1988, in their offices just off Fleet Street provided a salutary and even frightening insight into the kind of people who are running this multimillion-pound video industry which, in Britain alone, turns over some £700m a year in cassettes and rentals.

On my side at the hearing was Ian Watson, deputy editor of the *Sunday Telegraph* and on the other side was the British Videogram Association represented by its director general, Mr Norman Abbott; Mr John Gray, chief fund-raiser for the National Children's Home and Mr Graham Bright MP, whose Private Member's Bill became the Video Recordings Act 1984.

Such occasions can be quite nerve-wrecking and, just before we went into the chamber, I was offered a cup of coffee and expected to hold it steady as we all trooped in to find ourselves in front of about a dozen people, with only one woman, all sitting in solemn conclave around a large table. Every seat had a microphone in front of it since all the proceedings are recorded. We were invited to sit at two separate tables at the far end, where the cup of coffee remained untouched for most of the morning until Ian helped himself to it.

Mr Abbott opened the proceedings by saying that he had been up all night reading a transcript of the Hungerford inquest and that there was nothing in it which implicated them or *First Blood* in the Hungerford massacre as I had alleged. He had also brought along a video of *First Blood* to show them if they wanted. The main points of his opening remarks were that, far from being 'corrupt' and 'rotten' as I had claimed, they had developed a clean, well-regulated industry in which all their titles were certificated by the film censor with the clearest possible description of the contents on the packages. He also referred to our old friend the catharsis theory which, although stamped on from every side, continues to rear its ugly head.

(On the catharsis theory Dr Wertham, a New York consultant psychiatrist, said, 'This outlet theory is not only overdone: it is false. It is pseudo-scientific dogma. There is not a shred of clinical evidence for it. On the contrary the children are over-excited without being given an adequate release. Delinquent behaviour is not prevented but promoted.' Another survey of consultant psychiatrists, by the Royal College of Psychiatry, discovered that not a single psychiatrist believed that the viewing of scenes of extreme violence would enable a person to live out a horrific experience in fantasy or imagination and thus prevent them from carrying out such an act in reality.)[11]

Furthermore, Mr Abbott went on, this 'clean, well-regulated' industry gave 'vast sums' each year to charity and had happily complied with the 1984 Video Recordings Act which had set up a certification system for all videos for sale and hire and helped to clean out some thirty-nine 'nasties' which included *Driller Killer*, *Evil Dead* and *I Spit On Your Grave*. The best-selling video of all time in Britain, we learned, was *Watch with Mother*. All this was hardly consonant with an industry which was rotten to the core.

It was a low moment for me as Mr Abbott called his two main witnesses. It was all very well to sit down and poke about on a word processor keyboard, but now here I was going to have to face up to the consequences of my words; not something that often happens to journalists. I swallowed hard on a dry throat, knowing that this was going to be a long, stiff battle in which I might well get a good caning.

Mr John Gray was quite fulsome in his support of the video industry, saying that in the years 1987 and 1988 the BVA had given them £600,000. In cross-examination he declared himself quite happy with this amount, which I had described in my submission as being evidence only of a 'quite staggering miserliness', particularly when the industry's total income for that period was well in excess of £100,000m. Mr Gray added that some of the officials from the video industry had even come down and run a stall in one of their charitable fêtes.

Mr Graham Bright MP said that what I had portrayed was wrong since the video industry was trying to bring in self-regulation and had shown nothing other than co-operation with the Bill. Since his Bill had become law the video nasties had disappeared from the shelves and now the industry did not purvey anything illegal. 'Any video containing gratuitous violence has been outlawed.' He added that the children had been doubly protected.

By now I really was at my lowest point. I just could not believe that we were using the same language in that room. Was it possible that we were talking about the same society? *All gratuitous violence had been outlawed? The children had been doubly protected?* Is it possible that I had been going to a different video-shop from everyone else? What about all that NSPCC research on how even the youngest children had gained access to eighteen videos?[12] What about the list of sixty top video rentals I had with me? Was there really no gratuitous violence in the number one that week, *Robocop*, the story of a sort of mechanised Rambo who embarks on a relentless and non-stop orgy of violence? Was there really no gratuitous violence in almost forty others featuring violence and death in the top sixty video rentals that week? Just who was kidding whom? A headache began unravelling in my brain. I just wanted to pack up my Biro and go home.

At the start of my cross-examination of Mr Abbott I tried to clarify what his industry's view on the effect of screen violence was. In his original complaint about me to the Press Council he had said that the newspaper had 'published an unfair and misleading article about the effect of violent videos.' Now in a second and more detailed submission their position seemed to have changed to a more Olympian stance. 'The BVA does not claim that violence in films has no effect in real life. Nor have we ever argued to the contrary. We do note, however, that for every expert and every research project that supports one side of the argument, another can be found to support the other – with equal-seeming authority and conviction.'

So what was their position? Well, that any form of art can promote any form of good or evil, we suppose. Was he aware that *every* research project both here and in America had found a link between televised and social violence? No, he was not. Could he name any of these experts who had denied that there was a link? No, he hadn't come prepared for that kind of discussion. Just the *names* of these experts? No.

He had made much of the video certification system, but did he know that, according to research done by the NSPCC, 50 per cent of all children interviewed, between the ages of 7 and 17 had seen an 18 video? No. Did he know that 43 per cent of these children had seen at least four? No. Did this seem like protection or, as Mr Bright had it, double protection? He wasn't sure. Did he have any children? He had two grown-up children and two young grandchildren. Would he want his grandchildren to see any of these films? No. Their parents would stop them from seeing those rated 15 and 18. Would all parents protect their children in this way? Responsible parents would. Are all parents responsible? He couldn't speak for them.

I then referred to the new releases and asked if he had seen *Killer Klowns from Outer Space*? No. *Scumbusters?* No. I then moved on to the top ten of video rentals for November 14 which he had supplied, with clear satisfaction, in his own submission. Had he seen *Lost Boys* which was the number three? No. He had listed it as a U, but it was a 15. It was a mistake. Had he any idea what it was about? No. Would he believe me if I told him it was about dope-smoking teenage vampires? No reply. Number four was *The Untouchables*. Had he seen it? No. Would he believe me if I told him it was about gangsterism and that, in one scene, Al Capone smashes in a man's head with a baseball bat on a dining table? A shrug of the shoulders. Number five, *Stakeout?* No. Had he seen *Black Widow*? No. Did he know that it was about a woman who married a series of men and kills them for their money? Is it? It is. And did he know that his number ten, *Someone to Watch Over Me* by Ridley Scott, also director of the repellent *Alien*, begins with a man being stabbed repeatedly in the chest and throat? Really?

It did not bode well then, did it, that, in the top ten of your industry, in a list supplied by yourself, that you have films about witchcraft, vampirism, gangsterism, serial murder and psychopathic stabbers? No reply.

I then moved on from the top ten that the BVA had supplied and produced a list of the current top sixty video rentals that my local video shop had supplied. I asked him if he had seen the number one, *Robocop*. He had not. Number three, *Predator*? No. *Flowers in the Attic?* No. *Death Wish 4 – The Crackdown?* No. Was he aware that Leslie Halliwell, in his film guide, had described

Death Wish II as a badly-made exercise in the most repellent acts of violence? No he was not. Had he seen *Retribution*? No. Did he know that it was a horror splurge? No. What about *Witchcraft*? No, he hadn't seen that either.

At this point Mr Abbott complained to the chairman who interrupted me, saying that I had made my point. I withdrew, after pointing out that, of the top sixty rentals that week, around thirty-five were exceedingly violent and a further eight were horror. (It seems one in five rented videos are horror.)

Later in my summing-up I defined rotten as decomposed, morally, socially and politically corrupt, disagreeable, impure. I further defined the core of any industry as being its product. On this evidence, I argued, it was both fair and right to describe the video industry as being 'rotten to the core'. Mr Abbott had come along to defend his industry, but had brought practically no arguments with him, I continued. In all aspects of research into violence on the screen he had admitted that he knew nothing. He could not name any experts who denied that there was a link between violence on the screen and in real life. Furthermore, we had now established that he had not even seen the films which he had come to defend with such vigour. These films represented a blizzard of violence in our land. Their key themes were always terror, vengeance, murder and death. The council should not find for these people or there would be no holding them if they were given a consoling pat on the head and I was given a smack on the wrist. They represented the most serious menace ever mounted against our children who were all clearly at risk.

Mr Abbott declined to sum up and the hearing was over. His two witnesses had already gone so, with Ian Watson, we went to a pub in Fleet Street where, after all the nasty things I had said about his industry, Mr Abbott did buy me a pint of beer. Soon the three of us were chatting on first-name terms in the most cordial manner and he struck me as a decent, civilised man who would no more watch one of his violent videos than he would start a fight in that bar. Somehow he had got caught up in something which he knew very little about and, inheriting the traditional time-worn arguments and ideas of the video industry and those who made those wretched films, just carried

on defending them without thinking or questioning them over-
much.

Later, over lunch in El Vino's, Ian said that here was a case
of a man who just found himself stuck in something and had
never really asked himself what it was all about. It was all to do
with money, Ian suspected. An old editor had once told him
always to follow the money and he would never go far wrong.

Business as Usual

As it turned out the Press Council rejected the complaint
against me and the *Sunday Telegraph* for publishing my article on
the video industry. In its adjudication it said: 'The article made
strong criticism of videos and the video industry, but the
passages to which the complainants took exception were largely
matters of opinion. The newspaper and the writer were entitled
to express their opinion as they did. The criticism, while harsh,
did not go beyond the limits of fair comment in an article of that
kind.'[13]

But, in the wake of Prince Charles's criticism of the video
industry – and the Press Council adjudication – did that lead to
any modification of the video industry's output? Did they
attempt to prune their diseased list? Did it lead to withdrawal of
Rambo III, which was about to be released? Did they take *Taxi
Driver* off their shelves? Was *Critters* taken off? Not a bit of it. It
was very much business as before and surely the only conclusion we can draw from their unwillingness to do anything at
all about what they had been doing in the past was because the
overriding consideration was the overriding power of money.

So, yet again, we have managed to move closer to the
extraordinary and elusive identity of the evil that we are seeking
to expose in this enquiry. It is becoming clear that the acquisition of money is central to the Man of Lawlessness's operations and, to that end, he will keep whirling lassos of deceit and
shifting positions in front of many mirrors as he takes control of
the most powerful media known to man.

But he does not want to acquire money for its own sake; a
Himalayan range of money is useless to him in itself: he needs
the money to encourage and woo his unwitting lieutenants who

will, in their turn, put the finest veneer on his work, which is to
encourage lawlessness of every kind. Disorder and breakdown
are his very raison d'être, but he cannot work in a vacuum. He
does need people.

But we are also beginning to see other surfaces on the
multisided prism of his personality. We are beginning to
understand that there is nothing parochial about his work; that
it is, in every sense, global and that he is as interested in the
violence of the backyards of a South African township as he is in
disorders in the streets of an American ghetto – *as long as it is
violence and the greater and more mindless the violence the better*. By
feeding on these particular acts of localised violence he can then
create a general atmosphere of global violence which will, in its
turn, create planetary rings of violence, within which social and
world breakdown will move closer and closer.

His ultimate goal is social breakdown everywhere and politicians like Enoch Powell, with his skill at using the media and
his periodic prophecies of racial violence, are the greatest
blessing to the work of the Man of Lawlessness. (The more he
prophesies racial disorders the more self-fulfilling such
prophecies become.) But they will only be fulfilled if we fail to
understand the real nature of racial disorder; the way in which,
for example, isolated acts of black crime are being presented,
because of the fatal distortion of Romantic emphasis and
selection, as the total black reality.

The continual presentation of unsavoury details as being
representative of the usually healthy general picture is the Man
of Lawlessness's most popular sleight of hand; a trick which he
has used with the most devastating effect in Ulster. It is when
people *believe* that they are being threatened – despite the real
evidence to the contrary – that they will fight back or indeed
retaliate in advance. The continual shuffling of deceiving
illusions is very much the name of this game.

And when our streets are engulfed in racial disorders and
running with 'rivers of blood' you can only predict one thing
with complete certainty: Enoch Powell will be interviewed in
front of the television cameras and he will be saying 'I told you
so. I've been telling you that this was coming for years.' And we
shall all commend Enoch for his prophetic foresight when, all
along, the real villain had still not been identified as he was out

in the torn streets looking for yet more racial disorders with which to fuel the escalating conflict.

Yet surely the most breathtaking quality of our Man of Lawlessness is the way in which he can overcome reason and deny the evidence of hard fact. On the issue of violence on our screens every body of research and every carefully conducted scientific experiment has come out against his activities, so what does he do? Nothing. He just carries on as before, making violent sequel after violent sequel for the cinema and video industries, while also ensuring that in both Britain and America there is an act of violence every sixteen minutes on our television screens with a murder every half an hour.

When Prince Charles attacked 'this incessant menu of gratuitous violence' particularly in video in late 1988 what happened? Nothing. The following month produced an even greater avalanche of violent videos.

All these films are works of beauty and instruments of the most desirable education to the Man of Lawlessness. He uses them to stuff children's minds with violence and brutality which will then re-emerge in verbal and physical forms. He uses them to create impulses towards the morbid and the macabre, which will pervert their innate sense of decency and infest their sleep with the most lurid nightmares. These films will help him create a whole new generation who will think, if not act, like Travis Bickle and Rambo. These films will create illusions of terror and build imprisoning walls of fear. In this world the constant sounds of fighting will be the only real music. In his world the one all-pervading atmosphere will be that of paranoia and fear. These films will continue to shock, excite and thrill until, before anyone is aware of it, they really will have come true and we shall have a whole generation of disaffected, alienated, violent youth rampaging through our streets.

The French criminologist Gabriel Tarde (1843–1904) codified the three laws of imitation in our societies:
1 Men in cities imitate one another in proportion to the closeness of their contact. This is fashion. The superior is imitated by the inferior.
2 Crimes were once largely the privilege of royalty, but they seeped down through society until everyone was at it. Indecent assault on children was found at first in the great cities, but later

spread beyond them. Fashions such as dismembering corpses began in Paris in 1876. Vitriol-throwing began in 1895. Both fashions soon spread.

3 When two mutually-exclusive fashions come together, one could be substituted for the other. So there might be murders by knifing and murders by gun – as the one decreased the other increased.

Tarde believed that crime started as a fashion and became a custom. We are not very big on vitriol-throwing or corpse-dismembering these days, but if we look at Tarde's basic laws and set them in a modern context we begin to see other issues.

If closeness of contact is a factor in imitation, then we now, thanks to television's global village, could not be more intimate or closer to *everyone*. Every glue-sniffer and rapist is our neighbour now and we *know* how to pour glue into small polythene bags and how to inhale from them; we *understand* that if we buy some lighter fuel and sniff it we shall get a lively, if dangerous, buzz; we are *aware* that all you need to make a petrol bomb is a milk bottle filled with petrol with some strips of cloth stuffed in the mouth and we are being *told* again and again that 90 per cent of all muggings are successful. And how did we arrive at this information? Because our neighbours in the box in the corner of our living-room told us. Our friends from the village hall.

Through television the crimes of the few become central to the thought patterns of the many. When we are repeatedly told of child sex abuse it becomes a familiar part of our mental landscape; when the murder is reconstructed for the television news cameras we are being invited to enter into the world of the murderer and when we are shown the knife or the bloodstained anorak, to see if we can identify them and help the police with their enquiries, then we are, shockingly but thrillingly, a part of that world. As we explore this world we come across the gang tearing across the country, committing violent crimes in its wake; we meet the junkie taking his fix in a derelict house; we happen on a street riot or a bizarre murder. Our ideas about this world are framed accordingly and this world is in essence nothing less than the creation of the Man of Lawlessness. It is what he set out to build for us – his chosen people – and we can either enter into it by putting on our bovver boots and becoming an integrated lawless citizen or else we can sit back, wringing our hands and cringing in our new fear. Either reaction makes the Man of Lawlessness happy.

Furthermore, when we, the inferior, look up to our screens we have any number of superior role models to imitate. We have any number of fashions we can follow. We can smoke our cigarettes like Brian Ferry or try to emulate Terry Wogan's hair-do or talk in the deep authoritative manner of the respected American television announcer, Walter Cronkite. But the young are not interested in imitating them: they are *b-o-o-o-o-r-i-n-g*. The young are interested in imitating the violent and inviolable supermen . . . Sylvester Stallone, Charles Bronson, Arnold Schwarzenegger, Clint Eastwood . . . these Romantic studs with their fantasies of violence possess the waking dreams of the young and, while all cannot get their hands on weaponry, they can get their hands on knuckledusters, clubs and Stanley knives. They can fight, too. They can become vigilantes on behalf of their home team. They have seen their heroes extract revenge, so now they are going out to do the same, creating mayhem, terrorising people, smashing windows wherever they go. I have never seen a teenager walking home with a video of *Watch With Mother* in his hand. Teenagers are largely interested in violence and, thanks to the money-mad moguls of Hollywood, that is largely what they get.[14]

So violence – the preserve of the fashionable few like Stallone, Bronson and Eastwood – is already becoming the customary practice of the many, according to the principles enunciated by Tarde. The supermen's fashionable and stylised assaults on the screen become the rough-and-tumble battles on the streets. And so, too, do the muggings and the rapes which are so relentlessly portrayed that we can understand 'how terrible they really are'.

The classic example of the way evil is promoted under a cloak of the purest hypocrisy is the BBC television programme *Crimewatch*, watched by nearly a quarter of the adult population of Britain. *Crimewatch* has an arrest rate of about three a programme, which is the justification for reconstructing crimes in the most careful and shocking detail for a quarter of the population. Rapes, burglaries and assorted robberies all receive the same careful attention. One reconstructed robbery had the criminal producing a shotgun with the viewer looking up both barrels just as the assistant manager of the building society had done. It was so dramatic that the officer in charge of the case admitted to having jumped in fright at the first showing.

There were no arrests immediately after that programme, but could such a dramatic reconstruction have demonstrated to the young, the rootless, the mentally and morally vulnerable, just how to terrify the living daylights out of someone holding large amounts of cash? Maybe and maybe not, but the certain upshot of the programme was that, once again, violent crime had become another part of the mental furniture of the population. Once again the apprentice criminal was being fed with criminal ideas and shown ways of putting together his future tools.

(Anyone who doubts that the young do not pick up on every detail of what they see on television should watch the BBC's *Top of the Pops* on Thursday night, then go down to the local disco where they will see the dance routines imitated in the most elaborate detail.)

Many like Dr Clifford Hill, a consultant sociologist with the Home Office, believe that the media is generating crime and corruption on such a large scale that they are already threatening the very fabric of our society. He said that great changes had been wrought in our family, our schools, our courtrooms and our churches. And every change has been a change for the worse.

> It may well be that our freedoms are being challenged to an extent unique in history. When the level of the breakdown of social order reaches a certain point a situation is created wherein left-wing revolutions occur or right-wing dictators after the pattern of Hitler may arise and pose as social saviours. They may be eagerly supported by those who see no other alternative to the chaos in society, and thus they achieve power.[15]

The Case of Football Hooliganism

It is, of course, easy, if not glib, to *mutter* apocalyptic visions and prophesy social instability. It is all very well for the hot

polemicist to paint multicoloured nightmares about marauding hordes of violent teenagers tearing up our streets *except that is
already happening*. In both Britain and Europe our soccer thugs
have been going on the most destructive rampages, fighting and
destroying, even killing people as they did in 1985 in Heysel
Stadium in Brussels when rioting (Liverpool) fans caused the
death of thirty-four (Juventus) supporters.

These drunken Vikings, quivering with tribal hatred and
smashing their way through the city centres of Europe, are
probably the finest creations of the Man of Lawlessness's lathe.
These are very much the products of all the media technology
that he has managed to colonise; people who, practically all
their young lives, have been fed with dangerous concepts of
masculine individualism from *Clockwork Orange* through to *First
Blood* and *Colours*. Just in the last two decades they have grown
up in a culture which has increasingly glorified cold-blooded
and ruthless killing.

You prove yourself by showing how tough you are in a fight.
You impress others by demonstrating how many you can
wound or hurt, if not kill. You are as capable as the next man in
extracting the bloodiest revenge. You are a warrior now, my
boy. It is time to stand tall. You are a man.

But as we *are*, just at the moment, standing next to the Man of
Lawlessness's lathe, we could not expect it to be as simple as
that. Nothing is simple in his work and we must always
remember that he loves nothing more than to work with
illusions. As he fed the soccer thugs with the ideas that made
them what they are, then, at the same time, he also made them
famous and very much aware of their notoriety. He built them
up from without and within.

How many times now have we seen the footage of the riot in
Heysel Stadium, which is wheeled out again and again on the
flimsiest pretext? To become such a regular item in news
bulletins is fame indeed and soccer thugs revel in such attention
as is clear when, after some fans are arrested, newspaper
clippings of their activities are often found in their pockets.

Ever since the first tentative and slightly bloody appearance
of the soccer hooligan on the terraces in the early 'sixties the
Man of Lawlessness has made sure that most fights and punches
were publicised and dramatised in the media. Nearly every

small flurry and punch-up was focused on – often at the expense of the game – by the television news.[16] Any skinhead with a flag around his shoulders and a safety-pin through his nose, busy giving someone a good kicking, was more likely to make it on to the news round-up than the goal scorers. Routinely we were shown clips of fans fighting and routinely Jimmy Hill appeared in front of the cameras wringing his hands and telling us how hooliganism was ruining the game. All this, he kept insisting, was nothing to do with television and, while he kept reassuring us on that point, all those small acts of delinquent rebellion on the terraces, fed ever more and more by abundant media publicity, became declarations of war on the streets. Soon, fed by more of the same, those declarations of war became marching armies, looting and pillaging whenever they came together for a few cans of lager and a snort of amyl nitrate. Nourished by the Man of Lawlessness's constant spotlight they had become their image. They were e-e-e-e-e-v-i-l, as Millwall fans love to chant. They were warriors protecting 'their turf'.

Proof of the deep levels of distortion involved in this process, of the way that illusion can overtake reality, came a few years back when 150 British soccer fans arrived in Greece to be greeted by no less than 1,500 Greek policemen and six television cameras. Throughout the subsequent match the cameras concentrated on this terrified little group, too scared to hiccup, let alone start any aggravation by acting up in front of the cameras.

Not since Alaric and his boys set off to sack Rome had there been such excitement before the campaigns had actually begun. Virtually every battalion acquired its own diarist in the shape of a newspaper reporter or a television camera. In one full page of the *Sunday Times* (June 19th, 1988) we learned about how one thug got on the train at Victoria; how he hugged his girlfriend goodbye; how he got drunk and sniffed amyl nitrate in Dover; how he began shouting obscenities in Ostend; how he subsequently vomited over his shirt and roamed the Stuttgart streets, nearly being arrested before circling lots of screaming fights.

As if that deeply fascinating story had not been enough for one Sunday morning we were also treated to the names of each gang working its way around Stuttgart. (There were the

Intercity Firm (a hundred West Ham thugs); the Headhunters (several hundred Chelsea supporters); the Intercity Jibbers, the Zulu Warriors, the Bushwhackers and the Baby Squad (a group of Leicester fans ludicrously described as teenagers who provide crucial reinforcements when the top gangs are under attack.)[17]

Such slavish media attention adds to their own sense of notoriety; it makes them appear hard cases both in their own minds and in the world's eyes. These nobodies have become somebodies. Ted from West Ham had become Clint Eastwood. Tony from Liverpool had become Rambo. Peter from Cardiff had become Charles Bronson. And there they were on their way to attack a whole city, dominating practically every front page and news bulletin in the land.

Using principally the medium of television the Man of Lawlessness seized on them *and gave them to the whole world*. Football and the media came together in a passionate embrace and created the ugly offspring of terrace hooliganism, seizing on every fight and pitch invasion, then transmitting it everywhere. At the beginning of a recent English soccer season the *Straits Times* in Singapore, some 6,700 miles away, wrote in a leading article: 'The new British football season will be viewed with interest and concern throughout the world. Yet the sad fact is that almost before a ball has been kicked in anger, the symptoms of yet another malodorous season are already beginning there . . . football is besmirched by violence both on and off the field and now stands on a knife edge.'

Then the season began in Britain and the first Saturday brought the predictable disorder. Police arrested 236 youths at Euston Station, including sixty juveniles, all wearing Birmingham City blue, after they had run amok among families queuing for bank-holiday trains. The attack *before* the match had begun coincided with soccer's lowest first-day attendance since the war.

Singapore had been interested in all this because *Match of the Day* and *The Big Match* were the most regular views that many of the people there got of British behaviour. The *Straits Times* therefore concluded that their own black weekend when four players were sent off, twelve cautioned, a referee allegedly pushed and spat at and the pitch invaded by 200 fanatics mimicked Britain, 'Where major sport has become an excuse for tribal savagery.'

Some seventy nations put British football on their screens and violence has become endemic wherever the game has been shown. In Stockholm, football fans formed a Black Army, closely modelled on Manchester United's Reds. But already the nail-bombs that empty Dutch stadiums and the firebombs that burn down their stands, the match-day fatalities at grounds in Greece and Italy, the beatings-up of referees in Asia and death-tolls at riots in Italy are beginning to exceed even the excesses of British hooligans.

There *are* some television executives who have understood the role they are playing in this global contagion. Jeff Foulser, the executive producer of London Weekend's *Big Match*, said: 'Unless it is of major news value, our policy is not to show fighting in the crowd among a bunch of yobbos. I'm convinced the riots in our inner cities – at Brixton and Toxteth and Bristol – started in small pockets and grew out of publicity. People copy what they see on the box.' The BBC are slowly catching on – the cameras were told not to focus directly onto the Hillsborough tragedy because, at first, it was thought to be a riot.

But by now it was all too late, too late. The demons of violence had erupted everywhere, while early in 1989 we had another classic example of corrupt telemagnewspeak. Football manager Brian Clough ran on to the pitch at the end of the match at Nottingham and hit four of the pitch-invading fans. He was duly fined and banned from the touch-line until the end of the season, but that has not stopped this incident being repeated again and again on our screens. We may even have seen the footage of the Heysel Stadium riot at least a hundred times. Again and again – no matter what the news justification might be – the images of violence are shown, and again and again they are being mimicked throughout the world and all this will continue until word goes out that it is time for it to stop.

Yes, the Man of Lawlessness has come to love the soccer hooligan as his very own – in a sense they were his modern media first-born – and such is his skill at creating them that, to this day, barely anyone has managed to locate and identify the real dark and foul caves of Romantic alienation in which these thugs were born. Politicians in particular have managed to introduce a veritable shoal of red herrings into the issue as they flounder around talking of solving the problems with such means as travel restrictions, membership schemes, identity cards, passport confiscation, reduction of alcohol sales and more intelligence-gathering about hooligan activities by the police.

None of these suggestions will have any impact on the soccer hooligan whatsoever. Anyone who is in any way serious about confronting the soccer hooligan – and even effecting a change in his behaviour – has merely to address himself to these thugs' ideas and find out their source.

An idle study of television programmes might be a good start, but a half-hour browse in their local video shop might be a better one. It is becoming clear that a lot of blame also rests squarely on our squalid ideas of what makes news. Newspapers have made their contribution too. All need to be looked at, but the diligent and insightful investigator will eventually always come to stand at the foot of the shadow of one huge man with one dark philosophy.

7

A Gargoyle Art

In which we examine the powerful subtlety of the lie – Look in astonishment at the Queen's ninety-two pregnancies – Find a familiar face at the bottom of it all – Give an ironic chorus of approval for the tabloids' desire to serve us – Find yet another tissue of lies wrapped around the Yorkshire Ripper – See how the spirit of lawlessness has colonised the ancient hills of coal – And note the gathering of an enormous power.

The Primacy of Truth

A lie is a false statement; something which is opposed to – and destructive of – the truth. Much of the media insists and believes that it always proclaims the truth when, in so many ways, it is merely promoting lies. Almost every study has shown that there is no such thing as truth in the media's presentation of reality. It likes to think that it is holding up a mirror to the events of the world, but the result is a false and distorted illusion; a lie.

The old prophet Isaiah had a useful lament which could be applied to the modern world of communications: 'So justice is driven back, and righteousness stands at a distance; truth has stumbled in the streets, honesty cannot enter. Truth is nowhere to be found, and whoever shuns evil becomes a prey' (Isa.

59:14–15 *NIV*). The New Testament tells us that the pinnacle of all evil is the liar and Satan is the liar *par excellence*. 'When he lies, he speaks his native language, for he is a liar and the father of lies' (John 8:44 *NIV*).

Truth, however, is one of God's most abiding qualities; the attribute which gives Him the greatest pleasure. Job reminded us that there was no need to lie for God. Truthfulness is the mark of the real believer. We are back again to the words of St Paul: 'Therefore each of you must put off falsehood and speak truthfully to his neighbour, for we are all members of one body.' (Eph. 4:25 *NIV*).

There is nothing more important than the cause of the truth in any civilised society. It is the very lubricant of our communion one with another. The British courtroom insists on 'the truth, the whole truth and nothing but the truth'. The very worst thing a member of parliament can call another is 'a liar', since such an accusation breaks the trust necessary for any meaningful communication. We can only trust one another if we believe that we are speaking the truth. Lying destroys the possibility of that trust and makes all our efforts to communicate with one another pointless. It is the truth which sets us free. But how do newspapers, in particular, enshrine this lie which is destructive of all our attempts at sensible and important dialogue?[1]

There is a broad body of evidence of the way that newspapers tell lies, in which the so-called quality newspapers have sometimes been no less culpable than the sleazy tabloids. The *Sunday Times* – which once liked to trumpet itself as one of the great newspapers of the world – clearly bought the forged Hitler diaries for serialisation without investigating them properly. When they were exposed as fakes the proprietor of the newspaper, Rupert Murdoch, said: 'After all, we are all in the entertainment business.'

There used to be an amazing journalist on the *Daily Telegraph*, one Raphael Dunvant, who once sat outside Buckingham Palace all night, waiting for the Queen, and was struck by lightning, assaulted by a soccer hooligan and attacked by Tony Benn. Mr Dunvant, it emerged, was a fictional invention by the *Daily Telegraph* hacks, doubtless wiling away a spare hour before the King and Keys pub opened next door in Fleet Street.

When the *Daily Mirror* bought up an exclusive interview with the widow of a Falklands hero, the *Sun* responded with 'a world exclusive' of its own. This had been fabricated by John Kay in the newspaper's office, with the help of two secretaries who imagined the sort of things a grieving widow might be worrying about. It was only thanks to a secretary that the Press Council investigated the matter. The *Sun* continued to defend itself by saying that its quotes were lifted from other press and television interviews. Later the Press Council deplored this 'insensitive deception of the public'.

The Royal family has become the most popular target for British tabloid fiction writers, though they have still a long way to go before they catch up with the French press which, at the time of writing, has reported the Queen pregnant ninety-two times, abdicating sixty-three times, divorcing Prince Philip seventy-three times and expelling Lord Snowdon from the court 151 times. The new superstar Princess Diana is now suffering from a whole series of phantom pregnancies, continual bouts of anorexia and terminal marital rows with Prince Charles.[2]

America has had its own problems, too, as when Janet Cooke of the *Washington Post* won a Pulitzer Prize for a fabricated story about an 8-year-old heroin addict, 'Jimmy's World'. The story turned out to be a fictional composite located so convincingly in the streets of Washington that it fooled the Pulitzer Board and the editors of the *Washington Post*.

Henry Porter, a journalist who wrote an exposé of Fleet Street's penchant for making up whoppers, concluded, 'Newspapers lie to entertain, to compete with one another, to propagate their political convictions and persecute those with whom they disagree. And when there is no obvious reason, journalists continue to lie out of indolence and habit.'[3]

But Porter's attack is misconceived and largely untrue. Standards of accuracy are scrupulous and high in most sections of the British press and it is perhaps worth recalling that the Hitler diary forgery was exposed almost immediately on its publication. There was no attempt whatsoever to perpetuate the fraud and the *Sunday Times* itself made a full editorial apology the following week. Raphael Dunvant was similarly exposed and stopped while his 'lies' can hardly be said to have had disastrous consequences. Similarly Janet Cooke was also unmasked and dismissed.

(Henry Porter knew so much about his craft that he interviewed and ran a story on 'Meryl Streep' when it was, in fact, a look-alike secretary sent along by the *Daily Mail* just to wind Porter up.)

Apart from comics like *Sunday Sport*, British journalists do try and get it right and no one ever takes any notice of the French press anyway. And possibly the sleaziest newspaper in America – the Miami-based *National Enquirer* – insists that its reporters tape-record all their facts from at least two separate sources.

No, the lie in the newspaper world is infinitely more subtle, complicated and destructive than a handful of journalists trying to make a name for themselves by making up fairy-tales. The lie which burns at the heart of our communications system stems from the innate Romanticism of the newspaper world and the way this philosophy engages with reality. Therein lies the real attack on the truth.

The sleazier the newspaper the more it becomes engaged with the most basic principles of the Man of Lawlessness since, embedded in the very core of the tabloid press, are all the abiding Romantic themes of sexual perversion, morbidity and violence. Working in persistent and tireless pursuit of these themes the tabloids engage with and grossly disfigure the very face of the world. These newspapers come to sum up our ideas about the world and those that derive their ideas from reading them soon come to believe that we live in a very poor world indeed. The elements mined by the tabloids do exist in reality, but only as the tiniest fraction of the whole and, in this savage engagement, a complicated and lovely world becomes a fallen and perverse world riven with doom, pain and fear; an alien place dancing with erotic demons and divorced pregnant princesses; a home for pederast vicars and screaming terrorists; a fearful place of sudden death and violent criminality which, in the seeds of the tabloid pages, represents the ultimate dream of how the Man of Lawlessness wants the world to become.

Calling Black White

And, in the best manner of horror films which feature so
strongly in his work, this nightmare and global growth will keep
feeding on and replicating itself until the world really is a
doomed and dark place in which the lie will stop being a lie and
become a balanced reflection of reality. The Man of Lawlessness's ambition is finally to turn his lie into the truth.

He is working constantly towards this goal and no mistake.
Just the briefest examination of the tabloid formula shows his
dark influence on almost every page. Turn and turn again and
we get glimpses of the same scurrying elusive figure who
controlled the Moors Murderers, killed John Lennon, attacked
the President of the United States and actively fomented a war
in Northern Ireland. Those with eyes to see and ears to hear will
locate him soon enough, presiding over a vast and powerful
communications empire, with all his destructive powers
running at full stretch and operating at new heights of
unmanageability.

See him on page one, page three, page four, page seven, page
eleven . . . cataloguing the cruel, glorifying the violent, emphasising the bizarre and detailing the perverse. And all this
activity comes at the expense and denial of a peaceful, ordered,
normal world. No, the lie at the heart of newspaper practice is
not so much deliberate inaccuracy or falsehood as the Man of
Lawlessness's selective and systematic distortion of everything
he comes near.

In this way the sense of horror – and our new fear – becomes
more intense daily. This climate is continually reinforced by the
increasing linking of *local* lives to *national* events. The gruesome
headlines become part and parcel of all our lives. Just as the
execrable gossip columns, about which celebrity is doing what
to another, have become a substitute for community gossip so
this catalogue of violence serves to define all our sense of values.

Prince Charles, in the 1978 British Press Awards, put it this
way:

Regrettably it does not make news to know that fifty Jumbo jets
landed safely at London Airport yesterday, but it does make news if
one doesn't. I still believe, however, in the necessity every now and

then of reminding people, metaphorically, that vast numbers of Jumbos do land safely – for the simple reason that we are all human and the maintenance of our morale needs careful consideration.

But the language and grammar of newspapers – particularly of the tabloid variety – just do not have the ability to remind people of human continuity or an outbreak of peace. Neither are they there to maintain our morale since there is nothing they love more than to remind us of the extreme peril of our every position. Even if they attempted to do so they would cease to be what they are. It is in the very nature of the beast that it can only feed on disorder and failure; on disappointment and grief. This beast becomes serenely happy when it is contemplating a meal of the violent or the perverse and the more perverse the perversity and the more violent the violence then the more appetising the beast will find it *and* the more likely he will be to over indulge.

But the truly evil quality of this beast in question is that it seems to have no self-knowledge at all. Not only is it blissfully unaware that it has become a harmful menace to every single man, woman and child in the country, but, in the face of every fact to the contrary, it still stoutly maintains that it is actually performing a public service. Here hypocrisy is the appalling and unforgivable sin.

There is little our tabloids love more in the whole wide world than a very brutal rape, particularly if there is more than one man involved and the girl victim is very young. Their public posture in presenting such bestiality – with huge headlines and the largest graphics – is always one of sanctimonious horror, but the clear effect is the sexual titillation of the reader. Every conceivable aspect of the rape, every grisly detail, every known angle is presented voyeuristically so that 'we may know about these monsters'.

And yet by some obscure reasoning process these newspapers also then appoint themselves as the guardians of public morals, even suggesting that they have taken over where the Church has failed. They run steaming editorials attacking violence, pornography and the sexual exploitation of children. The *Sun* runs an editorial extolling the virtues of the family. The *Daily Mirror* runs an editorial ticking off Sylvester Stallone for all the violence in his Rambo films.[4] Yet these outbursts of editorial moralising are almost always surrounded by rape and violence and promises of easy sex with near-naked pneumatic young women inviting the readers to join in their sexual fantasies. 'I Long to Make Love to a Whole Football Team.'

Then, as we take a closer look at the pages of these pedlars of cant, we find that they are also openly advertising sexually explicit telephone calls and 'Strictly XXX Adult Only Videos' – which are not covered by the 1984 Video Recordings Act – and include such films as *Desires within Young Girls*, *Waves of Lust*, *Girls of Passion* and *Sexual Desires* which, apparently, is about how 'bored housewives satisfy their uncontrollable desires at all-action parties where anything and everything goes'.

But the tabloid apologists tell us that this country is not a concentration camp in which we are forced to read the *Sun* every morning before breakfast. We actually pay money, of our own free will, to revel in the gutter with them. This is the way we choose to be entertained and the tabloids are only behaving in a tabloid way. It is just all harmless fun.

But, in reality, there is nothing at all harmless about this fun. Far from laughing, we are, in fact, being threatened and attacked deep within the harmful caves of the Man of Lawlessness. There is no love, tenderness or truth in these caves. Here physical contact often comes through violent and perverted acts; here all relationships are corrupt and rotting; here we are all back at the writing-table of the Marquis de Sade in that Charenton asylum. Continue walking through the fetid air of these caves and, sooner or later, you will come to the foul and horrific lair where all the flowers are dead, the old are being mugged in their very living-rooms while innocent children are being tortured and then murdered only to be carried out again and buried in a crude grave on Saddleworth Moor.

The Yorkshire Ripper

One of the Man of Lawlessness's quite special creations was Peter Sutcliffe, who was born in June 1946 and grew up in Bingley, Yorkshire. He was, by all accounts, a shy self-contained wallflower while young; easily influenced and always

picking up other people's expressions. He developed an obsessive interest in a wax museum in Blackpool, according to one
account of his life, *Somebody's Husband, Somebody's Son*, by Gordon
Burn (Heinemann, 1984), where there was a Chamber of
Horrors, including the standard tableaux on Murder in the
Bath, the Blood Hook and Jack the Ripper. But also in the wax
museum was a Museum of Anatomy where wax torsos of
'bodies' had been cross-sectioned and there were glass cases
containing decayed sexual organs and diseased scrotums.
Figures had been disfigured with venereal sores. Sutcliffe was a
regular and fascinated visitor of these exhibits.

This fascination with the macabre is likely to have fuelled
another of his activities, since it emerged that Sutcliffe was the
Yorkshire Ripper who, in a trail of terror over three years, had
killed some thirteen women and attempted to kill another seven
in what can only be described as a most brutal and frenzied
manner.

But it is not Sutcliffe's Romantic attachment to the macabre
which is the important issue here, so much as the press's
Romantic attachment to *him* and, on the basis of a Press
Council report into the affair, we now have the clearest picture
of the way in which almost all sections of the press behave when
they are on the scent of a monstrous evil.[5]

Carlyle's suggested title for a history of newspapers was
Satan's Invisible World Displayed and nowhere have the state and
practitioners of this gargoyle art been so thoroughly displayed –
and condemned so comprehensively – as in the Press Council's
report on the Sutcliffe affair. It amounts to the most scathing
indictment of British newspapers and journalists that has ever
been published. It portrays a press which inexcusably im-
perilled a fair trial for Sutcliffe and it discloses – with photostats
– the traffic in blood money which newspaper after newspaper
offered the murderer's relatives and friends. It also turns a
spotlight on the sickening behaviour of reporters and photographers who laid siege to the mother of a victim and Sutcliffe's
wife – harassing them, the Press Council found, 'scandalously
and ferociously'. The report is possibly the best-ever exposure
of how efficiently and relentlessly the mind and influence of the
Man of Lawlessness works in discipling his people.

Within a day of the arrest hundreds of reporters were

swarming into the Bradford suburb of Heaton. There were thirty-two from the *Daily Mail* alone; fourteen from the *Sunday People* and eight from the *Daily Mirror*. In total there were 200 press people staying in the Norfolk Gardens Hotel. The *Daily Express* was ordering bucket after bucket of champagne, believing, mistakenly, that they had signed up Sonia, Sutcliffe's wife.[6]

Two days after the arrest, the Press Council, unhappy with the early reports of all this journalistic activity, announced on January 7th, 1981, that it was going to conduct its own enquiry and began amassing evidence and statements in May at the end of Sutcliffe's trial. It was not until November 1982 that the complaints committee could complete the enquiry and arrange to publish its report, when the Attorney General assured the Council that there would be no further appeal to the House of Lords. The enquiry occupied the committees for twenty-eight full days; they and the full Council had studied 350,000 words of summarised evidence and comment. The report, adopted unanimously by the Council and published on February 4th, runs to 80,000 words in eighteen chapters and seventeen appendixes.

At the heart of the report, according to the account of Ken Morgan, the director of the Press Council, is its section dealing with cheque-book journalism. It shows how the cheque-book has replaced the notebook in covering crime and unearths widespread examples of payments and offers which led to a wave of public revulsion, demonstrated by thousands of names on petitions calling for payments to criminals' families to be outlawed. Letters condemning the practice came from politicians, women's organisations, newspaper readers and even the Queen.

The Council found that payments had been made to people who were, or might reasonably have been, witnesses in Sutcliffe's trial and that there had also been payments to Sutcliffe's relatives and friends. The Council had long condemned payment to witnesses, particularly after the Moors Murders Trial when the chief prosecution witness was found to have been in a newspaper's pay throughout. In a Declaration of Principles, the Council had also forbidden payments to be made to criminals themselves.

In the Sutcliffe enquiry, as it unearthed the sordid story of offers and payments, the Council asked the people concerned to condemn, defend or explain the practice. But some editors were not at all co-operative or forthcoming in their explanations of cheque-book journalism, the Council discovered. It often required prolonged and detailed questioning to obtain this information, often given unwillingly, about their own news-paper's attempts to buy the stories of people connected with the case. Sometimes details of such attempts – or even that they were made at all – came to light as a result of enquiries the Council was making elsewhere.

Well after editors of all national and regional newspapers in Yorkshire had replied to most of its enquiries about payments and offers, the Council obtained from Mrs Sonia Sutcliffe a variety of letters and notes from newspapers, news agencies, publishers and agents and broadcasting organisations – many of them making offers or suggesting arrangements to buy the wife's story. 'They cast a new light not only on the scope and scale of offers but also on some editors' earlier replies,' said Ken Morgan.

The Council also observed that there had been more wide-spread public criticism of the press for offering payments to relatives or associates of criminals – stigmatised as 'blood money' – in the Sutcliffe case than in any previous one. The Council shared the public's abhorrence and distaste for press conduct that enabled those connected with a criminal to profit from the connection.

Just as it is wrong that the evil-doer should benefit from his crime so it is wrong that persons associated with the criminal should derive financial benefit from trading on that association. What gives value to such stories and pictures is the link with criminal activity. In effect the stories and pictures are sold on the back of crime. Associates include family, friends, neighbours and colleagues. Newspapers should not pay them, either directly or indirectly, through agents for such material and should not be party to publishing it if there is reason to believe that payment has been made for it. This practice is particularly abhorrent where the crime is one of violence and payment involves callous disregard for the feelings of victims and families.

In its verdicts on the activities of some newspapers the Council censured the *Daily Star* for paying £4,000 to a potential witness, Miss Olivia Reivers, the woman in the car with Sutcliffe when he was arrested; and the *Daily Express* for its offer of £80,000 to Sonia Sutcliffe when she was a potential witness. It said that it could not accept the statement by the then editor, Mr Arthur Firth, that it has never been the *Express*'s policy to pay money to criminals' relations, nor his explanation for the misleading answers he gave the Council when he said that he had 'forgotten' that the paper considered offering money during the two days after the story broke. The lapse of memory was astonishing, said the Council, which deplored the attempt made to mislead it.

Similarly, it criticised an attempt by the *Yorkshire Post* editor, Mr John Edwards, to mislead it by an assurance that no payments were made to the Sutcliffe family or friends when an offer had been made to Mrs Sutcliffe in the newspaper's letters to her solicitor. It also criticised the *News of the World*'s lack of candour in leaving the Council to discover the full nature and extent of approaches it made to Mrs Sutcliffe. The Council also condemned a *Daily Mail* reporter who asked a police superintendent to pass a note offering £5,000 to a potential witness, the prostitute who was with Sutcliffe when he was arrested, just as she was about to begin a press conference at Sheffield police headquarters. (She was later bought up by the *Daily Star*.)

Approaches were also made to Mrs Sutcliffe by the *Daily Express*, the *News of the World*, the *Yorkshire Post*, *Woman's Own* and the *Observer*.

The longest adjudications against individual newspapers were on complaints made by Mrs Doreen Hill, mother of Jacqueline, the final victim, that the *Sunday People* and the *Daily Mail* made payments to witnesses and offered 'blood money'. The *Sunday People* was condemned for making payments to Mr Trevor Birdsall, a friend of Sutcliffe, who gave evidence at the trial, and by making a contract with Mr Birdsall's friend, Mrs Gloria Conroy, effectively to buy his story.

In the case of the *Daily Mail*, the Council upheld Mrs Hill's complaint that the newspaper paid Peter Sutcliffe's father £5,000 when he could reasonably be expected to be a witness. But the Council's most serious view was on the newspaper's

contacts with Mrs Sutcliffe. Sir David English, the editor of the
Daily Mail, said that he had decided very early on that he would
not be paying any money to Mrs Sutcliffe, but nevertheless
continued making offers to her over three months in the hope of
obtaining an interview without payment.

Yet when the Council discovered the various offers that the
Daily Mail had put to Mrs Sutcliffe, the editor said that the
newspaper had merely entered into 'a ritual of negotiations' to
try to get background information, to find out and 'spoil' what
its rivals were doing, and to make its rivals pay more should
they intend to buy. The *Daily Mail*, as the editor put it, intended
'to work towards a confidence-building situation where we
might get an interview with Mrs Sutcliffe without paying any
money to her'.

The Council gave careful thought to whether it could accept
that the *Daily Mail* did indeed decide in early January 1981 that
it would not pay Mrs Sutcliffe any money or whether it only
decided to say this much later. The Press Council decided to
accept assurances from four editorial executives that they knew
of the editor's decision not to pay at an early stage in January. It
added: 'The effect is that it concludes also that a group of senior
editorial executives, including the editor, not only set out to
deceive Mrs Sutcliffe but their conduct had an effect of
artificially creating and sustaining a cheque-book journalism.'

The judgment ended: 'In the Press Council's view the
explanation offered by the newspaper amounts to a confession
that the *Daily Mail* was guilty of gross misconduct.'

Moving on to the way that newspapers combined to prejudice
Sutcliffe's trial the Council said: 'In most newspapers the
material, the tone and the display of the coverage combined to
create the general impression that the man who had been
detained, even though he had not then been charged, was
beyond doubt the killer of thirteen women and girls and that a
trial was no more than a formality.'

Some editors had expressed their concern very early. Reporting a warning by the Solicitor-General to newspapers about the
right to a fair trial, only days after the first stories appeared, *The
Times*'s leader had taxed the press and television with having
little to be proud of. The *Guardian*'s leader had begun: 'A man is

clearly guilty until he is proven innocent ... is the only conclusion to be drawn from the extraordinary hysteria ...'

In other statements to the Council, editors stressed the duty they felt to set public alarm at rest by linking the arrest with the Ripper murders, the uninhibited announcements and jubilation of the police and what one of them called 'error by example'. Some newspaper editors were holding back in the interests of fairness and a fair trial until they saw what had been shown on television or heard what was on the radio. Some broadcasting editors said that their coverage had been constrained until they saw what the early editions of the newspapers were running.

The most embarrassing part of the report, as far as journalists are concerned, describes the sickening hounding and besieging of people whose misfortune it was to find themselves involved in a major story. The Council took two examples, Mrs Doreen Hill, mother of Sutcliffe's last victim, and that of Mrs Sonia Sutcliffe. Mrs Hill gave hers in a Radio Four *Checkpoint* programme:

> We couldn't even think straight and then suddenly, I suppose within hours of finding out about Jacqueline's death, we were besieged at the door, by the telephone, by different press members. They must have realised what a state we were in, and at first we were quite polite in saying, no, we did not want to see anyone. In the end, we had to get a policeman at the gate and get all our telephone calls intercepted. We ended up getting our number changed anyway. It was like being in prison really. We were in here and we could see all the press, the television crews as well, outside ... I suppose it's their job, but they should understand what people are going through.

In one respect Mrs Hill was fortunate: she had on hand a solicitor and family friend, Mr Anelay Hart, in whose office her daughter Jacqueline had worked. The report quotes his account of what happened when the police decided to treat Jacqueline's death as a Ripper murder enquiry.

> That was the signal for hordes of media men to descend on the home of Jack and Doreen Hill. There were TV cameras, photographers, reporters, the lot. Their telephone began ringing

incessantly. Notes were being continually pushed through the letter-box. As you will realise, Jack and Doreen were so overcome by shock that they simply could not cope. Jacqueline's grandma, Mrs Florence Hill, who had gone to the Hill's home to look after them, telephoned me for help.

. . . My wife went down to the Hill home. She asked the media to leave the Hill family alone, asking them how they would feel if they had daughters of Jacqueline's age and this had happened to one of their daughters. Some of the media men said that they had daughters of Jacqueline's age and they sympathised, but they had to be there because their editors had so instructed them.

The other no-less-harrowing story was that of Mrs Sutcliffe who wrote a letter to Ken Morgan in which she spoke of 'this thoroughly moralless profession – the press – have prevented any hope of my ever picking up the threads of life and raising a family of my own.'

She described 'the despicable conduct' of reporters and cameramen when they laid siege to her in her parents' home when her husband was detained.

Hordes of reporters clambered one over the other, banging at the door, window and letter-box; shamelessly yelling that they would pay more than the next man or woman for my story. The scene was akin to a frenzied auction, with wild attempts to outbid each other in shouts of 'I will top any sum the rest of you care to name.' Not only did we have to keep the curtains continuously drawn, but we were not even able to leave the house to do our shopping. Our oppressors fared rather better. To accommodate this media mob some enterprising person found room among the streetful of press cars to set up a caravan, selling food and hot drinks to provide the said gang with which to continue their abysmal performance that freezing January.

The Press Council's condemnation of the conduct which both women had described was the strongest it had ever made of journalists in the field. The relatives of the victim and of the accused had been subject to wholly unacceptable and un-justified pressures by journalists anxious to interview or photograph them or bid for their stories. It was best described in the old phrase 'watching and besetting' and its targets were people in deep personal grief or grave anxiety who were harassed by the media ferociously and callously. 'There is no redeeming feature about behaviour of this kind.' Ken Morgan said:

> Looking back on the enquiry it was a fascinating but pretty saddening experience for anyone concerned with the reputation of British journalism and journalists. There was nothing, or at any rate very little, to laugh at at all. The nearest thing to a joke was Lord Hailsham's reference, to a cartoon of a police helicopter coming down on the Arctic waste while one Eskimo said to another: 'They are looking for an impartial jury.'
>
> There is, I am afraid, no doubt that on three counts – possible prejudice to a fair trial, blood money and harassment – conduct in Yorkshire and what was published throughout the country offered ammunition to those who would like to see legislative controls on what newspapers and journalists may do and what the press may say. The reaction was not limited to one pressure group or one political viewpoint. The petitions from the public were signed in the thousands. Conservative back-benchers tabled a motion calling for legislation to make cheque-book journalism illegal. SDP members tabled another calling on the press and other media not to pay accused persons and their families. Labour MPs called for cheque-book payments in the UK to be outlawed – and to be taxed at 100 per cent if they came from foreign sources. The press would be wise not to underestimate the pressure.

So we have seen then, in the broadest and fullest detail, a portrait of a pack on the hunt of the most enormous evil. There is nothing encouraging in the story at all, relating as it does, how truth was the first to the wall as journalism became involved in deceptions and lies of every kind in its relentless pursuit of the barbarous details of Sutcliffe's carnage. Overtaken, as it has been by the central emotions and principles of the Man of Lawlessness – who loves little more than to embrace violent and perverted serial murder – journalists were prepared to resort to any trick or deception to come close to the monster who, in his turn, would help them to sell newspapers.

Within forty-eight hours of his arrest they had driven a coach and horses through the contempt laws, forcing the Solicitor-General to remind them of 'the vital principles embodied in English law that a man accused of a crime, however serious, is presumed innocent and entitled to a fair trial.' They had also, in effect, anointed crime by handing out large sums of money to persons associated with the murderer. They had been brutal and heartless in their harassment of the bereaved. In just about everything they had done they had outraged all the normal canons of decency and, in so doing, had shown themselves true disciples of the Man of Lawlessness who, being the champion of lies and the sworn enemy of truth, was very pleased indeed with all their activities.

The Tale of Aberfan

But it is not just individuals that the press can watch and beset. Sometimes they can watch and beset a whole village as they have done now in Aberfan, a small Welsh mining village.

Aberfan is a raggle-taggle of grey, slate terraces, pub and chapel, which sits on the side of a brambled valley slope in South Wales. As a village it contains all the perfection of the ordinary with perhaps its most distinctive smell being that of brewing tea. Here ordinary people had been living out their days under the shadow of the pit until one damp morning in 1966 when the unthinkable happened. An enormous amount of water built up inside a coal-tip overlooking the village and sent a mountain of slurry down on to the village school, killing 116 children.

I was in the offices of the *Western Mail* in Cardiff at the time, just starting as a reporter on the Thomson training scheme. We knew little of the details from first reports. All we heard was that something had happened to a school in Aberfan, so I drove up there with another reporter. I can still remember that morning in the most vivid detail, journeying up through the melancholy valleys with their old abandoned mines and deserted chapels. The whole place might be one huge museum and, just moving along through the wide alleyways of the ruined landscape, you could see how completely the old order had broken down. From 1926, when the miners fought and lost a long strike, the coal industry had slipped into an irreversible decline. Everywhere there were empty coal-trucks sitting rusty and brooding on the old days. King Coal had finally died and now we had come to the most tragic chapter in the history of the valleys.

As we drove down the twisting road leading into the village a policeman was standing at the side of the road directing traffic, his eyes red from too many tears.

My colleague ran off and, uncertain what to do, I walked down towards the school, finding a woman, her hands in the pockets of a brown mackintosh, standing on a wall. I asked her what had happened. She did not reply so I asked her again.

'The children. They're all in there. They're all under that black stuff.'

I took out my virginal notebook with pen poised to ask further questions but then I put them both back into my pocket, those awful words burning into my mind like acid. *The children? They're all in there. They're all under the black stuff.*

I wandered away from the school, being sick repeatedly. *They're all in there.* My vision swam as I looked up at the monstrous black shape of the killer tip still shrouded in the early morning mists. Men were shouting and running around with shovels. It was the terrible cost of that bastard coal again.

I never did write a word about the disaster, staying clear of the action and standing, ill and frightened, at the top of the hill looking down at the smashed school. Some 300 miners were digging down through the slurry as if they were all burrowing and struggling through some obscure battlefield in the First World War. Their warm breath plumed dragon-like in the cold air. Their boots stuck in the black swamp. Buckets were being chained by hand. Every thirty seconds a whistle blew and the men stopped working for ten seconds: standard mining rescue technique for listening for sounds of any survivors.

Those ten-second silences were the longest that any would ever remember. Even twenty years later I can still hear those silences. They were like great prayers in this valley of death: great upsurges of silence when all that you could really hear was the savage crumbling music of your breaking heart. Dear Jesus, miners were always prepared for trouble but not for this. Not for *this*! Not their babies in their classrooms; finished before their young lives had begun.

That day was the longest ever. The Secretary of State for Wales, George Thomas, and an ashen-faced Lord Snowdon came and went. Groups of men and women were standing everywhere, stricken, silent, full of the most unbelievable pain.

Body after body was dug out of the slurry with one teacher being found holding two children in his arms and trying to protect them with a blackboard.

And then came the other members of my newly-chosen profession, some by car and a few by helicopter. They came pouring off the train in Cardiff and piled into taxis asking to be taken to Aberfan. They bought up phones in the village. They asked for ages, names, photographs, any available details of the dead. They came shouldering their television cameras and some were ordered back to London. One television crew had actually broken into the chapel of death where the dead children were being laid out on pews. Photographs were set up with crosses made of helmets and miners' shovels. And I was expected to do all this also! Instead, confused and a little angry by now, I went down to the local pub.

The excellent Christopher Booker, whose strictures on the media are among the most accurate and savage ever to appear in public print, made some telling points in his column in the *Daily Telegraph* in 1988, following an air crash on the M1. On the media coverage of this event he wrote:

> As soon as a disaster occurs, even while people are still being rescued, while relatives are still wondering wildly what has happened to those they love, the television crews, reporters and cameramen are converging on the scene in their hundreds, to provide round-the-clock coverage of every detail of what has happened, which continues unabated for days.
>
> Then there is the 'instant expertise', the desire to begin speculating at once on the cause of the disaster. Not only is every genuine expert in sight brought before the public for interrogation, often long before they can possibly have the information necessary to make a proper judgment, but politicians, presenters on the *Today* programme and men in pubs suddenly reveal an astonishing concern for the finer technical points of engine shut-off, signalling lights and the workings of the bow doors, which makes them feel immensely knowing and important. Then, as the first shock recedes, there is the demand for 'instant emotion', the rush for 'human stories' from every possible angle on everyone remotely involved in the disaster.
>
> There are the rows and recriminations, milked by the media for all they are worth – was some minor Royal 'tactless', should a

Minister have gone on holiday, was this person or that to blame? – all of which help to provide new headlines and new twists to the story. Meanwhile, at the centre of it all, of course, is the reality of what has happened to all those directly involved – the victims, the survivors, the doctors, the nurses, ambulance men, firemen, living through one of the most intensely emotional experiences of their lives.

In fact the whole drama is really unfolding on two quite different levels. On one hand there is the real drama, involving people as directly and profoundly as could be. All around it is this other, much more unsubstantial drama being played out, reported and discussed by all those outsiders who, in one way or another and for all sorts of motives, are feeding on the real drama.

Later that night in Aberfan – and none too sober – I walked back up the hill to look down on to the digging which was continuing in that broken school. With the giant sodium lamps it looked like a gaudy broken-down circus with all the rescuers moving around, black on yellow in the huge pools of light. I sat high up on the slope with another man, watching the work, both of us crying. We tried the odd word, but nothing came out and we waved one another quiet.

Down below the parents were queuing up outside the Moriah chapel to witness the ultimate obscenity; to identify their children laid out on the pews of the chapel of death, some still clutching the items they had died holding, others with their eyes clogged up and their mouths jammed full of coal slurry. The parents queued right through that savage night until the savage dawn when the last of the twenty-eight adults and 116 children had been dug out. The cost of coal again, some said. Aye. The terrible cost of that bastard coal.

But I was not only crying for those children and their parents – any one of the parents would have given anything to be on that chapel pew rather than their child – I was also crying for myself too. I had only been in the job for a few weeks and did not quite see how I was going to stay in it for a few more weeks. I had even been told to go around the parents trying to get photographs of the children which, for about five baleful minutes, I actually did. How could I go on doing this for a living?

How was I going to carry on in a profession whose most basic mechanisms I so bitterly despised? How could I become another of these bloodhounds in search of the troubles of the world, hurrying to disaster, feeding on grief and invading privacy? Well I did keep doing it and my work and my attitude to it became the central ambiguity of my life.

Luckily, I never came near to a story of the size of Aberfan ever again. And I rarely did any serious news stories as such. I did once cover an air crash for the *Sunday Times* in Belgium, but was so ill after seeing a severed hand in a field I was never sent on a serious story for them again, particularly as I had hardly excelled in my work in Northern Ireland. I had also discovered a talent for writing diaries, a nothing art about nothing.

Yet while I never had the stomach for the big news story I have always admired those who did and it has never been the slightest part of my argument that huge disasters such as Aberfan should be ignored. Clearly, here is an event of enormous public interest and we journalists keep telling ourselves that, through such reportage of such disasters, it ensures that they do not happen again. Well, that's what we keep telling ourselves anyway . . .

Neither, in this instance, am I complaining about the manner in which the press tackled the story since most were as upset and sensitive to the family difficulties as any human being could be expected to be. (Most of the scandal concerning the way the chapel of death was broken into was caused by one TV crew and the French press.)

My most bitter complaint – particularly with regard to Aberfan – is that once the press had got in there, *they never left again*. They watched and beset this beleaguered village continuously for years. And still they keep on raking over the ashes of a cold disaster, using the flimsiest of pretexts – usually an anniversary – to find a new angle, a new row, any new excuse to go there and gaze again at the face of the most appalling tragedy and sudden death. They have never allowed the village to mourn in peace and dignity. They effectively prevented the village from ever recovering its former stability and became, in the end, a disaster almost as big as the killer tip itself.

From the day the tip came down almost every hiccup in the village became the focus of worldwide publicity. There was Princess Margaret's disastrous toy appeal which all but buried the luckless village all over again with dolls and teddy-bears. There was an appeal fund which led to endless internal rows between the villagers. The £2m raised was an amount which these decent, ordinary people just could not cope with. There were quarrels, bickerings and endless wild words which were all duly reported. Every week we heard of a new row and a new point of view – all shouted to the world in banner headlines.

Then came the longest tribunal in history, which lasted for five months, hearing 136 witnesses and listening to 2,500,000 words set out in 4,500 pages of transcript. Parents stood outside the tribunal holding up placards before the television cameras asking: 'Is my child only worth £5,000?' Family was set against family. Few could even agree on the time of day and in the end £550,000 was spent on the community centre, £100,000 on a memorial garden and £150,000 towards the cost of making the tip safe. Those in the school who were unaffected were also given £200 each which, invested in unit trusts until they were 21, actually lost money.

Money, money, money. Suddenly money was all-important and while the quarrels about it continued in the village the most urgent articles were being written in the press and the most vital programmes were being made for television – all saying that these children should not have died in vain. There were calls to reclaim the valleys and economists wrote of the need for the provision of multipurpose complexes and new socio-economic strategies.

And the result of all these articles and programmes was that the valleys went plunging remorselessly towards their death until today the Rhondda valleys have become the new sick man of Europe with the highest premature death rate, the most diseases of poverty, the most without an inside toilet and the highest unemployment. But Aberfan did get three new squash courts, a badly-needed ski-slope and a swimming pool.

All this, you might say, is par for the course given a disaster of this magnitude. But still the press kept coming back, focusing on a few big-mouthed individuals or straining over any new hairline cracks in any tip within a hundred miles of Aberfan when, in September 1981, their great dreams of great distant news stories were again revived. It was reported that an underground fire had been discovered near to the school playground in Aberfan.

Playing on the old mythic terrors all the newspapers again had a wonderful time rolling out their wretched clichés about how fear was again stalking the valley of tears; how death had come back to the death school. Of course, had it been a real fire then it would have been a real story, but it was not a fire at all – as I discovered when the *Observer* asked me to go back there to find out what was going on.

The newspaper reports that week had been describing in graphic detail an underground blaze which was again threatening the school, but 'this underground blaze' turned out to be no more than a *heating* which, at its highest, was 150°F while a fire needs at least 400°F just to get started. But three trees had been charred as was a patch of ground and it was agreed to reroute an empty underground gas main whose existence had been heavily featured in the reports.

I was present on the grey afternoon when some parents met some engineers in the yard of their new school under the eyes of the local television cameras. The parents were told that the best technology was available to locate the heating and contain it. But still they insisted that everything and everywhere should be checked – particularly under the school. As the conversations continued I came to see that the parents just did not believe what the scientists were saying to them. They wanted to check and see for themselves. I felt sad just then because I understood that not only had they once lost their babies and then become undermined by money and the media, they had lost something else. These poor people, who had grown up in the shadow of the chapel and in the fear of God, had lost their faith, too.[7]

This had been my first time back in Aberfan since the day of the disaster so I walked back through the village to find that it had changed only in detail. There was a pretty memorial garden and a community centre where the school once stood. The tip had been terraced with trees planted on it, but the village was much the same. The grief was still much the same, too. Up in the cemetery the children's graves were a blaze of colour. Parents still came up here every week and some every day. I watched from a distance as one man came up to the tombstone, changed the flowers, changed the water and then stood for a full five minutes just looking at the tombstone.

Yvonne, Jeffrey, Julie, Susanne, Jean, Janette, Robert, Megan, Islwyn, Grahame . . . the loss still flooded out of those headstones. And there were dark accusations, too. 'A heart of gold stopped beating, two little hands at rest. Why did you have to break our hearts to prove you need the best?'

In a strange sense my career in regular journalism began in Aberfan and ended there, too. Back in 1966 I was a sick and useless greenhorn, but by 1981, with my first book written but not yet published, I was back again and saw that it really was time that I came to terms with the central ambiguity in my life. It really was not for me to go to Aberfan as a journalist and then start complaining about the weasel words of other sensation-seeking journalists who were continuing to undermine the stability of the place. I, too, had gone there and watched a grieving parent. I, too, had not really left this blighted village alone.

And, as much as anyone, I knew the colossal hypocrisy of all arms of the media; how each and every one of them was more than happy to point an accusing finger at almost everyone except themselves. It really was time to stand up straight and, within a few weeks of that visit to Aberfan, I left the *Observer* and never wrote another word for that newspaper again.

8

The Electronic Pulpit

In which we delight in meeting Billy Graham in Bristol's Holiday Inn – Travel up to London to listen to Luis Palau – Discover from a Welshman with an American accent how he learned the right way to tie up a package at five in the morning – Go to America for a round-up of the electronic evangelists and to hear about the king of sleaze – And see how the electronic church is not really a church at all.

A Life in the Day of Billy Graham

Besuited American youths with short hair and Weetabix muscles were bustling politely through the crowd of some 30,000 this dull afternoon on May 12th, 1984, in Ashton Gate stadium, Bristol. Walkie-talkies crackled with static and at least 100 photographers were milling around the great be-flowered stage on the football pitch. A red carpet stretched across the halfway line. Dark, fat clouds began chasing one another over the very roof of the sky as the 2,000-strong choir began singing 'All Hail the Power of Jesu's Name'.

Today Billy Graham was starting one of the biggest evan-gelistic crusades ever set up in this country. Even in such a large stadium, on such an unpromising day, the atmosphere was thrilling. The very air was thick with rising and falling

burblings of excitement. Great spasms of emotion were rolling around and around the crowded terraces. 'We are here to
welcome Billy back,' Gavin Reid told us over the microphone. 'Some of us think that he belongs here.'

Television cameras were dotted around the dais and, we
learned, video-cassettes of the service were going to be delivered to meetings in the local churches. There was a message
from the Archbishop of Canterbury: 'My prayers are with you
as you begin this mission.'

I was sitting with the others on the press bench where we had
all been given the best seats, 'media packs' *and* even been
excused the collection. 'We are sending a collection bucket
around, but you keep your heads down and pretend that you
are working,' one of the stewards told us. 'We don't want you to
pay anything. It is our delight that you could come. We know
that you will be blessed.'

Next to me was a reporter from the *News of the World*. I
wondered aloud what possible interest that newspaper could
have in a religious meeting like this. They always said that no
self-respecting haddock would want to get itself wrapped in the
News of the World. Ah, there was a lot of interest it seemed. 'I was
out chasing some nude murderer in the New Forest,' he said.
'Then I had a call from the office telling me to drop everything
and get down here. I've never been to a meeting like this before.
What happens?'

It turned out that Billy Graham had been meeting Rupert
Murdoch of late and the newspaper proprietor had even shown
the evangelist around his offices. The editor of the *News of the
World*, Nick Lloyd, had also offered Graham the use of his car
and chauffeur, but Graham had declined it. Yet Graham had
written an article for the *News of the World* and now Murdoch
had decreed that his newspapers should give the evangelist the
fullest possible publicity. As further proof of the earnest of this
decree, a none-too-sober woman turned up at Ashton Gate
from the *News of the World*'s magazine and, after fumbling
interminably and unsuccessfully for something in her handbag,
looked up and around her and asked what was going on. She
had never been to one of these 'dos' before. A steward gave her a
media pack.

This pack, I discovered on riffling through it, had everything anyone wanted to know about Mission England and Billy Graham. It gave a full biographical account of William Franklin Graham with his educational qualifications; the names of his children (all now married); his books and his many awards and honours. He has regularly been in the top ten of the most admired men in the world; been in America's top fifteen best-dressed men and, in 1975, was elected the Greatest Living American by the contestants of the Miss National Teenager pageant. He has preached to more people than any other religious leader.

He has achieved this largely through television. 'Television is the most powerful tool of communication ever devised by man,' he once wrote. 'Each of my prime-time "specials" is now carried by nearly three hundred stations across the US and Canada, so that in one single telecast I preach to millions more than Christ did in his lifetime.'

Meanwhile, back on that press bench in Bristol we were being fed with more bits of information. There were 31,000 in the stadium that day, we were informed on a bit of paper, with 2,000 in the choir, 570 coaches, 5,000 coming by car and four special trains. The clear strategy was that we should never walk away complaining that we had nothing to write about.

The 'opener' was provided by George Hamilton IV, who sang a few rounds of his Rocky Mountain theology. 'In just a minute Dr Graham is going to bring his message.'

And then, in just a minute, Dr Graham came on to the stage and brought his message, the odd word distorted in the amplification system:

I want to speak to you as if this was the last sermon I will ever proclaim. May we be conscious of no one except Him. Something like this may never come again. For God so loved the world he gave His only begotten son that whosoever (that includes you) should not perish but have everlasting life.

Remember the tapes at Watergate. They had everything recorded in the rooms in the White House. They had it all on tape. God has it all on tape. When you stand at the judgment of God He will say to the angels: 'Let's listen to the tapes.' . . . God did not make you a robot. You can do what you like and there's nothing that God can do about it. Man broke God's law and that's sin. We have all sinned. We are all under judgment and under condemnation.

He had begun with warm, soft, involving words, but as he went on the tone became more urgent. *The wages of sin is death. Hell begins here, but hell is to come as well. You won't find the answers in drugs or sex. Change your mind, your heart, your way of living.*
Such injunctions are always haunting to the religious imagination and that old oratorical magic was still clearly magical. The hand was raised, the finger was pointed at *you* . . .

So now I am going to ask you to get up out of your seat and say, by coming up here, that you are going to open your heart to Christ. You want to start again. Jesus called everyone publicly. He hung on the cross publicly for you. There must be discipleship. From now on Christ is the first in your life. You must get up and walk. It will take two or three minutes. And you will receive a prayer and some literature . . .

And, with the organ sorrowing softly, they began getting up out of their seats, drifting forward in ones, twos and small groups. That afternoon 2,352 came forward, according to another bit of paper later sent to my home. The next day there would be 2,172. The next 2,642. All figures were added up, analysed and fed into a computer. The commitments on this date are 8.8 per cent. The percentage commitments of total attendance are 8.3 per cent. 'Anything over 5 per cent is exciting.' The cumulative total commitments so far are 7,166 . . .
That summer's campaign, Mission England, was being staged in six separate football stadiums at a cost of £1½m. Some 60 per cent of the costs were gathered in the first three weeks of the campaign – largely from gifts from local churches. 'You can say that we are very, very excited,' said Larry Ross, the executive in charge of what they call media relations. 'You boys from the press have been very, very good to us.'
Billy Graham, perhaps more by accident than design, has developed something of a presidential aura and it was very difficult for anyone from the press to get a personal interview with him that summer, largely because he had a serious sinus operation at the beginning of the campaign and needed to conserve his strength.

I did, however, get a surprise phone call in my London home, early one morning, saying that, if I hot-footed it straight down to Bristol's Holiday Inn, he would see me for half an hour. The hotel suite – which had been converted into a temporary Mission England office – was abuzz with computers, word-processors and shaded-in maps. Everywhere there were clean-cut smiling American youths.

Billy Graham himself turned out to be a truly engaging man; one of the purely nicest people that I have ever met. It was his modesty which most took me aback; the way he genuinely seemed to want to know what you knew. Indeed his sheer sense of faith and holiness kept taking my breath away. As we chatted he was a continual picture of sunny and easy affability with piercing blue eyes and an immense nose, full of line and character. He was surprisingly tall, but walked and sat with a marked stoop in his shoulders. There was also a tinge of the hippy in his gingerish hair which was slightly long at the back and stretching well down over his shirt collar.

He spoke first of how much he missed his wife who had been recovering from an operation and how he loved her a million times more now than when they first married. 'Now that the children have grown up she travels with me a lot. Without her I don't know what I would do.'

We discussed the conservative nature of the people in Bristol, who are not known for any outbreaks of Pentecostal joy, and then I asked him about his curious relationship with Rupert Murdoch. Well they had first met in Australia, he said, and had been friends for a number of years. Murdoch believed that the Church had failed to respond to the needs of the working class, so he saw it as the function of his newspapers to provide those needs. I said I didn't understand any of that, but we let it pass.

When Graham had arrived in London, Murdoch had hosted a lunch of editors for him. Nick Lloyd, the editor of the *News of the World*, was there, but we all knew what the *News of the World* was about. Wasn't there some kind of contradiction in him, a mighty man of God, writing for such a newspaper? Didn't it give the rag some form of legitimacy? 'I just don't know,' he replied, leaning forward, his eyes a hard blue of questioning innocence. 'But I will tell you that I wish he would drop those page three photographs.'

We might recall that much of Graham's early fame grew out of his relationship with newspaper magnates. When he first started in California, Hearst sent out a telegram to all his newspapers with just two words: 'Puff Graham.'

Then we spoke of England and how much he enjoyed being here. He had been on television so much in America they had heard most of his sermons. Now he could use his favourites again. He also explained that he was going to Alaska when this campaign had finished, then to Korea and the Soviet Union. 'I am just waiting to see if I can do it physically. I want to set up contacts between the Americans and the Russians. Such contact has never been more important.'

Did he think that his evangelistic activity in the country would lead us back to God? 'I don't know. We'll have to wait a long time – maybe six months – to see how it all works out. We'll have to pray about it, too.'

Mission Saatchi

In tandem with Mission England during that same summer was Mission to London led by the Argentine evangelist, Luis Palau, the new superstar of the evangelical movement. This sleek and glossy campaign involved 2,000 churches which raised £1½m for the month-long series of meetings. Some £300,000 had been spent on advertisements and newspaper space, £280,000 on the hire of the stadium and £75,000 to £80,000 on building the stage and the PA system. The twenty-five strong staff had sent out four million leaflets and 25,000 car stickers.

It was not part of the Palau strategy to hide any lights under a bushel. Mission London had set out to ensure that every Londoner had heard of him by the time he had left and, to this end, there had been a carefully orchestrated campaign which, changing gear as smoothly as a Rolls-Royce, had begun by asking who was Palau, later being replaced by other posters urging people to bring their doubts to him at the Queens Park Rangers football ground. The campaign was masterminded by Sales Promotion Agency, a wholly-owned subsidiary of the then image-makers of the Tory party, Saatchi and Saatchi.

'Look this way, Luis.' 'That's it, Luis.' 'Hold it there, Luis.'
A stammering flash of cameras. The unwinding squeal of the
camera motors. The chirruping clicks of the shutters. 'That's
fine, Luis.' 'Over there, Luis.' Another stammering flash of the
cameras.

And so it came to pass that, after repeated promises from
Saatchi and Saatchi, one Luis Palau had come to town for his
first press conference of the visit to present the Gospel to Fleet
Street.

He was a small, tidy man with a Bible under his arm and a
smile of the most perfect brilliance etched on his teeth. He held
his back ramrod erect, while his hair was short and combed
immaculately. He spoke with a slight Spanish accent.

Now, after a photo-call in the street, he was ensconced on a
table with other leading church luminaries in a posh suite in the
Strand Palace Hotel. There was the Rev. Gilbert Kirby, Peter
Meadows and a Welshman with an American accent, Harvey
Thomas. On one side of the table were the glinting arc lamps of
the Thames television cameras while, scattered over the seats,
were perhaps eighty hacks from various arms of the media.
Palau was still smiling.

Harvey Thomas introduced everyone and straight off Palau
explained that he was off his head with excitement about
everything. They were going to videotape all the meetings of
Mission to London and send them off to all parts of the empire.
They were also going to use satellite and all worthwhile media
to proclaim the message of Christ.

He was clearly a great media enthusiast and had said on
previous occasions that it was created by God to proclaim the
good news. 'Any means in today's media is worth taking,' he
had said on the BBC's *Everyman* series. 'God allowed the
production of radio, television and magazines not to sell
bars of soap but to tell the truth of God to millions in the
world.'

But wasn't there a danger that he himself was being mar-
keted like a bar of soap? 'Well I just want a maximum number
of people to meet Jesus Christ,' he added. His organisation,
which is based in Portland, Oregon, reaches fifteen million
people in his daily broadcasts. He has already held ninety-six
mass crusades on four continents, given out sixteen million

brochures, forty-five films and ten books. No opportunity is lost in getting his message into the media.

Perhaps mischievously, I asked him if he would like to write an article for the *News of the World*. 'I'd love to,' he said. Perhaps he thought I was one of the commissioning editors. 'I should be honoured to write for the *News of the World*. My father used to have it at home and hide it from me unfortunately. Just give me the chance. I'd love to.

'This is not a sales job but the opportunity to proclaim Christ.' He held his Bible aloft. 'This is the word of God. You can trust it 100 per cent. The Bible is the inerrant word of God. The Bible is as much as I need to know for my walk with God. I hope you will all come to my meetings. You will all have passes and special sections to yourselves.'

I noted that, during the questions, Harvey Thomas was sitting there, also with a permanent smile like some cat that had made off with all the cream, visibly recording all Palau's words on a tape-recorder, almost as if he was letting the hacks know that if they misquoted Luis, then Harvey had got it all down on tape and there'd be a complaining letter to their editors faster than blinking. It's an old pop-star stunt, long dropped by pop stars, but now used by many politicians who, sadly in some cases, have yet to master the art of operating a tape-recorder.

Harvey had always said that he believed in the modern approach; that you had to set it up well. Certainly this press conference had been set up well, since we'd been given coffee, chocolate biscuits and a book on Palau's answers to tough questions. We had also been given another of those enormous media information packs (about four times the size of Billy Graham's) which contained every conceivable item of information about him except his sins. His wife's name was Patricia Marilyn Scofield and he had four sons – Kevin, Keith, Andrew and Stephen. He joined overseas crusades in California for ministry to Spanish-speaking people and, in 1966, held his first major evangelistic crusade in Bogota, Colombia.

At the stadium the following Thursday there was a very mixed bag in the audience as they waited to listen to the word of Señor Palau. There were Americans in stetsons and tartan trousers and fresh-faced youngsters from local Christian fellowships, all gazing up at the massed ranks of the 400 choristers. Up on the podium, underlined by a line of glossy house plants, a young man said into the microphone: 'Reach out to the people sitting on either side of you. Tell them what you have been doing for the last few days.' The great and sudden buzz was as if a swarm of ravening locusts had just descended from the dark skies.

A pop group followed, complete with 'Top of the Pops' haircuts and electronic keyboards. Strobe lights flashed along with the amplified beats. The keyboard man was told to wind it up. 'Can we have an extended welcome for . . . LUIS PALAU!'

It's so *exciting* to see you all here tonight! I feel that London needs Jesus Christ. Will you say 'Amen' to that? I hope you'll all develop a passion for souls and pray for God to come down with *maximum power*. Best of all pray that the Almighty should bless British journalists everywhere. Especially the BBC camera crew which is recording tonight's event, while another team is broadcasting this live, coast to coast, back in America.

His message is the orthodox Christian message of salvation through the death of Jesus Christ. And he usually tries to approach the issue by talking about the problems and concerns of his audience. More often than not he begins with a joke or story, gives a Bible reading, outlines the problems with examples and statistics before concluding with a message that the root of this problem can only be tackled with the help of Christ, who can only be known by faith.

Also the media are hardly ever forgotten.

After his address he was back in his brightly-lit dressing-room – PR men, minders and American executives in tow. But he looked brighter than his years and *he was still smiling*. How did he do it? 'I'm sort of an impatient man,' he said disarmingly. 'Maybe that's my quality. I'm impatient and pushy.' He complained that one-to-one conversations took too long. He wanted to reach *millions*.

'Palau wants to be liked and was totally co-operative with a lot of appreciation expressed after the filming,' Norman Stone, the director of the BBC crew which made the film of the Palau crusade, told me. 'He has a Latin charm with the gift of the gab, but he is not as formidable as Billy Graham. But he is hungry to be known and wants to assume Billy's mantle. They've already been calling him the Latin Billy Graham. But if you wanted to understand the publicity machine around him then you should talk to Harvey Thomas.'[1]

The Tricks of the Trade

I located Harvey Thomas in Smith Square where his full-time job is as public relations consultant to the Conservative Party and his work for Mission to London is unpaid. It turned out that he was an old media hand who had spent fifteen years as 'a media executive' with the Billy Graham organisation, learning all the tricks of electronic evangelism and every aspect of world communications. 'The Graham organisation was incredible and knew the media inside out,' he said. 'They taught you everything from how to look good on television to the proper way to tie up a package. I'm not joking. One of their men came into my hotel room at five in the morning and showed me the right way to tie up a package.'

Thomas first met Palau in Baton Rouge in America's Lousiana some fourteen years before. Palau knocked on the door and walked into the backstage room. 'Friends I want you all to meet Luis Palau,' said Billy Graham. 'He's going to take over the burden of world evangelism from me.' After leaving Graham in 1976 Thomas first introduced Palau to this country in 1977 and now, still speaking with an American accent, he is also publicity chairman and strategy planner for Mission to London.

Thomas reels off statistic after statistic about the campaign. He understands completely how the budgets break down. Some thirty-one countries will be listening to the services by satellite radio. There is a staff of twenty-seven in City Road and, at the end of the campaign, there will be fully-audited accounts. Everyone to do with these campaigns is nervous of the charge that they are making money. (Palau received no fee for his work in London, though at the end of the crusade he did receive an unsolicited gift.)

Such techniques as he learned on the evangelistic circuit Thomas now uses on behalf of the Tory Party. He has his own

television studios in Smith Square where he teaches MPs and
Euro-MPs how to look good on television. He also set up some
of the big electronic Tory rallies as when, to a great fanfare,
Margaret Thatcher was wheeled in before her ecstatic troops
looking for all the world like Boadicea who had lost her chariot.
He also developed the rising and falling podium – so no one
looked particularly big or small – and the invisible autocue for
the speech-makers.

He was also responsible for the disastrous youth rally when
the nutty disc jockey Kenny Everett urged Thatcher to bomb
the Russians. 'I'd prefer to forget about that one,' he said with a
small cough.[2]

The Electronic Church of America

The electronic church in the US, with the full backing of all new
media technology, is, thus far, a largely American phenomenon
with thirty-six wholly religious television stations and 1,300
radio stations. Some commentators now see the electronic
church as the most important cultural force in American life
and, thanks to cable and satellite, we shall doubtless soon see its
resurrection in between the advertisements on our screens in
Britain.[3]

'Some Christians are getting excited about the possibilities of
satellite,' wrote Roland Howard in *Strait*, the Greenbelt magazine. 'This is because at present Christian programmes have to
meet certain broadcasting standards to be given air time. They
rarely do. Now almost all they have to do is buy their way into a
satellite and they are free to propagandise until the sheep come
home. Apparently they believe that, once deregulation occurs,
the world is His oyster.'[4]

Aden Murcutt, executive director of Christian CVG television, said 'Satellite television is the greatest opportunity that
this country has ever had. The British depend on TV. They are
lost without it . . . they trust it totally.' Dales TV have been
involved in broadcasting since 1985. They spent £300,000 on
broadcasting in one year, stopping after 'disappointing' results.
They are determined to try again.

The phrase 'the electronic church' was coined in the

'seventies by an evangelist, Ben Amstrong: 'In this vision I saw the electronic church as a revolutionary form of the worshipping, witnessing Church that existed many centuries ago . . . as in New Testament times, so in the electronic church worship once again takes place in the home.'

And so it happened that a whole host of coiffed and charismatic leaders began bobbing up on American television screens – one hand holding a Bible aloft and the other reaching out for untold bundles of dollars. All these new preachers needed was not so much a knowledge of the Bible or any generous expository gifts as a good set of capped teeth, a toupee which did not look like a toupee and the ability to look good on television. Together they created the electronic church and stood in their electronic pulpit to address a combined audience (formerly known as a congregation) of 115 million. Some television ministries claimed twenty million viewers alone.

But the snag was that this new church was not really a church so much as a new and vigorous branch of show business. The services were slick and fast-moving with celebrities interviewed, pop groups raving and chorus girls dancing. The preacher was always full of smiling bonhomie – when he was not actually weeping about something obscure – and there were lots of cutaway shots to audiences who were also smiling – unless they were weeping about something even more obscure. There were religious chat shows, soap operas and panel games. Prizes came in the form of package tours of the Holy Land and luxury personalised Bibles. Free gifts came in the form of 'Jesus First' pins.[5]

But behind the show business was the real business and, lo, the money did pour in. The total annual revenue of the electronic church is estimated at $500m. In 1980 the top four preachers brought in a quarter of a billion dollars. The next five grossed $100m. Jerry Falwell alone raised one million dollars in a week.

Mailing lists were put on computer tapes so that each member could be addressed personally. They set up huge retailing operations in books, records, T-shirts and devotional tapes. Any harmless enquirer became a potential customer. The declared aim was always to raise more and more money to buy more and more television time.

The great speciality of these electronic evangelists in their electronic pulpits was simple solutions to complex problems. Any ailment from apathy to Aids could be cured – sometimes just by laying your hands on your television set. The enemies were Communists, humanists and homosexuals – 'God made Adam and Eve not Adam and Steve.'

Their political stance was somewhere to the right of Clint Eastwood. The New Christian Right was created in 1980 to ensure a right-wing president and a right-wing Congress. Just so that there would be no 'mistakes' in the elections Jerry Falwell and Co. had all the right names and addresses on their computerised files – the moral majority.

But these preachers clearly had an abundance of charisma which Max Weber had called 'those special gifts of the body and spirit'. They wanted to touch what William James had called 'the hot places in a man's consciousness'. They not only wanted your bucks; they really did want to save your souls and the leading lights to rise out of the electric seminary were:

★ Jimmy Swaggart, a long, tall Texan and cousin of that old rock 'n' roller, Jerry Lee Lewis, who spent an hour on most Sunday nights playing the piano and singing sweetly on his televised show when he was not booming in rage at something like some Old Testament prophet who had just missed the last bus to the promised land.

Verdict: All in all Jimmy is a very enjoyable demagogue with a tendency to sweat too much, but with a most promising patter in hard-selling expensive, personalised Bibles. Unfortunately, he was caught out doing something he ought not to have been doing with a whore in a Baton Rouge motel.

★ Robert Schuller, the smiling, soft-spoken, blue-gowned preacher in his Crystal Cathedral in Los Angeles, who speaks and exudes so much sugar he could sweeten every cup of tea in the world for the next decade without the sugar plantations making any further contribution. Everything is unblemished and radiant with light in the Crystal Cathedral. People do not drop litter, dribble or pick their noses in the Crystal Cathedral. Oh no, sir. Robert is particularly fond of celebrities like Cliff Robertson and Efrem Zimbalist Jr, using them for advertisements to try and drum up bigger audiences. (The last time I saw Cliff Robertson he was in an advertisement for time-share flats in Florida.)

Verdict: Robert is comforting to listen to, but he is far too sugary and, at times, there is the unfortunate aura of the sleeping-pill about him. He is just a bit too good to be true and could usefully roughen up his image a bit by, maybe, putting a bit more of the Swaggart zap into it.

★ Jerry Falwell, the nice man with a fat face and a little fat smile, who clearly understands the media as evinced by his *The Old Time Gospel Show* which is seen on 374 stations nationwide. Everything is superbly high-tech on this programme. Cameras scan the audience and seem to try and embrace everyone. Again and again they frame Jerry's face in close-up as he reads from the Bible. Chromo-key scenes, usually from the Holy Land, fill the screen behind his head. Printed words also appear synchronised with Jerry's voice as he reads.

Verdict: Jerry has been trying very hard and his undoubted sincerity makes up for his lack of intelligence. He does give the comfortable impression that he has managed to tie up every corner of the parcel safely, so that nothing will fall out, but this smugness also tends to add to the expectation that he is going to nod off in his rocking-chair at any second. But he would surely make all his teachers a little happier – and his classmates a lot less nervous – if he did not keep up that little fat smile all the time. He *must* learn to frown a bit.

★ Pat Robertson with his 700 Club. 'To say that the church should not be involved with television is utter folly,' Pat once said. 'The needs are the same, the message is the same, but the delivery can change . . . It would be folly for the church not to get involved with the most formative force in America.'

Pat does not believe in folly and so, interspersed through the message, there are segments including news stories, documentaries and taped re-enactments of people who have been driven to the edge of despair only to be saved by the 700 Club. A woman is plagued by paranoia and anxiety. She believes that her own children are trying to kill her. She sees the 700 Club. She allows Jesus into her heart. She is saved.

Verdict: Pat is a patently good man, but they rather stopped taking him seriously when he took himself off into the 1988 campaign to become the Republican candidate *and got nowhere*.

Americans do not like failures – not even in the electronic church where he who is last will be last for ever and ever. Amen.
★ The handsome and charismatic Jim Bakker – accompanied by his adoring wife and spiritual partner, Tammy Faye – began the *Praise the Lord* programme as a chat show. Gradually the show transformed itself into something new and even more grandiose, Heritage USA, a spiritual recreational centre in South Carolina. Families could go to this religious theme park for a day out with the Lord and it is still visited by around six million people a year, second only to Disneyland and Disneyworld. Here pilgrims can pray in the Upper Room, modelled after Jerusalem, attend recordings of the *Praise the Lord* television shows or simply enjoy the various features of the theme park.

Verdict: Brother Jim and Sister Tammy began their ministries well enough, but Brother Jim got caught up in an old scandal and there were allegations of blackmail. Then it turned out that Sister Tammy had a drug problem.

Tammy may well get back into the electronic pulpit, but Jim had been caught with the worst possible marked deck of cards since, in American eyes, sin is always equated with sex and, when it comes to that, there is never much forgiveness about. This is a shame because Christianity is about nothing if it is not about forgiveness.

The real problem of the electronic church was not so much its massive talent at raising huge amounts of money – or even the human weaknesses of some of its main celebrities – as the crucial shortcomings of the media in which this church has been built. The message was all right; it was the media in which it was delivered that was palsied.

It was the penny newspapers in the 1830s in America which first created the cosmos in which news about nobodies living in nowhere was flashed across the country for the interest of other nobodies living in nowhere. In 1844, the telegraph extended this cosmos of fire, flood and murder. Later came the radio. These media were not without their failings, but there was a lot that was benign about them – particularly radio. Yet there is nothing at all benign about television, which must rank as the most purely aggressive medium of them all, creating and

churning out an atomised world which is superficial, fragmented and discontinuous. Every moment is wrenched out of
context in this irrelevant and incoherent world. Thousands of
images are poured out in shots that last on an average 3.5
seconds. No sooner is one item presented than it is barged aside
for another item. Like us, Americans eat their dinner watching
news of murder, terrorism and rape, barely lifting an eye or
missing a munch. We all watch the beautiful commercials with
the same quiet disinterest. We all became desensitised prisoners in a cave of fragmented illusions in which every 3.5 seconds
has the same status and importance as the previous 3.5 seconds.

All this chaotic imagery is actually hostile to a religious
sensibility. This slide into endless and fragmented illusions is
inimical to any sense of meditation or spiritual depth. The
church and television make the most deadly pairing since
Cleopatra took the asp to her bosom. Television substitutes
theology with the spirit of the game show. Any sense of mystery
is drowned by advertising slogans. The call to repentance
assumes the same level as the Pepsi ad. Any feeling for the
sacred is destroyed by banality. Television is not interested in
the past or what might have been; it is only concerned with the
now. By its very nature it is incapable of taking up a logical
position or developing a rational argument.

There is also no sense of consecration in the corner in which
the television stands. The corner of the living-room or plinth
above the breakfast table are not special places set aside for
God. The electronic church demands none of the important
spirit of corporate worship; that sense of unified wonder when
we are together in a consecrated place and down on our knees
meditating on a holy God's first desire that His people become
holy, too. Neither is there any spirit of caring fellowship here –
without which no real sense of Christianity can ripen and
flourish.

Indeed, God takes a most visible second place to the
preachers of the electronic church whose intensity, body language and looks we attend to closely. The presence of God is
dwarfed by Oral Roberts's University, Jerry Falwell's Library
Baptist College, Pat Robertson's CBN University and Jim
Bakker's Heritage Park.

Neil Postman, in his excellent *Amusing Ourselves to Death*, summed it up well when he wrote: 'The danger is not that religion has become the content of television shows, but that television shows may become the content of religion.' He added that God does not play well on television.[6]

The electronic church is a privatised vision of the American dream, in which the love offering is a cheque – the greater the cheque, my beloved viewers, the greater the love. This is a church in which worship has been replaced by a vidicon tube sending 714 lines into a co-axial cable to be fed into a cathode-ray tube. This is a church in which the secret, intimate dialogue of the confessional and ministerial pastoring has become an exchange of letters with a word processor or a computerised tape. This is a church in which the word of God has become a day out in a theme park where you can pray in a building which *looks* like Jerusalem. This is a church which has traded in the cross for a television aerial. All this is possible, my dearly beloved, because this church is not a church at all.

Each of us has his own personal vision of the Church. Some see a vigorous Church as the surest sign of the hope of the resurrection. Others see the Church as a mystical and devotional body with all its members bound to one another in the love of Christ. For others, the Church is the centre of all life, a ministry of great and inspiring words in which the pulpit is the centre of all poetry, philosophy and drama. I cherish the dream that, one day, the Church will again become a powerful platform for witness; that it will again become truly prophetic.

But this church, which is not a church at all, does not even start to realise any of our faintest dreams or hopes. The electronic church has no vision or courage. If we ever decide to wait for this church to witness and become truly prophetic – in an age which has been created and informed by our Man of Lawlessness – then we are going to wait a very long time indeed.

Half an hour in front of almost any American television channel would suggest that, apart from any other considerations, there is nothing at all Christian about any part of its operations. It has, by any standards, become a crude and uncontrolled outpouring of crime, beatings, murder, drugs and adultery. Another University of Pennsylvania study found that crime occurred ten times more often on the box than in real life, with five acts of violence an hour on adult programmes and eighteen violent acts an hour on children's programmes. Victims of crime accounted for more than half of all characters portrayed each week. In one week just one American television station showed 300 killings, mostly in children's viewing time. That same week the various channels serving a large American city displayed 8,000 acts of violence.

The thirst for sleaze in American television has become virtually unquenchable. Chat shows are continually looking for those victims and perpetrators of violence and sexual abuse willing to be further abused before a national audience. 'Wife-beaters and beaten wives, rapists and rape victims, trans-sexuals, cross-dressers, racists, one-legged Lesbian nuns and homosexual priests parade across the screen from early morning to late at night,' David Blundy reported from Washington.[7]

> One host who has won a vast national audience is Morton Downey, a chain-smoking, foul-mouthed braggart who harangues his guests, jabbing them with nicotine-stained forefinger and shouting, 'Bullshit!' and 'Scumbag!' He had his own brother, who suffers from Aids, on the show and accused him of being a homosexual. 'Do you have sex with men?' he screamed at his brother. His studio audience, composed, it often seems, of fat-bellied, beer-swilling men with tattooed biceps, cheers him on with shouts of 'Mort! Mort! Mort!' The programme teeters on the edge of physical violence.

In a programme by the acknowledged king of sleaze, Geraldo Rivera, a white racist guest was assaulted by a black guest. A chair was thrown at Rivera, breaking his nose. The audience loved it and the programme broke records in the ratings. With blood dripping from one nostril the unstoppable Rivera went on to tape another show about sexual scandal in Washington.

Rivera moved into his own social twilight zone, hosting programmes dealing with trans-sexuals and their families, teenage prostitutes, swinging sexual suicide, mud-wrestling women, mass murderer Charles Manson, serial killers, kids who kill, battered women who kill, male strippers, white racists, kids abused by priests, patients abused by doctors, animals abused by scientists.

Real-life crimes proliferate, especially on Rupert Murdoch's American television network, Fox. Scenes of violence and sexual abuse were re-created in gory detail as victims eagerly described their experiences. His programme *The Reporters* re-enacted the sexual assault and murder of a woman in Tampa, Florida. It showed a picture of the corpse.

The programmes all have one thing in common: lots of dollars for the companies that broadcast them. Lotsa dollars. They were cheap to make and regularly commanded vast audiences and advertising revenue. Oprah Winfrey, a black chat-show hostess, dealt with such subjects as subservient women, infidelity, threesomes and wife-beaters. Her formula was so successful she earned several million dollars a year.

So when we look at this sordid panoply, it does not take too much time to work out that the real architect and philosopher of this type of programming is our Man of Lawlessness whose greatest delight it is to revel in perversion, morbidity and cruelty. This is the man whose favourite method of communication is through physical violence and raging incoherence. Here his mind and philosophy are on naked display.

And what does the mighty electronic church have to say about the way the Man of Lawlessness has put his foot on the neck of America and is laughing as the very blood and breath are draining out of the country's body? Well, the mighty electronic church has very little to say because, apart from the fact that it has yet to identify and recognise the Man of Lawlessness, it is interested, too, in making lots of dollars and creating its own form of show business. It has entered, too, into the chaotic cosmos of television. The electronic church has very little to say about anything at all that happens on television because, in all essentials, they are both in the same racket.

If we are now becoming persuaded that the media does enshrine seriously evil principles which are having seriously evil consequences for the world, then we cannot expect this church, which is not a church, to make a stand and denounce these evil harvest fields of the Man of Lawlessness. This is also because this 'church' is too busy massaging and exploiting the media to play a prophetic role and denounce it and all its works. The electronic church is too busy ingratiating itself with the Man of Lawlessness. The compelling and attractive conclusion is that the leaders of the electronic church do not attack the media because they are desperate to appear on it; they want to become involved in the action. They *believe* in it.

Following the sexual scandals, the electronic church lost a lot of its popularity in America, but the industry continues to thrive. Explicitly evangelistic and based on showmanship, the spiritual ends justify the emotional means and bring in millions of dollars. Tony Campolo, professor of sociology and evangelist said, 'If the nature of the medium lends itself to simplistic amusement, then the Man of Sorrows with all his profundity must adapt when he comes across on the screen.' Campolo suggests that evangelistic television simply does not work and added that he had met very few people who had become Christians through television.[8]

We might, in conclusion here, remember that Jesus was not a showman or a crowd-pleaser. He never exploited emotions or ignorance. Neither was he interested in cheap prizes or days out in a theme park. He also never appeared before a television camera or spoke into a radio microphone or was interviewed by a newspaper reporter or wrote a book. Yet the words and ideas of this lonely Galilean still ring down through the centuries, calling us urgently to prayer and to repentance that we may be ready for His return.

9

The New Political Dictator

*In which we meet the Right Honourable Harold Wilson, with his
wife and dog, for a 'photo-opportunity' – Read how Supermac
came to learn how to fly – Listen to Margaret Thatcher talk about
her new hairstyle and hear how Arthur Scargill keeps his intact –
Learn about Neil Kinnock in his student days – And again go to
America to see how politicians there are so much more carefully
stage-managed than they are here.*

The Photo-opportunity

It was the summer of 1970 and we had all parked our cars
outside the high walls of Chequers, the Prime Minister's
country home. About seventy of us, reporters and photographers, were then herded through the outlying fields until
we all converged on a wooden stile in a hedgerow. Behind every
bush there was a security man and, although summer, it was
still quite cold this Saturday morning. We stood around with
shoulders hunched and hands thrust deep down into our
pockets, our warm breath pluming in the cold air. The country
was in the grip of election fever. The question was, just when
was Harold Wilson going to call it?

In many ways Harold Wilson, the man for all seasons, was a
master of the media, particularly television, which he regarded

as the key to his becoming Prime Minister. 'Television had one great advantage for the Labour Pary,' he had once said. 'Most of the press were against us. And if the right-wing press were tempted to say about me – "This is a terrible man, looks like an ogre, his voice is terrible" – then you go on television and people say, "Oh look, he is an ordinary chap like the rest of us."'

Wilson was always keen to project a youthful, classless image, particularly following the stodgy grouse-moor Toryism of Harold Macmillan. He also desperately wanted to come over as an ordinary chap, so, in public, he always smoked his class-less pipe rather than his preferred cigars. His wedding-ring was always prominent in interviews. The man in the Gannex raincoat also had a carefully publicised love of HP sauce together with an assiduously maintained Yorkshire accent.[1]

Wilson had also long admired President Kennedy's ma-nipulation of the media, actually travelling to America after he became the Labour leader to spend some time with Kennedy. It was on such trips that Wilson learned the art of writing speeches in a way that made them irresistible to the media.[2] They would be spiced by attractive phrases and short, punchy paragraphs which could be lifted on to the news-bulletins without reference to anything else. Such lifts were later to become known as 'sound bites'.

There was hardly anything he would not do to drum up publicity and manipulate the media. He appeared on television joking with the Beatles. He rang up the BBC, cajoling and bullying them if there seemed a popular programme on polling-day which would keep his supporters home. Well what should the BBC put on? '*Oedipus Rex* – Greek tragedy.' He was perhaps the only politician who deliberately acquired a sense of humour to help him in his efforts to seduce and beguile the electorate while he was on the box. He arranged to be filmed and interviewed while on holiday in the Scilly Isles, even chartering a boat at his own expense for the cameramen and reporters. He said repeatedly in private that a political leader should always come over as being as reassuring as the family doctor and it was to maintain this image of trust that he constantly strove.[3]

He actually enjoyed being on television and was good at it. What he really hoped for was that he would be able to use it as another arm of government. He wanted to appear on it as often as possible and, in his first eighteen months in office, he managed a major appearance a month. But in this endeavour he was later to be thwarted, particularly by Sir Hugh Greene, the BBC Director-General, who instituted a new scheme for ministerial broadcasts. Then the Prime Minister could speak to the nation only when the BBC saw fit and invited him. Only the BBC decided if the Opposition should have a right of reply. This was a decision which, perhaps more than any other, changed the relationship between politician and television in this country. With that ruling the new medium of television began to become both an ascendant and dominant force in British democracy.

And so we were back this cold morning in the grounds of Chequers with the sun trying but failing to break through the thick, grey sky. And then, lo, Harold Wilson, hand in hand with his wife, Mary, followed by Paddy, their Labrador dog, suddenly appeared out of the wood as in a vision. But there were no rumblings of Metro-Goldwyn-Mayer thunder or great pillars of fire in this vision – just Harold and Mary ambling down the path towards the wooden stile where Mary was looking increasingly nervous and ill at ease, while Harold, one foot on the stile with an open-neck shirt, held his pipe and displayed his wedding ring as he moved his smiling face with Martian eyes, sagging eye bags and chubby jowls through an arc of 180 degrees so that every camera could get a full frontal shot of the great man out with his wife and dog for a morning walk.

Questions were shouted at him about the forthcoming election, but he ignored them all with a smile and one of those mysterious puffs on his pipe. Mary seemed to be getting more and more worried, at one stage thinking that she was patting the dog's head when, in fact, the dumb beast had turned around and she was patting his behind.

And then they turned around and walked away again with the dog. The cameramen all kept banging away as The Couple disappeared into the wood. You could easily work out the thinking behind it all. Our Leader In A Sylvan Setting Taking a Quiet Moment From the Problems Of Saving the World. It was much the same idea as that photograph of Kennedy walking on the beach with his dog – Kennedy's favourite photograph.

There was now nothing for it but for we assembled hacks to

slip away for some quiet pint in some quiet pub where we could telephone the office and tell them that there were no words in it. So what was it all about? Well, that was a 'photo-opportunity' that was; another nothing moment in the endless series of nothing moments, which is modern political campaigning, when the politician no longer so much bothers to make a speech as simply poses, against an attractive background, for the sole benefit of the cameras. These days one picture is seen as being worth a thousand speeches.

The TV Image and Political Power

The relationship between television and politicians in Britain is a strange and almost unbelievable story of role reversal, which, in another context, might make a good story line for one of those weird, highly implausible plays by Harold Pinter. In essence it is the story of the way a deeply frivolous and harmless medium of the lightest entertainment first emerged in our households and how then, over a period of nearly sixty years, it grew in power and confidence to the extent that, these days, no politician dares make a move or speak a word without first thinking how it will appear or sound on the small screen. Television is now at the very core of political power in the land. There is no doubt that the essential superficiality and crassness of modern television is firmly in control of British democracy and that this democracy is suffering grievously because of it.

But on the account of Michael Cockerell in his magisterial *Live from No 10* (Faber and Faber, 1988) television could not have had a blander beginning in this country as when it began with its weekly *Picture Page*, introduced by Leslie Mitchell, when among those interviewed were a fairy, a monkey, a string of onions, a Bond Street model, a sword swallower, a tray of muffins, a box of herrings and a silkworm. Early programmes included *Muffin the Mule*, Continental Cabaret and the excitements of live outside broadcasts from a wholesale dry cleaners and a paper-plate factory.

The Labour leader Clement Attlee thought it would have been better if television had not been invented. Winston Churchill agreed with him. Until 1948 an anonymous radio announcer in a dinner-jacket read the television news from behind the picture of a BBC clock. Any televisual incursions into general elections were forbidden and it was only after the votes had been counted that the BBC was allowed to mention that there had been a campaign.

It was not until 1951 that the political parties agreed to take a small step in putting the campaign on television by staging three party election broadcasts. Affable, tame interviewers were hired to ask affable, tame questions which had been agreed on in advance. But despite these small concessions Winston Churchill was back in office on October 26 and he was convinced that television had no part to play in politics. 'Winston never looked at television,' said his private secretary, Sir John Colville. 'He hated the lights, he hated the glare and he hated the heat.'[4]

But television refused to stay a supine puppy for ever – despite Sir Winston's strictures. In 1953, a new television magazine programme called *Panorama* began which was to become one of the most powerful platforms that British politicians ever found. Then some twenty million watched the Queen being crowned on June 2. And then came commercial television even though the great and good Lord Reith, former Director-General of the BBC, called it an unmitigated disaster for England – 'like dog-racing, smallpox and the bubonic plague'.

The first prime minister to exploit television fully was Anthony Eden, who alighted on it as a magnificent new method for issuing government press releases. By 1955 we saw our first television election. 'I attached first importance to television as a medium,' said Eden. After a series of slick appearances, watched by a third of the population, he was returned with a much increased majority. The Labour Party's televisual efforts had been disorganised and boring. Already the die was being set.

Eden regarded television as the new wonder drug and, in the early days, he appeared on it whenever he decided – to say almost anything he wanted. But already the tide was beginning to turn. The interviewer Robin Day arrived, armed with new and belligerent questioning techniques. ITN reporters began to ask more pointed questions. Then came the Suez crisis when Nasser seized the canal.

Eden spoke to the television cameras twice in four months, never answering a single question. Michael Cockerell said:

Two months after ordering the British troops into Suez he resigned. He was convinced that television, which he had been the first prime minister to seek to use as a tool of government, had in the end been used against him and contributed to his downfall . . . But within two years Harold Macmillan would transform the government's political prospects and his use of television would be a major factor in that transformation.

Harold Macmillan was the first prime minister to use the teleprompter or autocue which enabled him to read his notes – which were written on a sort of long sheet of lavatory paper – through a series of mirrors *and* look the camera straight in the eye. He also virtually invented the televised state trip – 'international relations made visible', John Whale called them – travelling to Russia and wearing a twelve-inch-high white fur hat to attract the attention of the television cameras. He was also always ready for a press conference in any airport lounge. Under his premiership television became the main soapbox of the hustings and Macmillan used the box to project himself to the people. He also learned how to be interviewed without looking like a freshly-dug-up corpse or screwing up his eyes to peer shiftily into the autocue.

By 1958 the number of homes with television sets had become seven in every ten. Television had become the public's prime source of political and social information. The green light was given for yet more politics on the screen *and* yet more searching questions.

In August 1959, Macmillan mounted his own television spectacular when he met the American President at London airport. Television cameras were invited into No. 10 to record the carefully-staged conversations. He was seen by the cameras to be on friendly first-name terms with the President. The country, he told us, 'never had it so good'. This was the unflappable Supermac. He was better known and better liked than any other previous prime minister in history. Supermac really could fly and a week later he called a general election winning a majority of more than 100. Hugh Gaitskell became the first leader of the British Labour Party to concede defeat on television.[5]

Yes, the great god of television gave a lot, but, as the politicians were also soon to learn to their cost, it took away a lot, too.

On July 13th, 1962, with the Tory fortunes on the slide, Macmillan decided on drastic surgery and sacked seven of his Cabinet in what became known as the night of the long knives. The main aim of the purge was to give the Cabinet a more youthful look so that they would come over better on television. 'No field of communications offers greater possibilities in the time at our disposal before an election to improve the public mood towards Government than that of broadcasting and television,' wrote William Deedes, one of the new ministers. 'Their impact on the public mind is immense. Though we have come a long way, there is still a tendency in many places to view the resources available with suspicion and to use them half-heartedly. The Government always has the monopoly of news value and to this extent a natural lead over other parties.'

Then Hugh Carleton Greene decided when the Prime Minister and leader of the Opposition should appear on BBC television. And along came *That Was The Week That Was*, a satirical series which regularly depicted Macmillan and his Cabinet as upper-class buffoons. The Profumo affair rocked the Government seriously and then Supermac was finally grounded by a prostate operation and resigned. And so the premiership of the first politician fully to exploit television came to an end.

His successor as Tory leader was Sir Alec Douglas-Home, who may have been the most untelegenic politician ever to get his face on the box. Part of his face had been paralysed by a wartime illness. His tongue tended to dart out like a lizard's in search of flies and his dress suggested that he spent all his time on the grouse moors. While Harold Wilson kept waving his slide-rule around and talking of the white heat of technology, Sir Alec admitted to using matchsticks to work out economic problems. Throughout his period in office Sir Alec feared television and, when the election came, was duly routed by the new and undisputed master of the photo-opportunity and the sound bite, Harold Wilson.

After an impressive residence in No. 10, characterised by constant publicity gimmicks and media manipulation, Wilson slipped on a few televisual banana skins. His own peak-time devaluation broadcast, when he famously referred to the pound in our pockets as being worth the same as before, caused him incalculable damage. By 1969 polls found him the most

unpopular prime minister since Neville Chamberlain and he
was finally unseated by Edward Heath, who had also been
busy mastering the new techniques of the electronic hustings
and deployed one of the most sophisticated television election
campaigns that the country had yet seen.

It was Heath who came up with the first televised walkabout.
He had a set designer on loan from J. Arthur Rank and a
professional lighting cameraman. Speeches were timed for the
TV news bulletins. In 1970 the party politicals were each
watched by 10 million people. There was to be no escape for any
of us since the Tories, under Heath, insisted that their party
politicals should be transmitted simultaneously on all three
channels. Research had found a clear link between voting
intention and watching television programmes. Television did
not so much make miraculous converts as confirmed prejudices
and impressions that had been built up on television in the
preceding years.[6]

But once in No. 10 Heath rejected television, regarding it
with a mixture of contempt and fear. In his first year he did just
three televised interviews and did not appear at all for his first
hundred days. He did, however, try a few heavily-hyped 'world
press conferences' as when he was trying to sell the idea of
British entry into the Common Market. 'There was confidence
all the way,' wrote Hella Pick in the *Guardian*. 'The suntan was
there, reinforced by a sailing weekend, there was a light blue
shirt and a darker blue tie to accentuate the blue eyes. Only a
Tory blue cornflower was missing.'

But for most of his premiership he laid low and paid the price.
Arthur Scargill, the miners' leader, who had a real and distinctive skill in using the media, led a crippling strike which caused
coal shortages and power cuts. After being an aloof figure for
almost three and a half years Heath was ousted from No. 10 –
again by Harold Wilson.

Wilson played a rather different game this time around, but
after a number of setbacks he again resigned on television.
'Television has undoubtedly had a good effect on politics,' he
told David Frost. 'All the people can hear the leaders of the
political parties and size them up. They can decide whether
what is being said is for political effect or whether it is real.' He
added that television was a very cruel medium.

His successor as Labour leader, James Callaghan, was again the supreme media professional, but he, too, finally came unstuck largely because of television. He had flown off to Guadeloupe for a summit in the middle of a freezing strike-torn winter. The continual pictures of Sunny Jim's permanent smile in the sunny Caribbean did little to develop our affections as we shivered back home, but then he added insult to our jealousy. On his return at the airport he denied that there was any chaos at home. Crisis! What crisis? Where had he been? It was a gaffe which was to cost him dear.[7]

But by now his office was being stalked by Margaret Thatcher, the best media manipulator of them all, who was already learning to wear less fussy clothes and soften her hairstyle and make-up. She had also consulted a voice tutor who gave her humming lessons to bring her voice pitch down. She had even been taught to move her weight from one buttock to the other during an interview to appear more interested in the questions. No opportunity was lost for a good plug. She was filmed doing everyday tasks like shopping and housework. She talked about her dress size and face cream.

Mrs Thatcher had also found a new media guru, Gordon Reece, a television producer, who knew everything about projecting an image. In Leicester she cut out her own dress pattern. She had her lungs tested in Milton Keynes. She coated chocolates in Bourneville. In Suffolk she spent fifteen minutes clutching a newly-born calf 'the wrong way' – according to James Callaghan. Reece was behind it all. The *Guardian* said: 'There was once a warrior Leaderene who frightened her followers almost as much as the enemy. Her tongue was a lash, her eyes chips of ice, her hair as stiff as an aardvark's bristle. Then one day she met a humble TV producer and a miracle occurred.'

'The truth is in this election the Tories are being sold as though they were Daz or Omo,' grumbled Callaghan, who lost to Thatcher by a 44-seat majority.

Once in office Mrs Thatcher intended to hold on to it and, to that effect, developed a most televisual style of premiership, flying to funerals and scenes of disasters, inviting cameras inside No. 10 for intimate tours, appearing on the Jimmy Young radio show, dolling up for appearances on *Panorama* and firmly seeing off the challenge of Michael Foot in the following election since the new Labour leader, with his long white hair, thick glasses and walking-stick hardly seemed the stuff of prime ministers, particularly on television, where he came across as a bit daffy and even dozy. His scruffy clothes led him to be dubbed Worzel Gummidge after the television scarecrow. One of Foot's colleagues derided his 'oxy-acetylene welder's glasses and the fact that on television he looked like a lizard who had just stumbled out into the sun'.

The successful Falklands campaign led to a revival in Mrs Thatcher's flagging fortunes – particularly after she was filmed in Downing Street urging everyone to 'Rejoice' on the night victory was announced. She also managed to enlist the help of President Reagan in one of her election campaigns as when she managed to turn a world summit in Virginia into an 'international photo-opportunity' and even got the President to pay a glowing tribute to her on television.

The final photo-opportunity in her struggle against Foot was that huge electronic rally masterminded by our old friend Harvey Thomas. Foot was routed and, when it seemed that she was going to be in residence at No. 10 for ever, the miners led by Arthur Scargill again threw down the challenge with a strike. Harvey Thomas guided her media appearances during this industrial conflict, insisting on back-lighting her in the studios to produce 'a softer and more attractive picture'. He also removed Robin Day's desk so that there would be no physical barrier between her and the interviewer. Day had to balance his clipboard on his knee and he later quipped that he planned to begin the next interview with her by asking, 'Prime Minister, what is your answer to my first question?'

The Media – A Forum for Negotiation?

But for much of the 1984 miners' strike Margaret Thatcher tried to keep a low profile, content, in the early stages anyway, to let the main protagonists fight it out with one another. And fight it out they did – in the press, on radio and on television.

This strike was the longest and most expensive in British history and in one detailed analysis, by Nicholas Jones, of the way it was conducted, we find a most dispiriting story of the

way in which progress to a solution kept breaking down, largely
because of the desires of the miners' leader, Arthur Scargill, and
the Coal Board chairman, Ian MacGregor, to negotiate
through the media. In this one strike the media clearly over-
reached itself, not content with reporting what was happening,
but, time and again, actually creating the news.

Furthermore, Fleet Street headline writers personalised the
conflict from the start – 'Mac the Knife is set to take on Scargill'
– and there is no doubt that the whole of the media actually
created the Scargill persona of 'part-monster, part-demagogue'
who, in the words of one delegate, had threatened to call more
strikes than there were numbers in a game of bingo.[8]

'How did a man like Scargill, whose judgment is so weak,
whose sense of what his members want is so flagrantly and
repeatedly in error ever become president of a great union?'
Paul Johnson wrote in the *Daily Mail*. 'The answer is simple:
the media, and above all the BBC and ITV, by their massive
exposure for this glib exponent of political showbiz, put Scargill
where he is. Media distortion of the relative weights of the
personalities within the union allowed Scargill, for a brief
instant, to blind many miners to their true interests and so win
himself the presidency.'

'One of the good things about Arthur is that he knows how to
get publicity,' Joe Gormley wrote in the *Daily Express*. 'He has
done it while repeatedly saying how appalled he is at the
media's behaviour. He realised ten years ago, I am sure, that no
publicity is bad publicity and decided to get his face in front of
the public. As a result he has created an image for himself. He is
now as much a household word, so far as the miners are
concerned, as I am. The problem he now faces is that the same
household word is not used for the both of us.'

'Scargill is one of the most remarkable, instinctive exploiters
of publicity in British politics,' Simon Jenkins wrote in *The
Times*. 'Neither the Coal Board nor the Government has anything to match.'

Obsessed by his own publicity, he kept cuttings of himself in
huge leather-bound volumes with A. Scargill inscribed in gold
on the binding. He monitored everything said about him on
television and somehow contrived to get on it at least three
times a week. He was also solely responsible for issuing press

statements on behalf of the union, writing most of them himself and chairing all news conferences.

Despite the media's constant attention he never lost an opportunity to complain about them, particularly after one photographer managed to get a shot of his hair lacquer spray sitting among his papers in his brief-case. In one hotel a television crew virtually camped outside his bedroom and another crew followed him into the lavatory.

'The capitalist media has played a role which would have impressed even Goebbels,' he told one miners' conference. 'Press and broadcasting have smeared and lied about our union, its leadership and members. It's no good just blaming proprietors and managing editors. Journalists, many of them here today who will say they support the miners, have allowed themselves to be used to attack us every day at every turn, as we fight to protect and sustain our industry.'

In the other corner, MacGregor was more than ready to compete with Scargill in public confrontation, backed up by a private consultant from Saatchi and Saatchi and twenty-three public-relations officers who were authorised to speak to reporters. MacGregor also recorded videotapes of himself to be sent to the miners, and throughout the strike the Coal Board spent £4,566,000 on advertising the Board's case in national newspapers.[9]

When the both sides did meet they were as often as not distracted by the media, leading to one famous occasion when Scargill and MacGregor actually agreed on *something* and they both stood together on the steps of a hotel to announce that their talks had been 'ruined by media harassment'. At one stage a cameraman was seen sitting in a tree outside a window and they also feared that limpet microphones had been attached to the windows of the conference room.

'Throughout the ACAS talks the NUM and NCB vied for publicity,' wrote Nicholas Jones. 'The rivalry was intense and their eagerness to follow the news so great that the negotiating teams even competed with one another for the one portable television set provided for those times when all the negotiators could do was wile away the hours in separate rooms as Mr Lowry and his staff pursued the path to conciliation.'

Premature publicity often brought new initiatives to a halt

and, while the media pantomime continued, the miners themselves were suffering the most grievous hardships.

But the central controversy of the strike revolved around the television pictures, shown night after night, of picket-line violence. Confrontations did indeed take place, but in the persistent pursuit of violence which, as we have seen, is crucial to the whole operation of television news, there is little doubt that the atmosphere on the picket lines was inflamed and distorted by the presence of the cameras. Such reports also crucially misrepresented the majority of the picket lines and served to reduce public support for the miners' cause to a minimum.

I spent two years living with the miners during that dispute for *Black Sunlight*, a novel I was writing set in the mining communities of South Wales.[10] I attended the strike meetings every Sunday morning and travelled on picket duty with the men. Such forays were unfailingly good-tempered and even amusing and, in the whole two years, the only act of violence I ever saw was a cold meat pie thrown at a policeman and missing him by about ten yards. It was almost unbelievable then to come home and see the violence on the television news whose scenes never once corresponded with the daily reality of the strike in the Rhondda. Towering over it all, yet again, was the incredible lie machine of our Man of Lawlessness.

Faced with such a powerful array of enemies it was always difficult to understand how the miners lasted so long on strike, particularly as they were, in the later stages, desperately short of money and were being offered huge cash incentives to return. The final days of the strike were characterised by blatant news management with the Energy Secretary, Peter Walker, persistently using the word 'senseless' in all his media interviews – it was a 'senseless' strike. Most of his statements were timed for the early evening news and one civil servant referred to Walker as the best press officer he had ever worked with. Probably more than anyone else he plunged a knife into the miners' resolve when, choosing that lean period for news immediately after Christmas – a time when the media will seize on any morsel – he announced categorically that there would be no power cuts in 1985.

Defeated and demoralised, the men returned to work understanding, with some bitterness, that their case had never been properly explained, particularly in the media, which, throughout their year of struggle, had persistently misrepresented and lied about their cause.

Meanwhile, Mrs Thatcher was now faced with a new contender for her throne in the shape of Neil Kinnock, who had replaced Michael Foot and, surprise, surprise, said that he owed almost everything to television. 'I got to be leader of the Labour Party by being good on television,' he said.

The Image Makers

The Rt Hon Neil Kinnock, BA Dip Ed, was a graduate of the University College of Wales, Cardiff. He was a strong-jawed, multifreckled sculpture of Welsh charisma whose passion for words was later only to be matched by his passion for the constituents he came to represent in Bedwellty, South Wales. Life has changed a lot for him since he was an undergraduate in Cardiff, living in a room where he would wake up at around seven in the morning and lie in bed serenading himself loudly with some Welsh hymns. I know all this because I was lying in the next bedroom to his since, as students together, we once shared the same house.[11]

A hurricane of energy, he was up before any of us, for ever rushing about getting everything organised since he was President of the Union, haranguer-in-chief in debates, and chairman of the Socialist Society. (No South African oranges ever managed to get in through the door when he was in charge.) He only ever managed to fit in the odd lecture which, perhaps, explains his none-too-brilliant academic record. In fact, few were more surprised than he when, on his second attempt, he did manage to get his degree. I shall never forget him, having got stuck into very many pints of strong Welsh beer, after he had heard he had passed, sitting in the gutter that night, saying to himself repeatedly and wonderingly: 'I've got a BA, I've got a BA.'

He was one of those people whom you either loved or hated and I loved him a lot. He had the most attractive human faults. He could get emotional and excited if you told him you had bought a new tie. He was also extremely sensitive to criticism, sometimes getting revenge years later. He never forgot – or forgave – an insult. He liked to play soccer with the boys on the beach, though you would never see him bare-chested in a swimming costume since he was not proud of his body. Once, in a student party, an ex-collier told him about his pit injuries and Kinnock burst into tears. But he always knew that he would become an MP; there wasn't the slightest doubt in his mind – though there was plenty in ours – and, with an undiminished vitality, he pursued and won one of the safest Labour seats in Britain.

The point of retailing all this is that I knew him as a great and warm human being. He had a brilliant anecdotal sense, a steady and unwavering commitment to his family and friends and a marvellous, ferocious idealism which, at times in our debating chamber, was quite thrilling.

Soon after he became shadow Minister of Education in 1979 I was a columnist on the *Observer* and was invited to a dinner at his house, which was not so much a dinner as a press conference since, also present, were the deputy editor of the *Guardian* and the economics editor of *The Times*. I distinctly remember the gentleman from *The Times* as he had a huge safety-pin keeping the fly of his jeans together. No worry about image with him.

What I did not know then was exactly how this dinner was to be a marker for his future since, almost from that date, just about everything he did was with an eye on publicity. Everyone was carefully nurtured and, if they did not respond as expected, they were frozen out. He lost links with his old friends and acquired a whole gallery of new ones, including Anthony Sher, Ben Elton and Tracey Ullman. Life was a battle with his image: the old ideals were pumped up and down to suit the public's likely perception of them. It was not so much a question of what he believed as of tailoring his beliefs to what he hoped the public believed. He began wavering on the issue of devolution and even started shifting positions on the bomb when, in university, he had given the clear message to anyone in the vicinity that he would dismantle the bomb with his own bare hands if only someone gave him the right spanner.

When the miners were locked in their long struggle he was so desperate not to be associated with Arthur Scargill; so worried about his image that he virtually disappeared out of sight for practically the whole of the strike, only to turn up at the picket line right at the end of the strike, when the miners were all but on their last legs – and then for the benefit of the television cameras.

In his first broadcast as Labour leader he was shown saluting the faithful victoriously with both arms, hugging his wife, talking with nurses and playing rugby – all set to the music of Brahms. He kept bobbing up on youth 'chat shows' talking with such as Peter Townshend of 'The Who'. He even danced on a pop video with Tracey Ullman and performed *Singing in the Rain* underneath a multicoloured umbrella for the TV cameras. He was also filmed falling into the sea, although that was an unplanned accident.

All these antics were not lost on Mrs Thatcher and, the more he show-boated before the media, the more she seemed to do so as well. She appeared on the *Michael Aspel Show*, with pop singer Barry Manilow, explaining in her new softened voice and beneath her new unfussy hairstyle, how she began the day at six in the morning listening to the news and the farming programme on the radio. Breakfast was a Vitamin C pill and a glass of sparkling water. On another programme she showed her clothes wardrobe to viewers – she always bought her under-wear from Marks and Spencer, 'doesn't everyone?' On York-shire television she spoke of her childhood in a very small home with 'no mod cons and an outside toilet'. She visited homes for handicapped children. She was filmed walking a dog on a beach.

But Mrs Thatcher has always understood television's power to deceive. She said:

> We live in a television age and television is selective. One camera shot of a pretty nurse helping an elderly patient out of an empty ward speaks louder than all the statistics of Whitehall and West-minster. Never mind that the hospital is being closed because it is out of date. Never mind that that a few miles away a spanking new hospital is being opened with brighter wards, better operating theatres and the very latest equipment. In today's world selective seeing is believing and in today's world television comes over as truth. I remember opening a beautiful new hospital. Virtually the only publicity was a demonstration outside – about cuts.

Yet, understanding the nature of the beast as she did, she was never slow to use it on her own behalf. Research by Saatchi and Saatchi had found that people believed that she did not care. In a subsequent speech to the party conference she used the word care eight times in one minute. Her opponents were never slow to proclaim a monopoly of care, but caring was what you did, not just what you said: the government cared about the old, cared about the disabled, cared about unemployment, cared about drug addiction, cared about Britain's world reputation and it was doing something positive about them all. 'We do not need lessons on care from other parties.'

Then she managed to turn her trip to Russia into a television spectacular. A series of telegenic locations were found in that country prior to her arrival and soon we were watching her in intimate discussions with Gorbachev, ending in a private dinner with brandies by a fire at a Moscow villa. She shopped; she went walkabout; she attended church – and the television cameras did not miss one step of her progress.[12] The *Observer* said that her *coup de publicité* was all due to her press secretary, Bernard Ingham: 'The Eisenstein of the photo-opportunity had pulled off the big one – the most successful exercise in public relations that Downing Street has mounted for years.'

By contrast, Kinnock's visit to Washington the previous week was an unmitigated shambles. Reagan, who was anyway an unabashed Thatcherite, could only spare Kinnock just less than half an hour and cameras were not allowed to film the two men together – the point of the trip. The White House even gave out a disparaging version of their conversation.

So the two great modern media manipulators of Britain then plunged themselves into a general election in which, according to Michael Cockerell, television *was* the campaign. Every word was videotaped by both sides and watched over and over again. Mrs Thatcher turned down the opportunity to debate with Kinnock on television. 'I fear such a debate would generate more hot air than light,' she declared haughtily.

Then the Labour Party entered the image game for real with film of Kinnock flaunting his youth and beautiful wife. Everywhere he went his arms were spearing the air in victory as if he had just scored the winning try for Wales against England. The party adopted the red rose as their emblem. Hugh Hudson, director of *Chariots of Fire*, filmed a tear-inducing montage of Kinnock in the valleys; Kinnock remembering the death of his parents; Kinnock's relatives talking fondly of him and, finally, Kinnock and his wife walking hand in hand on some Welsh cliffs.[13] In none of these exercises was there any mention of a policy or any sign of a manifesto, but they did manage to pump up his ratings by 16 per cent.

Mrs Thatcher meanwhile was breakfasting with nurses, dancing with residents of old people's homes and waving her handbag around in the Docklands. By turns she was a caring social worker, a world statesman and a simple housewife. She spoke a populist language and, in the end, won yet again hands down if only because there was still no one around as good as she at mastering the 'photo-opportunity' and the 'sound bite'. 'Television is the most powerful form of communication known to man,' she once told broadcasting executives. What she might well have added was that she, better than anyone, had learned how to use it.

The Televisual Charade

In this brief sketch of British politicians disporting themselves in front of the television cameras we have seen how television has firmly and decisively taken over as the power broker in British politics. We have seen the way in which traditional values have been traduced and policies trivialised to the point of extinction in favour of the essentially pictorial cult of the grandiose personality.

We have also seen how a good, ordinary human being has been presented as an extraordinary, sanitised 'product' which, as it happened, the consumer – formerly known as the voter – decided to reject because he believed that there was a better 'product' on offer. We have also seen how our political process – which decides nothing less than how our country is run – is being turned increasingly into another arm of show business. We have also, in the example of the miners' strike, seen how powerful and intrusive the media has become and how, at times, it can damage progress to peace and add substantially to the sense of conflict.

But while politicians look to the media to 'create' them then, so too, we have noted the quite positive way in which the media can 'destroy' them also. Positions can stand or fall on a few whims of the incredible image machine. Personalities are held up or annihilated in the mystic magic rays. Bob Geldof will

happily explain to you what happens when you get an abundance of the wrong sort of publicity. Look in the wrong
direction, swallow at the wrong juncture, allow a bead of sweat
to form on your upper lip and, no matter if you have the brain
the size of a small planet and you can out-argue Aristotle, your
career may be on the wobble and you may well have to find a
new one soon. Gerald Ford once said on US television: 'There is
no Soviet domination of Eastern Europe' – liberating Poland
and losing the election almost at a stroke.

But, more than all this, we have seen how all politicians come
shuffling eagerly to the television studios; almost prepared to
say anything at all to get those precious 10-seconds 'sound
bites' on a news-bulletin – anything, that is, except what a
rotten, corrupt and damaging process the whole televisual
charade has become. But, as we all know, if anyone did manage to
say anything as wonderfully stimulating as this on the box then
he would almost certainly not be invited back again, would
probably end up on the cutting-room floor and would also
run the risk of being broken on the anvil of obscurity for the rest
of his life. It does not anyway occur to politicians to criticise the
media, largely because they are so desperate to be featured in it.

The pattern for the future of our political systems – as laid
down by our new political dictator – is now clear. Rational
argument, complex answers and any sense of history will all be
swept aside in this new age of image politics. Linguistic dis-
course on the hustings will be replaced by the simple, but
effective, dynamics of advertising. All answers will be simplistic, if not monosyllabic, and any feeling for – or reference to –
the past will be substituted by the glittering immediacy of the
now. Confident burblings, combined with smooth images and
soothing music, will increasingly become the political order of
the day. Even the party divisions of right and left will become
more and more irrelevant since complex and sophisticated
viewpoints have no place in image politics whose one central
ambition is to attain power and then hold on to it by any trick or
devious stroke deemed necessary.

This new political dictator is clearly as crass and superficial
in his theory as he is powerful in practice. But all politicians will
continue to submit to his royal demands, hoping to be blessed
in return with the knighthood of a blaze of publicity and a

position in the centre of the stage of world affairs. They feel any sign of opposition is pointless. They feel that they *have* to live with him which is why they even invite him along with them on holiday – and pay for him, too.

Many of us still yearn for political leaders, unconcerned with their image, who will present closely-argued policies and detailed manifestos which will set out to improve the well-being of every member of society. But our new dictator is going to insist with increasing stridency and force that we are given political leaders who *seem* to be ready to improve the lot of every member of society, but, in fact, are merely concerned with their own lot, particularly the lot of their hair, their teeth, their sweaty brows, etc.

Virtually our only source of comfort in surveying the way the political process is developing in Britain is that in America – where much of these image politics have sprung from – the situation is far, far worse.

Over the Sea, but not Far Away?

Almost every American presidential candidate that there has ever been has concerned himself with his image. Thus, in the early days, presidents appeared with homely props like log cabins and coonskin caps – the symbols of the pioneer and the patriot. Eloquent and forceful orators like William Jennings Bryan and Woodrow Wilson created their own images with their voices alone. And then came radio. In 1924 there were three million radios in America; by 1935, thirty million. Over the course of 100 days in the campaign of 1896 William Jennings Bryan made 600 speeches in twenty-seven states and travelled more than 18,000 miles to reach five million people. In a single fireside chat while seated in his parlour, Franklin D. Roosevelt reached twelve times that number.[14]

Politicians started to take on 'political managers' who cut long radio messages into shorter versions. In 1928 the usual time purchased by candidates was one hour. In 1988 the typical political message was thirty seconds. The 1948 election was the first in which television played a part. The first generation of television advisers learned politics on the job. By 1964 the ad teams were on equal footing with the political operators in the campaign. As the teams became more powerful with each election, the candidate began to lose his identity – and control of his campaign. The ad men began to speak of themselves and the candidate as one. With the publication of Joe McGinness's book, *The Selling of a President*, a wickedly acerbic account of how the media experts got Richard Nixon elected into the White House, the age of the media handlers was born. The following year Hubert Humphrey's media director, Joe Napolitan, founded the American Association of Political Consultants and from there came some of the toughest and meanest graduates of this new school of hidden persuaders.

Perhaps our most chilling insight into the way our new political dictator works came in a 1988 book co-authored by Jane Mayer and Doyle McManus, which revealed how Ronald Reagan, a former B-movie actor was re-elected president.[15] In 1984 a recording was made of a meeting in the Reagan campaign headquarters which revealed contempt both for Reagan and the issues. A plan for overhauling tax was deemed unmentionable. 'We have to put it off until after the election,' said one of the chief aides. 'It's a question of politics – not policy. If there's any uncertainty about it, it can hurt us.'

They also all agreed that Reagan was not bright enough to understand it. 'We'd have to get five people with brains to sit down and cast a position by the President.' The same man added that there might be votes to be won from the women if the President spoke about 'wife-beating'. 'You just get the old man [Reagan] so upset he tells the health secretary: "I want you to spend $30m on it right now. I don't care where you find it."'

In what they concluded was a desert of ideas, the aides planned for Reagan at least to give the impression that he had a policy. One tactic they discussed was to get him to make a few 'sophisticated speeches . . . without really saying anything.' The message from the meeting was that the candidate was a mere cypher who, nevertheless, could be sold easily through the media.

But, as we know, Reagan was re-elected by a huge majority and went on to become one of the most popular presidents in American history. This, by any standards, was a triumph of public relations over every other consideration since he was also one of the laziest presidents in American history, given to many gaffes and with only the feeblest understanding of foreign and economic policy. It was undoubtedly his battery of public-relations specialists, speech-writers and political consultants who helped him to victory over George Bush in the 1980 Republican nomination contest and his victory over Jimmy Carter in the subsequent election. And it was undoubtedly the same gang who helped keep him there.

But there was also a sense in which this genial and likable man was his own media guru. He had after all spent most of his life in the business and knew everything about crowd-pleasing and the power of artifice to deceive. 'Politics is just like show business,' he said back in 1966. A former White House aide said of him: 'He's an actor. He's used to being directed and produced. He stands where he is supposed to and delivers the lines, he reads beautifully, he knows how to wait for the applause line. You know, some guys are good salesmen, but can't ask the customers to give them an order. This guy is good at asking for the order and getting it.'[16]

Trevor Macdonald of ITN said:

> Throughout the Reagan years access to the president has been controlled with studied skill and relentless vigour. The operation has been so successful that whatever news emerged from the Reagan White House, with very few exceptions, was determined, not by the White House press corps, but by Reagan's staff. Most of the time it was calculated not to illuminate international issues but to make the President look good. Reagan communication experts ensured that access to the President came only in carefully staged photo-opportunities.

The image was to be the message and it applied as much to those countless Rose Garden ceremonies as it did to the shouted questions from reporters, barely audible over the noise of the helicopter engines.

Reagan's image-makers were endlessly busy and partly as a result of this manipulation and partly through a kind of voluntary self-censorship, the American press all but gave up its responsibility to report what was going on during the Reagan presidency. 'Seduced by one of the most accomplished television performers in the modern history of the American presidency, and by the propagandistic skills of his staff, the press virtually signed off on its proper investigative role,' said Macdonald.

Of the Reagan presidency, Leslie Janka, former deputy chief press secretary at the White House, said: 'This was a public relations outfit that became the president and took over the country . . . the Constitution forced them to do things like make a budget, run foreign policy and all that . . . but their first, last and over-arching activity was public relations.'

When The Great Communicator finally did bow out on television, amid a shower of the warmest self-congratulation, his successor, George Bush, was already in the White House, thanks to much the same group of image-makers as had kept Reagan there. Bush had started off his bid for the presidency very low in the polls, but soon the wimp was transformed into the strong and caring man, again by projecting the carefully chosen image, again largely through that scourge of American civilisation, the political commercial.

The political commercial is now the chief platform for projecting political ideas in America, which is why very few ideas get through to the American public, since it is not so much the ideas that matter in commercials as the presentation of the image. Bush was repeatedly sold in short, sharp images of himself posing with his family and before the flag while all that we learned about what he stood for could have been written on the back of a postage-stamp. The commercials made him a familiar and well-known celebrity who, apparently, enjoyed cooking an endless supply of hamburgers for his kids on the Bush barbecue, never beat his wife or kicked the dog. He was the perfect, patriotic family man and the commercials not so much offered an image of himself so much as an image of the projected audience. How good he might be in the White House we were not even given the slightest clue.

Neil Postman[17] wrote:

> The television commercial is the most peculiar and pervasive form of communication to issue forth from the electric plug. An American who has reached the age of 40 will have seen well over one million television commercials in his or her lifetime, and has close to another million to go before his first social security cheque arrives. We may safely assume, therefore, that the television commercial has profoundly influenced American habits of thought. Certainly there is no difficulty in demonstrating that it has become an important paradigm for the structure of every type of public discourse.

Many worry about the barren import of such commercials and the former mayor of New York, John Lindsay, suggested that they should be banned, though an effective one was made directed at Bush by Senator Robert Dole. A beast crashed through the snow leaving no tracks behind it. The sell was: what kind of political animal walks through so many fields – ambassador to China, director of the CIA, chairman of the Republican National Committee during Watergate, Vice-President for eight years – and leaves no footprints in any of them?

Bush had all the clear definition of a pile of feathers, the commercial suggested. After twenty-five years in politics he was still an enigma; a man with no personality or ideas, who just ghosted through everything.

Bush's handlers responded to this with their own series of ads, presenting a new and firmer persona, giving us glimpses of the 'kinder and gentler' Bush – one who cared about the poor, the elderly and the environment. He was also told to get tougher on criminals so, in crime prevention, he kept saying: 'Out here we know what to say to violent criminals – Make My Day!' The audience would then pick up the chant. Make My Day! Make My Day! It was, of course, the famous line that Clint Eastwood uses while holding a Magnum 44 to that punk's head. We *know* that Eastwood is going to win the presidency by the biggest landslide in American history when he runs for the presidency. There are an awful lot of Americans who love Dirty Harry.

In any event the mix worked and Bush won, though, oddly, we still have very little idea what, if anything, he is up to. We still do not know what he's really like and doubtless we never shall. This really is a man who will not be leaving his footprints anywhere. All we know for certain is that his image was created and then accepted by the American voter on its face value.

With his skill at shuffling glittering images, the Man of Lawlessness had created a president just as surely as he had set out to attack the previous one. His influence was now reaching into every corner of American life. His power – as American youths like to say – had become truly awesome.

10

A Prophet and a Prophecy

*In which we add up what we have so far gathered and wonder
what it all means – We travel back to meet the effervescent and
tireless St Paul – Learn of the impending collapse of the Roman
Empire – Follow St Paul through Mediterranean storms
and along sunny Roman roads – Hear that he was a chronic
disturber of the peace – And ponder on his prophecy about a
great and mysterious tide of evil which would one day engulf
the world.*

At the End of the Trail

We started this enquiry quietly enough with an examination of
the circumstances of the death of John Lennon. But the sheer
scale of the terror soon began escalating in leaps and bounds
until, surely, we had traced what must be, without any exaggeration, the greatest and most unimaginable trail of havoc in
the history of the world. And at the end of that trail we have
found the Man of Lawlessness sitting in a forest clearing, the
bones of his latest savagery scattered all around his feet, hunted
down at last.

We began our hunt by assuming that there was someone like
him hanging around somewhere and, merely for convenience,
using the name of Man of Lawlessness as a metaphor for an evil

which we might, or might not, expose. We then decided that the evil which he represented could also, for the purposes of this enquiry, be said to be Romantic. We then defined Romantic and noted that, in particular, its principal characteristic was the persistent pursuit of violence. This was our first hard clue as to the nature of this essentially lawless personality.

After investigating the circumstances of the death of John Lennon, we then, in some detail, also looked at the attempted assassination of President Ronald Reagan and immediately uncovered evidence of a common mind and philosophy at work in both these shootings. It was our first real sighting of the Romantic Assassin. We then began examining the Romantic lionisation of the individual and found another important key to the philosophy under scrutiny since there was everywhere evidence of his presence in the Hungerford massacre. The other keyword in the operation of his work was alienation.

Now that we knew what we were looking for, our Man of Lawlessness began bobbing up everywhere with persistent and frequent showings, particularly in murder trials. But his evil activities were not only confined to individuals. He might even be able to conduct a civil war, we decided, as we were fitting together some new insights on the troubles in Northern Ireland. That's where the real evil of Ulster was lying and not, as some have supposed, in traditional religious enmities. We also soon began to work out that he could work both openly and un-detected since, such was his mastery at deception, he had deceived even those who were working for him. We had long known that when evil comes it always comes with evil's undiluted power to deceive.

We then documented the way in which he could cause the most awesome havoc and yet remain unexposed, as when he kept rolling great balls of racial violence through our inner cities. There was, for a while, a real possibility that he was going to get fingered this time and, indeed, the evidence was stacking up against him quite quickly – perhaps too quickly for his own liking – since no sooner were a lot of people asking some real questions about the real causes of the disorders than he relented and disappeared, leaving the disorders to clear up almost as quickly as they had begun. And when the cities were peaceful then so, too, did powerful men step up to defend his interests and deny any possibility that he had such a destructive influence.

The reason he was continuing to get away with it all the time – we began to suppose – was that he had an unparalleled ability to tell lies and so we began digging around trying to define the nature of this lie. We saw that he always managed to pervert the nature of reality by engaging his Romantic mind with it and, in the process, delivering an untruth which seemed to be the truth. Everything became twisted and distorted within the dark complexities of the working of his imagination. The Romantic Assassin was also The Great Perverter.

Some basic old-fashioned reporting began revealing more about our Man of Lawlessness's motives and modus operandi. We began to see quite clearly that the love of money was central to a lot of his actions and, indeed, the reason why he had acquired so many willing and powerful lieutenants to work on his behalf was the way in which he rewarded them with quite unbelievable amounts of money. Given such huge amounts of money, these lieutenants then all but stopped questioning their work on his behalf and also began pulling out the most plausible rationalisations for their work to continue.

This mounting body of evidence enabled us to work out precisely what he liked in matters of art. As one of his principal characteristics was the persistent pursuit of violence it followed that he most enjoyed continual and graphic representations of violence. Everything from the main body of the work of the cinema to the television news gave him great pleasure though, as we have also seen, few films can have given him quite as much pleasure as Alan Clarke's *Elephant*, where it was simply a 'story' of killing after killing, devoid of any plot development, music or dialogue – all of which our Man of Lawlessness finds boring and irrelevant.

Yet, as he has been so active and he has, from time to time, even been spotted, why then has he not been roundly denounced? How has he managed to get away with his violence for so long? The simple answer to that is that he has accumulated such a huge reserve of power that he is almost beyond criticism. Indeed he has so cleverly arranged his affairs that even leading churchmen have to find an accommodation with him. So, too, do the politicians. But it is not money these two groups are after so much as fame and influence. They have known all along that as long as they played ball with him – as long as they flattered and pleased him – then their careers would be seen to flourish and prosper. The attractiveness of their image, in the Man of Lawlessness's hands, would more than compensate for their deficiencies.

Perhaps it should also be said that even leading journalists have never been notable for their criticisms of the media either. Dog does not eat dog. Mary Whitehouse and Malcolm Muggeridge are perhaps our most famous media critics though I have always believed that the media allows their criticisms because the media is not terribly worried or threatened by them.

We see the broadest and darkest picture of a man who relentlessly pursues violence with a view to fomenting it; one who loves money and civil war; a supporter of terrorism and murder whose habitual stance is alienated. He will happily and fearlessly attack the highest and lowest in the land,but he is such a master of the darkest riddles that no one has yet been able to spot and identify him, particularly those with influence – our church leaders, politicians and journalists. There is a definite sense in which they are all acquiescing to the same lie.

St Paul and a Prophecy

So, we have now finally tracked him down, just sitting there and looking at us, fresh blood dribbling down the corners of his mouth. He sits there – a real, living and active presence – a portrait of the purest evil, easily the greatest single outbreak of violence and destruction in the history of the world. We are not quite sure what to say to him – or he to us. Having found him, what do we then do with him?

All we can really do is take comfort that he was finally going to emerge one day; that his brawling destructive entry on to the world's stage was foreseen, in great clarity and the most exact detail, by those men who once wrote the Bible. He was written about in both Daniel and Revelation but, if we are to know the basic nature of the prophecy, we should first look at the life and writings of St Paul.

St Paul was the biggest and brightest star in the Christian firmament. He is widely acknowledged as the first man to understand the life and death of Christ, writing nearly half the books of the New Testament. If Christ was the light then St Paul was the beacon. Aquinas called Paul the professor of the apostles and we know, from the story of his life, that he was a Jew from Tarsus; a man whose mind was on fire with new ideas at a time when the world was in ferment following the death of one, Jesus of Nazareth, recently put to death on a cross on a hill in Jerusalem.

Paul was a tiny man, weak in appearance, who suffered from a painful illness which may have been malarial but, when he was not actually teaching the word of God, he supported himself as a tent-maker. A man of tremendous and inexhaustible energy, he travelled throughout Europe, preaching in synagogues, revealing the most amazing mysteries of the Apocalypse and setting up the first Christian churches. For his pains this apostle of peace and love was clapped in irons seven times and scourged three times by local authorities. The Jewish synagogue authorities gave him the maximum 'forty stripes less one' no less than five times. He was stoned once and shipwrecked three times. One winter he was adrift and tossed in a storm for twenty-four hours until rescue arrived.[1]

The first we learn of him was that he was a proud citizen of the Roman Empire and that he hailed from the city of Tarsus, a flourishing and determinedly immoral centre of learning and philosophy. He was busy terrorising the followers of the Nazarene everywhere, entering homes, carrying off men and women and putting them into prison.

They were gleefully pagan times with the stabilising law and order of the Roman Empire collapsing fast. Temples were still going up to the old gods. Sacrifices were offered and sexual perversion rampant. Prostitutes did their business in the temples and the watchword 'freedom' was used to justify intercourse with them. There was gross unchastity in Corinth, theft at Ephesus and drunkenness in both.

Within this framework the teachings of the mad Nazarene had exploded with all the force of an anarchist with a bomb. He was a trouble-making revolutionary, destroying the Jewish faith and upsetting the peace. Life had been difficult enough without His going around performing His magic tricks. He had not been nailed to that cross a minute before time. His ideas were clearly going to hasten the collapse of the Roman Empire. And Paul was there in the forefront of this extermination campaign though he clearly did stop to think when he saw Stephen being stoned to death outside Jerusalem. As Stephen died, he prayed to the Lord that He would not hold this sin against his attackers. Just what were these Christian people all about? *Love your enemy?* They were all as brainless as waterfalls – or were they?

While about his business, as the bloody avenger of an outraged law, Paul received a vision of the risen Christ on the road to Damascus:

> Thus I journeyed to Damascus with the authority and commission of the chief priests. At midday . . . I saw on the way a light from heaven, brighter than the sun, shining round me and those who journeyed with me. And when we had all fallen to the ground, I heard a voice say to me in the Hebrew language, 'Saul, Saul, why do you persecute me? It hurts you to kick against the goads.' And I said, 'Who are you, Lord?' And the Lord said, 'I am Jesus whom you are persecuting' (Acts 26: 12–15 *RSV*).

He was actually blinded by Christ's appearance only to be healed later by Ananias. Like Moses, Elijah and John the Baptist he went off into the desert where, alone and clearly shaken to the core, he confronted himself and dedicated his life to the service of God.

For fifteen years he worked as a missionary in Arabia, Jordan and south-east of Damascus. Often with his faithful side-kicks he sailed the Mediterranean in sunshine and storm; trudged miles along old Roman roads, once rode horseback from Jerusalem to Caesarea. His first long, missionary journey took him to Cyprus – where he had a friendly meeting with the Roman governor in Paphos – and then he travelled up through the bandit-infested and dangerous mountains of Turkey to visit Perga. His moods were volatile and all we know about this part of the journey was that he parted company with John Mark.

They passed Lake Egridir and travelled up to the thriving city of Antioch, making for the synagogue where Paul began his address on Jewish lines, but concluded by declaring a belief in Christ. The next Sunday practically the whole of the city turned up, but Paul and his companions were forced to move on by the authorities. In Iconium they were threatened with a stoning. At Lystra there were angry mobs. Whenever Paul opened his mouth trouble followed just as surely as night follows day.

Paul wanted to create an empire for Christ; a universal Church which would absorb everyone. So he would settle in some spot and preach to anyone, including Athenian philosophers, Roman civil servants, the immoral hordes at Corinth, the workers of Ephesus and the drifting 'riff-raff' of any seaport. And everywhere he preached there was trouble.

Some time after returning to Antioch they heard that Jerusalem had sent yet more persecuting hounds after them. These Judaisers disturbed the converts in Galatia, denouncing Paul as a bogus apostle, insisting that he was leading them all up the garden path. It was then that he wrote his letter to the Galatians, which he probably dictated to Timothy or Silas, who wrote it down on papyrus.

He was, he told them with conviction and emphasis, a real apostle, appointed by God and that he had received his Gospel from God. 'O foolish Galatians! Who has bewitched you, before whose eyes Jesus Christ was publicly portrayed as crucified? Let me ask you only this: Did you receive the Spirit by works of law or by hearing with faith?' (Gal. 3:1–2 RSV).

Here he was making an important contrast between faith and law. If we believe in Christ we are set free. If you are led by the Spirit you are not under the law.

These letters were to become the most important feature of Paul's work, containing a lively and enduring testimony of faith as well as being a mirror of the living man, telling us of his enthusiasm and mysticism, of his hospitable nature and quite astonishing tenderness, of his genius for friendship as well as the way he could think in other people's terms. The letters also tell us a lot about his times as when, in the letter to the Romans, he paints a most lurid picture of pagan morals. But the letters were never literary or philosophical as such since they just set out to deal with immediate problems in a practical manner – only the letters to the Romans and Ephesians attempt any systematic arguments or philosophy.

After he left Antioch the Spirit moved him to go to Troas, near the ancient city of Troy. Here a Macedonian appeared to Paul in a dream and called him to come over to this country. He obeyed and this was one of the most decisive moments in history, since for the first time the Christian faith was being taken into Europe.

He sailed to Neapolis and began walking the Via Egnatia – or the Egnatian Way – to Philippi, about nine miles inland, where he founded the first Christian church in Europe. At Philippi Paul converted Lydia, a dealer in purple cloth, then the whole household. Then trouble began about money and Paul was thrown into prison. It was a familiar pattern. He always seemed to win them over at first and then they rejected him. What no one seemed to be able to do was to ignore him.

From Philippi, Paul – with Silas and Timothy – went to Thessalonica, a very large city where a new vigorous church sprang up, largely with Gentile converts, with a Greek culture and under the domination of Rome. Yet again the orthodox Jews began stirring up trouble against him. Paul was urged to move on for his own safety, but Silas and Timothy remained behind to tend to the young churches. Paul went on to Athens to found a church and he was appalled at what he found. Publicity – the journalism of the ancient world – was based in Athens. People only wanted to tell and learn something new. Every interest, every shrine, every glory of the city was pagan. In its theatre real people were being crucified on the stage for dramatic effect. The games were huge presentations of violence and eroticism. Paul soon left, anxious to go to Corinth where one of the liveliest of the Pauline churches had sprung up.

It was in Corinth that Timothy came to him with a report. The church in Thessalonica, he said, was sound and in good faith. They were mostly Gentile Christians, but there were many spiritual problems. They had been drawn into a huge net of needless anxieties as they contemplated the shape of things to come. Many of them had stopped working, becoming idle and listless, waiting for Christ's return. When would Christ return? Why would they have to wait for so long? Of would it be long? What would happen if they died before His return? How could they tell when the end was nigh? Such questions summarised the old Christian dilemma: caught between the sudden lightning of the First Coming and waiting anxiously for the thunder of the Second.

Paul dictated a letter to the church. He exhorted them to wait confidently for times and seasons which have not yet been revealed. He urged them to lead sober lives as 'children of the light' and not get overexcited. The new age had yet to dawn. They were to be watchful and sober. Hold fast to that which is good. Steer clear of evil. This letter is seen as having closer connections with the crisis in the church than any other. Here he was opening the door to a breakthrough in a trusting faith.

But he was to receive further news that, despite his letter, his new converts were coming to believe that the Second Coming was imminent. They had misunderstood what Paul had said and were now clutching this belief with a dogmatic certainty. So within a few weeks of his first letter, and not more than six months at the most, Paul wrote his second letter to the Thessalonians in which he defined most carefully the conditions that must precede the return of the Son of Man. At the heart of the letter is a prophecy and a warning.

At the time of dictating the letter in Corinth he may have caught sight of a vision, a shadow of shadows. He described the Man of Lawlessness, a great and mysterious tide of evil which was going to engulf the world as a necessary precondition to the return of the Son of Man. In full summary the prophecy says that, before the return of the Lord, evil will reach its climax under the leadership of the Man of Lawlessness. He will oppose Christ and be destructive of the very mind of God. He will make war on everything sacred and holy.

> Now concerning the coming of our Lord Jesus Christ and our assembling to meet him, we beg you, brethren, not to be quickly shaken in mind or excited, either by spirit or by word, or by letter purporting to be from us, to the effect that the day of the Lord has come. Let no one deceive you in any way; for that day will not come, unless the rebellion comes first, and the man of lawlessness is revealed, the son of perdition (2 Thess. 2: 1–3 *RSV*).

So the Man of Lawlessness will be ruthlessly exposed. This Man of Lawlessness will be the last and most famous Antichrist of them all. He will be made known before the end is near, but is doomed to ultimate destruction. But Paul then enters an important caveat. 'And now you know what is holding him back, so that he may be revealed at the proper time' (2 Thess. 2:6 *NIV*). This line has become known as the restrainer. Something will be lifted at the right time and the Man of Lawlessness will be revealed in his own season.

Paul adds that when he comes he will come with all the 'powers and miracles' of the lie. 'And with all the wicked deception of those who are to perish.' It will be a strong delusion 'to make them believe what is false' (2 Thess. 2:10–11 *RSV*).

After leaving Corinth, Paul went on to do some brilliant work in Ephesus before returning to Macedonia and Greece. Then, with a strong sense of foreboding, he went back to Jerusalem for the last time. As usual be became embroiled in a heated row after being accused of taking a Gentile into an exclusively Jewish part of the Temple. A mob was actually going to lynch him, but Roman soldiers took him to Caesarea where he was brought before Felix, the governor. He was locked up there for two years and finally sent for trial in Rome. That city always fascinated him. The pagan authorities were still persecuting Christians and he dreamed of setting up the standard of Christ on her seven hills.

But it was not to be. After an eventful journey, which included being shipwrecked off the coast of Malta, Paul did finally get to Rome where, under Nero, he was probably executed as a disturber of the peace.

The Face is Unveiled

So we are left, then, with the prophecy of the Man of Lawlessness and a simple puzzle. What does it mean? Skipping through other texts in the Bible, we find other similar apocalyptic visions of evil. And so, in Daniel, we were presented with the very incarnation of iniquity: a masterpiece of savage power complete with a horn, iron teeth, bronze claws and a mouth spewing out dark curses against God. He was the abomination of the desolation and we should be weeping in terror. Blasphemy was written in large letters, but there is no living sculptured personality here.

Further on, in Revelation, we encounter a form such as the world has never known. The sheer scale of the evil is such that the human mind cannot comprehend it. 'He was given power to make war against the saints and to conquer them. And he was given authority over every tribe, people, language and nation' (Rev 13:7 *NIV*). The imagery is as incredible as it is frightening. The beast has ten horned heads. He is the hard core of the tempest who was once thrown out of heaven dragging down a third of the angels with him. He has evil's unsurpassed power to deceive; just when we begin to relish our freedom we find that we are, in fact, working for him. He enfolds us and is within us. His intelligence is formidable and dazzling. He rules through error and exercises mesmeric sway over every home. He *even* makes us laugh.

These are the most powerful and vivid visions of evil to be found anywhere in the Bible, but just what are they referring to?

The words and imagery of John and Daniel are the words and imagery of Jewish apocalyptic tradition. The concept of a great adversary, who will bring down even God, is an ancient one, far older than even the Messianic tradition. In Ur-Babylonian myth we learn of Marduk and the Chaos-Dragon, in which a human opponent of God uses Satan as an instrument. Later this notion was turned into that of a Jewish pseudo-Messiah and was thought to have been passed down through secret oral tradition. In the Old Testament we find frequent references to Belial, someone who signifies a demonic presence.

Some scholars have argued that, as an educated Jew, Paul would have been aware of the idea of the great adversary, taking it from the apocalyptic tradition and dolling it up for his own purposes, i.e. to reinvigorate the confused and fearful Thessalonians and getting them back to work. Nothing could be less likely.

In everything he did Paul was his own man who would have felt no need to adapt the ideas of others, no matter how exalted the source. He always claimed to be an apostle appointed by God and working under the Holy Spirit and, whatever else such spirit-filled prophets do, they do not pinch other people's ideas.

Similarly, his excitement at seeing this vision of shadow of shadows suggests that it shaped itself in his mind at the time of dictation. It is a tremendous statement of absolute conviction. Furthermore, his vision differs in shape, detail and substance from those in the apocalyptic tradition. There is the problematic element of the restrainer and the promise that God will, in time, choose to lift it in the Man of Lawlessness's own season. 'And you know what is restraining him now so that he may be revealed in his time. For the mystery of lawlessness is already at work; only he who now restrains it will do so until he is out of the way (2 Thess. 2:6–7 *RSV*). Furthermore, Paul uses the phrase 'be revealed' implying that, when the time is right, this Satanic parody of the true Messiah, will be ruthlessly exposed.

Biblical scholars have long been busy trying to work out exactly what the restrainer might be. Large sections of Paul's teaching suggest that it actually might be the design of God. In 2 Thessalonians 1 (2–16) Paul said that God is purposely allowing men to 'fill up the measure of their sins' and large sections of his teaching (e.g. Rom. 8) are based on the supposition that God temporarily permits the victory of evil and the sufferings of Christians, but that vindication is near. The view that a predetermined period of sin and suffering (the 'Messianic' woes or 'birthpangs') must precede the end is another conventional feature of Jewish apocalyptic. (Matt. 24:6–12 and especially v. 22, also 1 Pet. 4:12–17.) Others have argued that the preaching of the Gospel is itself the restrainer and there is some evidence for this, too (Matt. 24:14).

But while there has never been any absolute agreement on the nature of the restrainer neither has there ever been any agreement on the identity of the Man of Lawlessness, but, throughout history, there has been no shortage of theories. Perhaps there is a sense that each age provides its own particular evil which then becomes, with some validity, that age's Man of Lawlessness. John said that history has been plentiful in its record of the many Antichrists (1 John 2:18). But the Man of Lawlessness will be the last and most infamous Antichrist of all. He will be made known when the end is near.

Thus far he has been variously identified as Nero or Judas Iscariot resurrected from the dead. Some recall the supreme blasphemy with which, in AD 40, Caligula set up an image of himself in the Temple and demanded that it be worshipped. Others have looked to Vespasian, Titus and Domitian – and the whole rotten and corrupt story of the emperors of Rome. Others have said that it was Luther or Calvin. Still more have believed that it was Bonaparte or Hitler. Many of the leaders of the Reformation – and indeed many of the Protestant leaders of Ulster – have argued that it was the Papacy.

But for many other important reasons all the other interpretations must also be wrong. Marcus Loane, sometime Archbishop of Sydney, wrote of the Man of Lawlessness:

> So the resurgence of evil will culminate in an attempt to drive God from his throne. There are always men who would like to lead God to the edge of the universe and bow Him out; but this act of usurpation will be the ultimate blasphemy . . . meanwhile His presence is hidden though His activities were potent as force in the world . . . the whole picture is heightened by the use of the bold phrase *the mystery of lawlessness*.[2]

We are almost certainly looking for a compound personality suggesting that more than one person is involved. Many scholars believe that he could only be an individual, but sheer commonsense tells us otherwise. No single figure could aspire to such corrupting power. No one person could attempt to drive God from His throne. We are almost certainly looking for a system which, although supported by people, has a sort of metaphysical flavour. This system will have the power to astonish and deceive, influencing people so that they move away from truth and come to believe in error. This system or rule will be a widespread and violent rebellion against the mind and very thought of God. In this system evil will become good and a worldwide moral collapse will take place. Sin will have reached its climax in the form of its greatest and most explosive lie.

Furthermore, we can be certain that Paul was referring to the last and supreme embodiment of evil. He will be the last and most famous of them all. Our Man of Lawlessness is therefore an eschatological personage; someone to do with the doctrine of death and last things; someone who will appear in the last times when good and evil enter their final great confrontation. Then the Man of Lawlessness will be slain by the return of Christ. The usurper will fall as if from a blast of fire from the mouth of a dragon. Luther's hymn: 'And word shall quickly slay him.'

So even by the simplest test of logic all previous individuals and systems become ineligible. If he exists at all then he can only exist in the present – unless he has not yet arrived though Paul told the Thessalonians that he was working, albeit in secret, at the time of his prophecy.

And what of the restrainer again? But surely the restrainer also cannot be human, since no human could hold back the work of Satan. One attractive suggestion is that the restrainer is the word and law of God. In the mysterious methods of His workings it is God who finally gives way to the Man of Lawlessness since this tide of evil somehow fulfils His purpose. This God Busy in the Adventure Playground school of theology says that He will lift His restraining hand gradually and somehow mobilise this evil in His quest to work out His original purpose in creating the world. When this evil has come to a certain point He will make a resolute move to contain it. He will send back His Son and the career of the Man of Lawlessness will have run its course.

This might be so, but surely it smacks too much of theoretical guesswork. We do not know God's mind. He does not think as we do. As the Thessalonians 'knew what it was' our best bet is also the simplest. By the restrainer Paul was probably and simply referring to the restraining power of law and order, especially as these were maintained by Rome. Paul had the greatest reverence for the law:

> Let every person be subject to the governing authorities. For there is no authority except from God, and those that exist have been instituted by God. Therefore he who resists the authorities resists what God has appointed, and those who resist will incur judgment (Rom. 13:1–2 *RSV*).

But he was worried as he was watching law and order break down. A revolutionary he most emphatically was not. The world, he said, was full of suffering and attuned to disorder. Roman law aimed at the triumph of right and the punishment of wrong. As it stood it was restraining a threatened outbreak of anarchy but, in time, this restrainer was going to be moved out of the way and the world was going to slip into lawlessness which would find a leader who would both enshrine and encourage these criminal principles. As lawlessness grew then a large mass of humanity was going to take a wrong turn. Light would become darkness. Everywhere people would descend into their own unrequited passions; they would follow their own desires. This process was already at work, but the leader had not yet come out of the closet. Who was he? Just quite how lawless could he be?

And so now we have nearly, but not quite, reached the conclusion of our enquiry and are left with some difficult but important questions. Is the Man of Lawlessness finally with us? Is it possible that the restrainer has been fully and finally lifted and that we are all now crashing down the road of lawlessness and disorder because the lawlessness, which has always been in the world, has finally found a leader?

Could it be that the mind of the modern media is, in fact, this long-prophesied personage and this season of escalating crime and terror is his season? Is this the man who has come to assume religious and political control of the world while bemusing the very elect of God? Is this the fearful outbreak of evil which was going to promote fear and make man's love for one another grow cold? Is the 'powerful and miraculous' lie, that was going to be attendant on all his activities, in fact be the Romantic lie of false emphasis and the persistent pursuit of violence? Is this the man who, with the very largest following, has finally come to teach that sin is pleasure and that pleasure is sin? Have we finally located him in all our homes and teaching all our children and, if that is indeed the case, then is it not fully and finally the time that we do what St Paul urged the Thessalonians to do – understand its mighty significance and prepare ourselves immediately for the Second Coming?

11

The Second Coming

In which we journey to Malaya and go through a strange and signal period of cosmic disclosure – Fly to California where the old visions come to trembling life again – Take a ship through the Greek Islands and get off on Patmos in the middle of the night – Examine current thinking on the Second Coming – And wonder how far away it might now be.

A Journey to the Past

From what we do know about the Man of Lawlessness, as revealed in the pages of the Bible, we also know that he is not discoverable by human search. He will be revealed when God decides, in his own season.

It is time then to begin rounding off this enquiry and to travel back to Malaya some twenty-five years ago when, during a strange and signal period of cosmic disclosure, the roots of this enquiry first took chaotic shape in my mind. It was a period of a few weeks when, or so I believe, God spoke directly to me and in describing the events of those few weeks I shall also, I believe, answer a key question which should arise from the way I actually began this enquiry. Why did I choose to use the word Romantic to describe the primary evil as it had first appeared?

The year was 1963 and I was teaching English with Voluntary Service Overseas in the town of Alor Star in Kedah, North

Malaya. The town itself was a ramshackle collection of shops, restaurants, houses and monsoon gutters, all plonked down in the middle of vast stretches of paddy-field since here we were in the middle of the rice-bowl of South-East Asia. Alor Star also had a cinema, a milk bar and lots of mobile food stalls down by the river. The residents were mostly either Malayan or Chinese with a smattering of Indian who, all in all, got on cautiously well, but did not mix with one another much.

I taught in the Sultan Abdul Hamid school, living in a room in the adjoining hostel, surrounded by posters of such as Ho Chi Minh and Mick Jagger. I lived with a mynah bird – for whom it was my daily duty to catch grasshoppers out in the lalang with a tennis racket – with books and papers scattered all over the place. Being something of a revolutionary straight out of university, I was, when not actually teaching or walking into town for something to eat, working on the great novel since I had always wanted to be a writer from that very first time I could think about anything. Apart from anything else, this work also helped to pass the time since, when school had finished, there was almost nothing to do in Alor Star, particularly if you had seen whatever was on at the cinema that week. Weekends were particularly empty.[1]

The novel was called *Squaredance* and was, as I remember, a rambling, undisciplined work about the often violent struggle between three men to come to terms with themselves and one another. It was set in the Malayan jungle and the plot, such as it was, explored the relationship between a young teacher (guess who?) and a broken old commodities broker which was gradually destroyed and overtaken by the cold calculations of a homosexual rubber planter. When this rubber planter was not seducing the local men he was given to periodic bouts of awesome violence. My themes were alienation, violence and arcane sexuality. Essentially it was derivative and, although I should not have liked to have admitted it at that time, it was a pretty good summary of what was going on in the fashionable modern novel since that is what I mostly read.

Writers like Anthony Burgess have often noted that words seem just to pour out of you in the tropics and so it seemed here since I had written well over 400 pages of my magnum opus with the struggle between my protagonists intense, if not murderous, with no resolution in sight. During breaks in my work I would often stroll around the town, just chatting to anyone at all. Everyone was amazingly friendly and I felt welcome wherever I went, even in the most distant parts of the jungle since there would usually be some child or other there whom I happened to be teaching at the time. One day I was introduced to a visiting European missionary by one of my pupils and we had a discussion about God. I remember that he was clearly a bright but rather testy man who wore a Malayan sarong. Quite soon he was losing his temper with my tedious questions and, when I persisted with them, he got quite nasty. 'Why is it,' I wanted to know, 'that you seem to understand and know God quite easily when I find it most difficult? Why does He reveal Himself to you and not to me? What's the matter with me?'

'Well I've got a few ideas on *that*,' he snapped back.

'Tell me, then.'

'Because you're a Romantic.'

I was genuinely puzzled by this response, but he refused to elaborate any further and left almost immediately. I never saw him again. A Romantic, though? Just what did he mean? Someone who goes around jumping into bed with a lot of women? Even despite my young years I had done an awful lot of that and, indeed, had spent quite a lot of my free time here – when I had a bit of money – travelling up over the border and spending a lot of time in the brothels of Thailand. Somewhat predictably, Henry Miller was also one of my favourite authors.

But within a week I was to find out precisely what a Romantic was since I had been teaching T. S. Eliot to the sixth form in my school and had asked the class to tell me in what way T. S. Eliot was different from the other contemporary writers. They all came back with much the same essay – possibly because they had all cribbed it out of much the same book – and every essay explained that T. S. Eliot's greatness was judged to lie in the fact that he had a Classical temper and had avoided all taint of Romanticism. They all then defined what this Romanticism was.

And, as I sat at my desk in my room, reading these dozen or so essays, there were certain key phrases cropping up again and again, of which the most common was – *A Romantic is one who indulges in the persistent pursuit of the morbid, the supernatural, the cruel, the perverted and the violent*. Perhaps because they also understood – because they were a bright bunch – that they had at last discovered just what Sir was up to they also seemed to take a great glee in spelling out what a Romantic stood for . . . the insistence on the primacy of sexuality, the importance of the imagination, the emphasis on the individual and the quest for the strange and the bizarre.

I finished reading those essays, put them to one side and sniffed. So *that* is what I was. Well, at least, I now knew. It was indeed as that missionary had so puzzlingly described me. I was a Romantic who was working on a novel which was nothing if not Romantic. I was a Romantic just as surely as I had a nose on my face. But, there again, so were very many other writers and artists, though just how many at that time I had not even started to work out.

I continued teaching in the school and working on my novel by night when, one day, in the middle of the day, I hallucinated. With the size and clarity of a huge cinema poster I saw a frozen picture of myself standing in the school playground with the three characters from my novel all holding me, their bodies bright and quivering like summer lightning. The homosexual rubber planter's mouth was open and salivating with his teeth bared like those of a vicious dog.

I returned to my room and was getting slightly worried about things. My manuscript, which was now several hundred pages long, seemed to be trying to tell me something. Sometimes I would sit on the end of my bed and just stare at it, chewing my lip and trying to understand what it was trying to tell me. It would not tell me, of course, so I continued to work on it with an enveloping sense of gloom.

About a week later I was sitting on the end of my bed again when the pages of my manuscript seemed to judder slightly as if electrified. I blinked at it a lot, but then decided to put it away in a drawer and stop working on it altogether. I had only a few weeks left before returning to Britain and was quite keen on getting out of Alor Star with my brain intact. I wasn't on anything by the way of drugs during that period either, which, given my normal excesses, was something of a change. The blunt truth was that I had virtually no money and could barely afford to buy the odd can of beer. Anyway, I preferred blowing all my money in one hit, on the last day of the month when I was paid – over the border in Thailand.

I could not give the book a rest, of course, since I was well into it and it was virtually the only way I had of passing time. So I decided instead to work for some kind of resolution by, if necessary, killing off my characters. But, somehow, and despite some chapters larded with the most lurid violence, my characters always seemed to be able to crawl back into the fray and kick lumps out of one another.

One night my mynah bird had died and I sat down at my desk again, rolled a sheet of paper into my typewriter, but no sooner had I lifted my hands than I let them fall again. There was a rustle in the sheaf of papers that was my novel and the sound scared me so much I jumped back and knocked over my chair with a resounding crack on the floor. I was tense and scared about what was going to happen. Something was going to happen. That was very clear. I turned around and looked back at my desk, my mind slipping and sliding around, parts of it moving up and others moving down like many planks on an invisible fulcrum. Even in the mental disorganisation of everything I knew that the book was going to attack me.

I lit a cigarette and pulled my fingertips across my eyes feeling very weary indeed. When I looked over at my book again I saw a fungus ball growing out of it. It was one of the most amazing things that I had ever seen. It just swelled and swelled remorselessly until it completely covered the lower half of the window. The ball glowed with a startlingly brilliant light and, in texture, it seemed to be made out of a translucent jelly with red, orange and purple veins running out of its heart and circling back into it.

Ideas were trickling along the veins like tadpoles, falling down to feed on the small, dark heart before swimming back up the veins again. Faces moved around in it, too. I stared at it for a long time. I knew what it represented immediately. This giant fungus was the poisoned and poisoning growth of my own Romanticism. I do not know why I understood this so clearly. I just did.

I tried to stand up, but my legs would not let me. I tried to turn around, but my body was frozen. The glowering fungus just hung there when, as slowly as it had grown, it shivered into nothing and, in a blast of warm air, the room went black. My body, released, collapsed back on the bed.

I was lying there twitching a bit – as if after some bad accident – when I felt fluttering movements around my arms, legs and chest. I sat up and gazed at the wall. It was no longer dark, but nothing made sense. The feeling was of a face smashed up against a mirror. The face had been broken into a fragmented image with the different parts of the mirror reflecting, in a hundred different ways, the numerous images of the same face. I tried to focus on the wall, but the galvanised forces of something were now in overdrive. I stood up, turned and caught sight of the pages of my manuscript. Then something hot and quick tore down inside me and the ideas of the book rose up out of the pages, sweeping through my mind and rushing around the room like a swarm of bees.

They massed in one top corner of the room, buzzing and swelling, then swept down through my brain again. It was like staring down a well with a furious gale blowing up out of it and I had to hold on to the top of my head tightly lest it blow off. Those ideas leaked out of every part of my body; through my fingers, eyes and ears; pouring down my cheeks and running over my chest. I tried to punch my unravelling head back into place with my fists, but only hit a sparkling, dancing jumble of nonsensical ideas reaching up out of books and films and plays . . . all travelling through and smashing up against one another in . . . my body where, deep down, yet more ideas were being generated which, in turn, whipped up great swirling tempests of yet more ideas. The Romantic meets his blitz. My own dogs had got me. Oh please, God, call off the dogs.

But He did not. In the following days, only ever occasionally aware of myself, I kept stumbling around the town seeing the most fearful visions. My pupils often found me standing alone and lost somewhere on the outskirts of the town and took me home. One night I stumbled down to the river-bank, my brain swelling and contracting inside my head like a lung, my hands pressing hard down on the top of my skull, scared stiff that my brain was actually going to burst. I lay down on the bank with my arms around my head and had a vision of the world.

I saw a silvery plain with hundreds, perhaps thousands, of small matchstick men milling around on it. Tiny ideas were flitting between their heads in looping arcs and lightning dashes. A cliff was overhanging the plain and all along the cliff-edge, dark and demonic bands of artists were loosing off volleys of wild, fizzing ideas which were shelling the people below. As the volleys became wilder and more intense the movements of the matchstick men on the plain became more and more agitated. They were rioting, jumping on one another and rolling around fighting.

The ideas of those on the cliff-edge were *Romantic* and, just lying there gazing at the screen of this extraordinary vision, I saw that the world was but a rising, multiplying jungle of ideas in which the artists were corrupt and busy corrupting the people.

The next time I became aware of myself I was walking along one of the town's back streets when the silvery plain returned, except that this time it was *me* standing on the cliff-edge with destructive ideas shooting out of my mouth and rocketing down on the fighting matchstick people below. This time my ideas were like conkers fastened on to a long piece of string, whirling down out of my mind and zipping straight back in again. So I, too, was just as corrupt as the rest of them.

I have never really understood how I got through the next few weeks since, long after the initial shock of seeing those visions I continued brainstorming, getting lost and being taken back home by sympathetic pupils. Always my hands were firmly clamped on my head since I continued having the sensation that my brain was going to explode. One afternoon I found myself walking along the main street trying to get back to my room, but that seemed to be beyond me since, no sooner had I decided where that room was and stumbled towards it, than I saw another part of my past or a book I had read or a film I had seen which had affected my behaviour. While pondering on these new revelations, I would stumble past my room and end up on the other side of town.

Even in all the chaos I could see that there was indeed a sense in which I was but a creation of all the Romantically corrupt books, plays and films of my time. The Romantic writer reinforces the debility of the Romantic reader and, within this wicked wheel of madness, surely lies the flaming force which is busy scorching the life out of the world.

One afternoon I was standing near a bus stop watching a woman with a large earthenware pot disembark. A Chinese man who had two children in one of my classes asked me about the forthcoming examinations and how I rated the children's chances. But I did not answer and just put my hands on my head as my legs took off for another ramble.

A few days later I was wandering around in Penang and things seemed to have gone quiet when I looked up at some trees. The very sky seemed to be breaking as if something was trying to burst through it when a tiny bright hole opened up. A shower of fat black ideas seemed to be pouring out of it. The black rain.

The night before I finished as a teacher in Malaya I was lying in my room with my brain still simmering from the shock of these new insights when I felt a warm, breathing presence within and all around me. The presence moved closer and deeper inside me and I abandoned myself to it. Tears bubbled up out of my closed eyes and I opened my arms wide feeling so warm, secure and trusting that nothing in that moment could have caused me any fear. The palm of a hand stroked my smashed brain which bubbled and moved around with its soothing presence. The presence became even deeper and more loving and I lifted my head to try and see it when it rose up out of my body, leaving me on the bed, alone.

A Commission

I returned to Britain a crushed and broken man. There can be few shocks in anyone's life quite so shocking as to find that, not only were your ideas up the wall, but that they were *dangerously* up the wall. I soon abandoned all thoughts of writing a novel, became a journalist (a profession I had always despised), got married and, at that time, wanted little more than the standard 2.4 kids with a standard semi-detached house and the usual mortgage. I had also begun going to church. Everyone became very worried about the loss of the rebellious twinkle in my eye and I still remember, one afternoon, Neil Kinnock saying, in exasperation: 'I just wish you would tell me what happened to you in Malaya. I'm sure I could talk you out of it.'

But I never did tell him what had happened to me in Malaya – and neither did I tell anyone else for almost seventeen years. I had rather reverted to my bad old self too – devoting most of my energy to wine, women and song and, later, a little bit of my energy to the *Observer* since I had become the diarist 'Pendennis' on that newspaper. It was with that hat on that I went to Jerusalem early in 1980 where, in The Garden Tomb, I met Colonel Orde Dobbie and his wife, Flo. They invited me back to the Tomb for a meal that evening and I don't know what came over me – as the shoplifters always say – but, for the first time, I told them my strange story about the exploding book and, most hauntingly, the black rain. Orde thought that God was calling on me to do something. I did not know about that, but, nevertheless, asked if I could be left alone to pray just next to the tomb before going back to my hotel. It was late and dark as I prayed standing just above the entrance to the tomb when there was a loud crack as of a bullwhip and the noise of a rushing wind. Startled, I opened my eyes and looked up. The pine needles just above my head were perfectly still. I knew then that God was at work in my life again.

Within a few weeks of being in Jerusalem I went up to York and met Canon David Watson, whose work at St Michael-le-Belfry had become such an exciting symbol of Anglican renewal. David turned out to be an absolute treasure and I still count meeting him as one of the great privileges of my life. We soon got to know each other quite well and it was while writing about him that I also went public about my Malayan visions in my column in the *Observer*. Yes, we could see another revival in Britain, I wrote – and there are great and good men like David Watson who could lead it – but the main obstacle to any revival in this country was that we had taken to ourselves a body of literature, a television service, most of the newspaper industry, together with a film and video industry which were all rotten to the core. That's what any revival had to get through and meanwhile we were all, so to speak, dying in this long season of black rain.[2]

I left the *Observer* soon after that column and wrote my first book, *Merlyn the Magician and the Pacific Coast Highway*, in which I described my travels around the world on a bicycle while looking for the meaning of my visions, which I described in some detail. During the writing of that book, which had taken me to California to live for four months, I felt that I was finally coming near to the real meaning of those visions, and events were beginning to throw up confirmatory evidence that we were indeed living in the Man of Lawlessness's season.

I had flown to California within days of John Lennon's being shot. Even as the first sketchy reports began coming in about the young assassin and his favourite paperback I knew exactly why Lennon had been shot, but at that time had, of course, no evidence. Just as I left California, President Reagan was shot and again, from the first reports about Hinckley's obsession with Jodie Foster, I knew the reason – and could have told the psychiatrists Hinckley's motive long before they worked it out – but again had no real evidence. The whole mystery of the black rain was now coming together and I knew so much about Chapman and Hinckley because, the more I read about them, the more I saw that they were me before I was struck down by those visions. In other circumstances it could easily have been me who had pulled those triggers. We had all been essentially the same immature, imaginative people, brimming over with misplaced defiance.

After I had returned to London and continued to work on the book I had to slip off to Greece for two weeks to cycle there for a new chapter when my wife noticed a report in a newspaper about St John on Patmos. I said that I might go there and, later, while interviewing a woman in Athens, she offered me the use of her house on Patmos. As it turned out I still decided not to go to Patmos, taking the ferry straight down to Rhodes. It was not until a week later, when I was on the ferry going back to Athens, that I began worrying that I was being pointed in the direction of Patmos, but ignoring it. I had no idea where I was since we were sailing through the 1,420 Greek islands and it was the middle of the night. But I could not stand all this sudden worrying any more so I went down to the purser's office on the ferry and asked him what was the next stop. Patmos. I gave up and got off the ferry.

However, I still did not understand the meaning of my pleasant few days there until I was discussing the form of the end of my book with the Rev. Owen Thomas who was then vicar of St Stephen's Canonbury. My problem was whether to

depict the media as the source of primary evil that I was coming
to understand it to be. He believed that it had all got too late for
evasions and that I should get stuck in. He pointed out that the
Revelation was written on Patmos which, among other issues,
was about the final and spectacular emergence of evil. Another
bit of the jigsaw had fallen into place.

Just as I finished working on *Merlyn* in London there was
further confirmation of the activity of this evil when most of our
cities exploded into a series of riots more or less at the same
time. It was strange and not a little frustrating again understanding the connection and causes of all these horrible events;
knowing that I had an insight which would explain them, but
that I lacked the one thing that I needed the most – hard
evidence for my claims. Even I knew that I was going to make
no progress at all by putting all the blame on the black rain.
People would not become convinced by mystical insights but
factual evidence. I had to bring home the bacon on the back of
careful research and painstaking investigation. In a sense it
would be a work of theological journalism and I knew I could
only ever do it as an on-the-ground reporter; not using the
well-worn theories of the academics, sociologists and politicians, but dragging it all out into the courtyard of cold fact.
That was the only way I should ever get it all to stand up. *If* I
was ever going to do it . . .

However, I kept cutting out bits from newspapers, making
notes from books and just filing them away. If anything caught
my eye which might one day be useful for this work I would ring
up whoever and ask if I could cover it for them. In this way I
followed the Billy Graham campaign around the country for
the *Sunday Express Magazine* and went to Northern Ireland for
the *Sunday Telegraph*. One day I might be able to do the job
properly and, if God had lit a fire in me – as David Watson used
to like to say – then I also had to rely on God's sense of timing. I
had to accept that the book would be written and published
when He decided that it was ready. But when, oh when, would
that day come?

While I waited for that day, I wrote other books which
explored and reflected on other aspects of those visions. There
was *The Electric Harvest*, a portrait of a society broken down by
media-generated violence; *Stained Glass Hours*, a modern

pilgrimage and an enquiry into the meaning of holiness in our society; *One Winter of the Holy Spirit*, a novel based on the life of Evan Roberts, a Welsh evangelist who was also besieged by visions of a coming evil; *Black Sunlight*, a novel about how this evil had already colonised the mining communities of South Wales who had given up on everything as they rolled over in front of their television sets; and *Fire in the Bay*, a novel in which, in the central and evil figure of the rich shipowner, Hamilton, I sought to give Romanticism a human face, as he spawned riot and created violence, controlled key figures with lots of money, was attracted to medievalism and given to perversion, worked for the nascent Nazi party and tried everything to gain possession of the Holy Grail which belongs only to God.[3]

They all reflected the theme of my Malayan visions and, in a sense, *all* my work has risen out of those fiery few weeks in those Malayan paddy-fields. But there was still that one book that I knew I had to bring home one day and it was the events at Hungerford that finally sparked it off when we stood looking at the ashes of Michael Ryan's home. I was standing with Robert Peart watching a policeman shovelling out the ashes when, just on top of a fresh pile, there was a familiar shape. I pointed it out to Robert who went over to a policeman and asked if that was a video-recorder. The policeman confirmed that it was.

Just standing there and looking at that charred recorder, all God's grief came flooding back to me. *Just look what they're doing to all my babies. You understand all this now. Just look*. I knew then that the time had come fully and finally to expose the man behind all this. I tried to tell Robert about it, but he thought I was mad.

I did not start the book immediately as I wanted to spend some more time in Northern Ireland since I have always believed that, somewhere in the mystery of the black rain, God always had in mind the tragic events in Ulster, that he wanted those beleaguered people to know that he had not forgotten them and would never, *ever*, abandon them.

Just after my return from Northern Ireland – when my visit co-incided with one of the most savage IRA campaigns for years – I finally got the all-clear from Hodder and Stoughton who had known that I had been thinking of this book for some time. And so finally I was ready. When I did sit down to write it

I did so without a pause and this has been the easiest and fastest book that I have ever written, probably because I had been rehearsing its arguments in my mind for more than twenty years and had been collecting a lot of material over that same period. Whether it is any good or not – and whether I was up to my task or not – other people will decide. My quiet prayer is that I have finally managed to honour my Malayan visions and that real historians, real sociologists, and real theologians will take up where I left off. I have only ever really seen myself as a reporter who, in the end, gave it his best shot.

The Oldest Story on Earth

But what I have also come to understand now – largely through conversations with Dr Iwan Russell-Jones – is that violence and lawlessness are central features of the Bible and that, as the Book of Genesis shows, they are the necessary and inevitable consequences of Adam's rebellion.[4] Adam's sin was that he disobeyed God and, in so doing, tried to be like God. His expulsion from the Garden of Eden put him at war with God. From this sin flow all the other sins of mankind and, in an important sense, there is no other sin. Cain's murder of Abel was a logical consequence of the Fall. Violence did not so much start there as continue.

The consequences of playing God are spelled out in stark terms. Men and women destroy each other and the world that God has made. From the perspective of the Book of Genesis, a tide of violence and lawlessness is let loose on the world precisely because of what man attempts to be, that is, independent of God. In the story of Noah we see judgment coming upon the world in the most devastating fashion. In the covenant which follows the flood, God places limitations on human violence and revenge (Gen. 9:6). This is a covenant which is understood to be with all mankind, not just the Jews, and there's a clear notion in it of the restraining hand of God. God sets up certain laws and principles in human society to stop us all totally devouring one another.

There seem to be times, however, when He simply allows us to go our own sweet way to destruction (Rom. 1:26–7). Perhaps it is precisely this freedom in which the Man of Lawlessness manages to work in all our lives and societies, brutalising our ideals and corrupting the best, generating colossal waves of violence and stoking up our new fear. He is an eschatological manifestation of what, without God, we are really all about.

The Final Battle?

But before drawing this enquiry to a conclusion there is one enormously exciting outcome of it all that must be canvassed. If my analysis of the nature of the Man of Lawlessness is correct; if my deductions about his activity in the world are accurate; and if this season of black rain is his season, then it must follow that God has finally raised the curtains for the Son of Man to make his reappearance on the world's stage. If . . .

Every Christian has always believed in the Second Coming. It is a belief that is central to the faith, and early Christians used to greet one another in the street with the word, '*Maranatha*' – 'The Lord is coming.' The return of the Lord has always been thought of as the logical and joyous climax of God's original purpose in creating the world.

The Second Coming is referred to 318 times in the 210 chapters of the New Testament. It is Christ's greatest and most repeated promise. 'I will not leave you as orphans; I will come to you' (John 14:18 *NIV*). Every New Testament writer, without exception, bears witness to this return. St Paul referred to it twenty-seven times, though Matthew also told us that any attempt to fix its date exactly was always doomed to failure. It is a secret locked in the heart of the Father.[5]

Every age has probably felt itself doomed and its children corrupted, but there can be no doubt that never in the history of this small planet have all our children been so systematically corrupted, attacked and even destroyed. Never has there been such a wholesale loss of social stability. Arnold Toynbee in his *Study of History*, described the breakdown of civilisation as being caused by three main defects: a failure of creative power in the minority, an answering withdrawal of mimesis (imitation) on the part of the majority and a consequent loss of social unity in the society as a whole. Yeats told of us of times when things fall apart, the centre cannot hold . . . and everywhere the best lack conviction and the worst are full of passionate intensity.

We see and feel all these characteristics just now and all we really know for sure is that it will all get far, far worse and that this storm of black rain will become as a hurricane before there is any likelihood that it will begin blowing itself out.

Even a random study of the Bible tells us that the times are right for His return. He will return when there are wars and rumours of wars; when there are famines and earthquakes. St Paul listed moral traits that would characterise the general conditions of the last days . . . love of self, love of money, boasting, arrogance, disobedience to parents, ungratefulness, lack of holiness, irreconcilability, malicious gossip, lack of self-control, hatred of the good, treachery, recklessness, conceit, love of pleasure rather than love of God, maintaining a form of religion when they have denied its power. We are more than familiar with most of these traits.

There will also be earthquakes (Luke); an increase in knowledge (Daniel); a revival in interest in demonic activity (Timothy); a stockpiling of riches (James); the people will be returned to Israel (Isaiah) and the Gospel will be preached to the whole world (Matthew).

Perhaps significantly all the wars, famines and earthquakes; all of St Paul's moral traits and all the other preconditions listed by the prophets and disciples of old have all been seized upon and amplified by the active and all-powerful mind of the modern media or else the Man of Lawlessness, as we have come to know him.

So could it be that the last and decisive battle between good and evil is finally under way and that we are already seeing our people and children dying in the opening stages of the battle of Armageddon? And could it be that this battle will only finally be resolved by the dazzling appearance of Christ accompanied by all His saints and armies of Heaven?

We do not know. It is, as yet, still a secret locked in the heart of the Father. But we do know that the murders will get more frequent, the massacres will get bigger and that this apostle of our new fear will begin eating deep into our very souls. We do know that a lot more of our children will die yet and that more than we dared think are dying already.

And as every one of us begins to feel the lash of this evil we should know that now is the time to hold fast to whatsoever is pure, whatsoever is lovely, whatsoever men are of good report. We should know that God may be even now preparing Himself for His final great struggle with His destiny. We should know that this is a time for the lighting of candles and the manning of the watch-towers. St Paul's call to readiness may now be more urgent and relevant than at any time in our history.

Since soon now – and sooner than anyone has yet imagined – these tidal waves of evil, in this long monsoon of black rain, may well be firmly and finally repulsed by the transcendental brilliance of the Second Coming.

Endnotes

1: The New Fear

1 During 1988 sex offences were up 9 per cent and violence up 11 per cent in Wales, according to leaked figures from the Home Office on March 17th, 1989.
2 Fear of crime has become a worse problem than crime, according to the Home Secretary, Douglas Hurd. *Independent*, March 17th, 1989.
3 The *Sunday Times*, January 8th, 1989.
4 The *Independent*, February 1989.
5 The *Daily Mirror*, November 27th, 1985.
6 The *Independent*, March 17th, 1989.
7 A book by Delwyn Tattum and David Lane shows that around a quarter of final-year primary schoolchildren may be involved in bullying other children for at least a year. The *Observer*, March 19th, 1989.

2: The Holiness of the Imagination

1 Paul Johnson, *Intellectuals* (Weidenfeld, 1988), p. 3.
2 Ibid., p. 10.
3 Ibid., p. 19.
4 I. W. Allen, quoted in Lester G. Crocker's *Jean-Jacques Rousseau* (New York, 1974).
5 Mario Pratz, *The Romantic Agony* (Oxford University Press, 1933). Still the best guide to literary Romanticism.
6 Shelley, *A Defence of Poetry*, 1821.
7 Quoted in *The Romantic Agony*.
8 Ibid., p. 139.

3: Myths Which Enable Murder

1 Duncan Williams, *Trousered Apes* (Churchill Press, 1971). An excellent short study of the influence of literature on contemporary society.
2 Malcolm Bradbury, *The Modern World: Ten Great Writers* (Secker and Warburg, 1988).
3 Ibid.
4 Os Guinness, *Dust of Death* (InterVarsity Press, 1973) is an excellent guide to the radicals of the counter-culture. It also contains a brilliant and penetrating analysis of the Christian response to violence.
5 Hilary Mills, *Mailer: A Biography* (New English Library, 1982).
6 Pendennis in the *Observer*, November 11th, 1979.
7 *Mailer*, op. cit., p. 224.
8 *Intellectuals*, op. cit., p. 337.
9 *The Outsider* (Victor Gollancz, 1956).
10 Ibid., p. 153.
11 T. E. Hulme, *Speculations* (Kegan Paul, 1926).
12 Pendennis in the *Observer*, December 7th, 1980.
13 Ian Hamilton, *In Search of J. D. Salinger* (Heinemann, 1988). Quoted on p. 132.
14 Ibid., p. 134.
15 Ibid., p. 155.
16 Ibid., reviews quoted.
17 J. D. Salinger, *Catcher in the Rye* (Hamish Hamilton, 1951).
18 Albert Goldman, *The Lives of John Lennon* (Bantam Press, 1988) and a 'First Tuesday' documentary by Yorkshire Television, *The Man Who Killed John Lennon* are my principal sources of information about Mark Chapman.

4: The Rambo Syndrome

1 Jack and Jo Ann Hinckley, *Breaking Points* (Hodder and Stoughton, 1985) provides most of my information about John Hinckley.
2 Quoted by Barry Norman in *Talking Pictures* (Hodder and Stoughton, 1987), p. 171.
3 Ibid., p. 171.
4 Most films listed here are taken from *Nightmare Movies*, Kim Fletcher (Bloomsbury, 1984).
5 Ibid.
6 A full treatment of modern British film-makers, 'Through a Lens

Darkly', is given by Norman Stone in the *Sunday Times*, January 10th, 1988.

7   Details of Nietzsche's life taken from *Encylopaedia Britannica*.
8   Jeffrey Richards, 'Is Superman a Gentleman?', the *Daily Telegraph*, August 31st, 1987.
9   Quoted in *Talking Pictures*, op. cit., p. 176.
10 David Morrell, *First Blood Part Two* (Arrow, 1985), and *Rambo III* (New English Library, 1988).
11 The *Independent*, January 19th, 1989.
12 The *Sun*, August 18th, 1988.
13 Author with Robert Peart, 'The Man Who Thought He Was Rambo' in the *Sunday Telegraph*, August 2nd, 1987.
14 Kirk Douglas, *The Ragman's Son* (Simon and Schuster, 1988), p. 451.
15 Full account by author in the *Telegraph on Saturday*, June 25th, 1988.
16 Leslie Halliwell, *Halliwell's Film Guide* (Paladin, 1988).
17 The *Independent*, September 13th, 1988.
18 The *Sunday Telegraph*, June 19th, 1988.
19 The *Independent*, January 25th, 1989.
20 The *Independent*, January 31st, 1989.

5: A Theatre for Terrorism

1   The *Sunday Times*, August 7th, 1988.
2   The *Independent*, August 15th, 1988.
3   Quoted in *The Media and Political Violence*, Brigadier Richard Clutterbuck (Macmillan, 1981), p. 89.
4   Lord Annan, *Report of the Committee on the future of Broadcasting* (London, HMSO), p. 270.
5   *The Times*, August 1st, 1988.
6   The *Belfast Telegraph*, August 11th, 1988.
7   Fenyesi, *The Quill*, July/August, 1977, p. 18, in *Media Development* Vol. XXXIV.
8   Krauthammer, 'Looking Evil Dead in the Eye', *Time*, July 15th, 1985.
9   *Media Development*, Vol. XXXIV.
10 The *Sunday Times*, August 7th, 1988.
11 RUC spokesman in interview with author.
12 *The Media and Political Violence*, op. cit., p. 91.
13 Barry White in interview with author.
14 Sartre's details from *Encyclopaedia Britannica* and *Intellectuals*, op. cit.
15 *Intellectuals*, op. cit., p. 246.

16   Andrew Stephen in the *Observer*, February 29th, 1976.
17   Tony McGrath in the *Observer*, May 10th, 1981.
18   Andrew Stephen in the *Observer*, February 29th, 1976.
19   Quoted in *Stained Glass Hours* (New English Library, 1985).
20   Richard Francis, *Broadcasting to a Community in Conflict*, pp. 14–15.
21   Mary Kenny in the *Sunday Telegraph*, November 15th, 1987.
22   *The Times*, June 4th, 1981.
23   *New Society*, November 25th, 1976.
24   *The Media and Political Violence*, op. cit., p. 89.
25   Patrick Bishop and Eamonn Mallie, *The Provisional IRA* (Heinemann, 1987).
26   Ibid., p. 94.
27   *The Media and Political Violence*, op. cit., p. 89.
28   *The Electric Harvest* (New English Library, 1984).

6: Riots on the Village Green

1   Mary Whitehouse, *A Most Dangerous Woman?* (Lion, 1982), p. 161.
2   Mrs Thatcher's speech quoted in *Live From No. 10*, Michael Cockerell (Faber and Faber, 1988), pp. 266–7.
3   *A Most Dangerous Woman?*, op. cit., p. 122.
4   Quoted in ibid.
5   Quoted in ibid.
6   Quoted in *God-in-a-Box*, Colin Morris (Hodder, 1984).
7   J. B. Priestley, *The Edwardians* (Heinemann, 1970).
8   Quoted in *A Most Dangerous Woman?*, op. cit.
9   Geoffrey Barlow and Allison Hill (eds), *Video Violence and Children* (Hodder, 1985), p. 166.
10   The *Daily Mail*, December 17th, 1988.
11   Quoted in *A Most Dangerous Woman?*, op. cit.
12   Quoted in *Video Violence and Children*, op. cit.
13   Adjudication printed in the *Sunday Telegraph*, February 12th, 1989.
14   Barry Norman concludes his *Talking Pictures* with these words: 'But no matter how much money Hollywood makes, can it, for very much longer, continue to ignore the accusation that it has taken over the most exciting new art form of the twentieth century and handed it over largely, if not indeed almost exclusively, to an endless exploration of the dreams, wishes, growing pains and masturbatory fantasies of teenage children?'
15   *Video Violence and Children*, op. cit., p. 170.
16   Violence has now moved squarely – and for the first time – into

Rugby Union. In the England versus Wales match in Cardiff Arms Park on March 18th, 1989, Wales deservedly won an exciting and dramatic match, but only the single fight between the forwards was featured in the BBC's 'Six O'Clock Violence' of that day.

17   The *Sunday Times*, June 19th, 1988.

7: A Gargoyle Art

1   These issues are raised and discussed at length in 'Lies and Lying', *Media Development*, 3/1986.

2   Don Rowlands in Ibid.

3   Henry Porter, *Lies, Damned Lies and Some Exclusives* (Coronet, 1988).

4   A *Daily Mirror* editorial on August 17th, 1988 called Stallone a 'Muscle-head'. 'He is muscle-bound from head to toe. And his biggest muscles are in his head.'

5   I have drawn almost totally on the account of the Press Council's report on Sutcliffe by Ken Morgan as it appeared in the *Journalist*, February 1983.

6   Gordon Burn, *Somebody's Husband, Somebody's Son* (Heinemann, 1984).

7   Reported by the author in the *Observer* September 6th, 1981.

8 The Electronic Pulpit

1   Both the Palau and Graham campaigns were reported by the author for the *Sunday Express Magazine*, June 1984.

2   Interview by the author.

3   Scandals in the electronic church involving Swaggart and Bakker led to a sharp decline in their viewers from 7,306,000 to 4,620,000 households, according to a report in *Christianity Today* (February 3rd, 1989). Schuller was complaining of 'crushing financial blows' and Swaggart's ministry income may have gone down by as much as $90m in the year. Nevertheless most leaders of the electronic church were still optimistic for the future of religious broadcasting in America.

4   *Strait*, Spring 1989.

5   Discussed at length in 'Religious Television Destroys the Sacred' by Susan Noone in *Media Development*, 2/1987, Vol. XXXIV.

6   Neil Postman, *Amusing Ourselves to Death* (Heinemann, 1985).

7   The *Sunday Telegraph*, January 1st, 1989.

8   *Strait*, Spring 1989.

8: The New Political Dictator

1   Michael Cockerell, *Live From No. 10* (Faber and Faber, 1988) p. 89.
2   Ibid., p. 89.
3   Ibid., p. 107.
4   Ibid., p. 14.
5   Ibid., p. 66.
6   Ibid., p. 158.
7   Ibid., p. 242.
8   Nicholas Jones, *Strikes and the Media* (Blackwell, 1986).
9   Ibid., p. 99.
10 *Black Sunlight* (Macdonald, 1987).
11 Pendennis, by the author, the *Observer*, July 1st, 1979.
12 *Live From No. 10*, op. cit., p. 299.
13 Ibid., p. 323.
14 Peter Pringle, 'Boys in the Back Room', the *Independent Magazine* November 12th, 1988.
15 Jane Mayer and Doyle McManus, *Landslide* (Collins, 1989).
16 Trevor McDonald, 'Opening Shots', *The Observer Magazine* (1988).
17 *Amusing Ourselves to Death*, op. cit.

10: A Prophet and a Prophecy

1   For the facts about the life of St Paul I have drawn heavily on *Paul: Envoy Extraordinary*, Malcolm Muggeridge and Alec Vidler (Collins, 1972), and *The Meaning of Paul Today*, C. H. Dodd (George Allen and Unwin, 1920).
2   Marcus Loane, *Grace and the Gentiles* (The Banner of Truth Trust, 1981).

11: The Second Coming

1   A full account of the Malayan visions and the author's world journeys on a bicycle searching for their meaning is given in *Merlyn the Magician and the Pacific Coast Highway* (New English Library, 1982).
2   Pendennis, April 6th, 1980.
3   *Fire in the Bay* (Collins, 1989).
4   Dr Iwan Russell-Jones is in charge of religious radio for BBC Wales.
5   J. Oswald Sanders, *Certainties of Christ's Second Coming* (Kingsway, 1977).